At Home in the Language of the Soul

At Home in the Language of the Soul

Exploring Jungian Discourse and
Psyche's Grammar of Transformation

Josephine Evetts-Secker

LONDON AND NEW YORK

Excerpts from:
The Red Book by C.G. Jung.
Edited by Sonu Shamdasani.
Translated by Mark Kyburz, John Peck, and Sonu Shamdasani.

First published 2012 by Spring Journal Books

Published 2021 by Routledge
2 Park Square, Milton Park, Abingdon, Oxon OX14 4RN
52 Vanderbilt Avenue, New York, NY 10017

Routledge is an imprint of the Taylor & Francis Group, an informa business

© 2021 Josephine Evetts-Secker

The right of Josephine Evetts-Secker to be identified as author of this work has been asserted by her in accordance with sections 77 and 78 of the Copyright, Designs and Patents Act 1988.

All rights reserved. No part of this book may be reprinted or reproduced or utilised in any form or by any electronic, mechanical, or other means, now known or hereafter invented, including photocopying and recording, or in any information storage or retrieval system, without permission in writing from the publishers.

Trademark notice: Product or corporate names may be trademarks or registered trademarks, and are used only for identification and explanation without intent to infringe.

British Library Cataloguing-in-Publication Data
A catalogue record for this book is available from the British Library

Library of Congress Cataloging-in-Publication Data
A catalog record has been requested for this book

ISBN: 978-0-367-47769-1 (hbk)
ISBN: 978-0-367-47770-7 (pbk)
ISBN: 978-1-003-03648-7 (ebk)

Contents

Dedication vii
Acknowledgments viii
List of Illustrations xiii

Prelude 1

Chapter One: Whence and Whither 13

Chapter Two: Native Rhetoric of Psyche 23

Chapter Three: Psyche's Grammar:
  Discourse of Analytical Psychology 63

Chapter Four: Whither of the Dream:
  Foretaste of the Terminus 91

Chapter Five: Whither of the Fairytale:
  Between Once Upon a Time and Ever After 135

Chapter Six: Whither in Myth:
  We Are All Part of It 165

Postlude 201

Notes 217

Appendix 241

Index 245

Dedication

For dearest Leah and Renee,
who are learning and loving language
with delight.

And for my patient children
who tolerated dictionaries at every meal!

Acknowledgments

Great debts accrue to more teachers, analysts, and friends than I can mention.

But I acknowledge special gratitude to Gillian Wilkins and Randolph Quirk who opened doors; for Sonja Marjasch and John Mattern who helped me through them; for Sandy, Johanna, Erika, Pat, and John who have accompanied and shared my journey into language.

For Murray Stein who believed that something was waiting to be said. And for sympathetic editors, my thanks.

To all my analysands, present and past, who have excited my experience of psyche, and my students who always enriched my joy in literature.

Grateful acknowledgment is made to the following publishers, persons, and institutions for permission to quote from the following:

"Ithaca" by C. P. Cavafy. Republished with permission of Princeton University Press, from *Collected Poems*, by C. P. Cavafy, edited by Edmund Keeley and Philip Sherrard, Revised Edition 1992; permission conveyed through Copyright Clearance Center, Inc.

"But" by Robert Coltman. Reprinted by kind permission of his illustrator daughter, Gillian McClure.

"anyone lived in a pretty how town." Copyright 1940, © 1968, 1991 by the Trustees for the E. E. Cummings Trust, from COMPLETE POEMS: 1904–1962 by E. E. Cummings, edited by George J. Firmage. Used by permission of Liveright Publishing Corporation.

Roy Daniells, "Deeper into the Forest." From *Deeper Into the Forest* by McClelland & Stewart in 1948. Reprinted by kind permission of his daughters Susan and Sara Daniells.

"Caul," "Away and See," and "River" from *New Selected Poems* by Carol Ann Duffy. Published by Pan Macmillan, 2011. Copyright © Carol Ann Duffy. Reproduced by permission of the author c/o Rogers, Coleridge & White Ltd., 20 Powis Mews, London W11 1JN.

Excerpts from "The Love Song of Alfred J. Prufrock" and "East Coker" from COLLECTED POEMS 1909–1962 by T. S. Eliot. Copyright © 1952 by Houghton Mifflin Harcourt Publishing Company, renewed 1980 by Esme Valerie Eliot. Reprinted by permission of Houghton Mifflin Harcourt Publishing Company. All rights reserved.

Excerpt from "The Love Song of Alfred J. Prufrock," "East Coker," and "Four Quartets" from *The Complete Poems and Plays* by T.S. Eliot. Copyright © 2011 by Faber & Faber Ltd. By permission of Faber and Faber Ltd.

Excerpt from *Doubts and Loves: What Is Left of Christianity* by Richard Halloway. Copyright © Richard Holloway, 2001. © Canongate Books Ltd.

Excerpt from "An Invocation" from *The Spirit Level* by Seamus Heaney. Copyright © 1996 by Seamus Heaney. Reprinted by permission of Farrar, Straus and Giroux.

Excerpts from *Opened Ground: Selected Poems 1966–1996* by Seamus Heaney. Copyright © 1998 by Seamus Heaney. By permission of Farrar, Straus and Giroux.

Excerpts from *The Spirit Level, New Selected Poems 1996–1987*, and Station Island by Seamus Heaney. Copyright by Seamus Heaney. By permission of Faber and Faber Ltd.

Excerpts from *New Selected Poems 1966–1987* by Seamus Heaney. Copyright © 1998 by Seamus Heaney.

Excerpts from *Tales from Ovid* by Ted Hughes. Copyright © 1997 by Ted Hughes. Reprinted by permission of Farrar, Straus and Giroux.

Excerpts from *Tales from Ovid* by Ted Hughes. Copyright © 1997 by Ted Hughes. By permission of Faber & Faber Ltd. All rights reserved.

The words from "The Great Hunger," "Lough Derg," and "In Memory of My Mother" by Patrick Kavanagh are reprinted from *Collected Poems*, edited by Antoinette Quinn (Allen Lane, 2004), by kind permission of the Trustees of the Estate of the late Katherine B. Kavanagh, through the Jonathan Williams Literary Agency.

Fiere by Jackie Kay. Copyright © 2011, Jackie Kay, used by permission of The Wylie Agency (UK) Limited.

Excerpt from "Aubade" from *The Complete Poems of Philip Larkin* by Philip Larkin, edited by Archie Burnett. Copyright © 2012 by The Estate of Philip Larkin. Reprinted by permission of Farrar, Straus and Giroux.

Excerpt from "Aubade" from *The Complete Poems of Philip Larkin*, by Philip Larkin, edited by Archie Burnett. Copyright © 2012 by The Estate of Philip Larkin. Reprinted by permission of Faber & Faber, Ltd.

The Child in Time by Ian McEwan. Copyright © 1987 by Ian McEwan. Reprinted by permission of Georges Borchardt, Inc., on behalf of the author.

Excerpt from *The Child in Time* by Ian McEwan, Copyright © 1987 Ian McEwan. Reprinted by permission of Vintage Canada, a division of Penguin Random House Canada Limited. All rights reserved.

No Passion Spent: Essays 1978–1995 by George Steiner. Copyright © 1996 by George Steiner. Reprinted by permission of Georges Borchardt, Inc., on behalf of the author.

Excerpt from *No Passion Spent: Essays 1978–1995* by George Steiner. Copyright © 1996 by George Steiner. Reprinted by permission of Faber & Faber, Ltd.

Excerpt from *Terrorist* by John Updike, copyright © 2006 by John Updike. Used by permission of Alfred A. Knopf, an imprint of the Knopf Doubleday Publishing Group, a division of Penguin Random House LLC. All rights reserved.

Excerpt from *Where Three Roads Meet* by Salley Vickers. Copyright © Salley Vickers, 2007 © Canongate Books Ltd.

Excerpt from "Midsummer" from The Poetry of Derek Walcott 1948–2013 by Derek Walcott, selected by Glyn Maxwell. Copyright © 2014 by Derek Walcott. Reprinted by permission of Farrar, Straus and Giroux.

Excerpt from "Midsummer" from The Poetry of Derek Walcott 1948–2013 by Derek Walcott, selected by Glyn Maxwell. Copyright © 2014 by Derek Walcott. Reprinted by permission of Faber & Faber, Ltd.

Illustrations:

Workshop of Albrecht Dürer. The Virgin and Child ('The Madonna with the Iris'). About 1500–10. © The National Gallery, London. Bought through the Art Fund, 1945.

Maurizio Cattelan: Him, 2001. Polyester resin, wax, pigment, clothing, leather boots, human hair. Number two of an edition of three. Installation: Partners, curated by Ydessa Hendeles at the Haus der Kunst, Munich, November 2003–February 2004. Photo by Robert Keziere. © Ydessa Hendeles Art Foundation.

Alberto Giacometti, Four Figurines on a Stand, 1950–1965, cast c. 1965–6 (1901–1966). Purchased with assistance from the Friends of the Tate Gallery 1965. Photo © Tate. © The Estate of Alberto Giacometti (Fondation Giacometti, Paris and ADAGP, Paris), licensed in the UK by ACS and DACS, London 2020.

Robert Therrien, No Title (Table and Four Chairs), 2003 (1947–2019). Acquired jointly with the National Galleries of Scotland through The d'Offay Donation with assistance from the National Heritage Memorial Fund and the Art Fund 2008. © ARS, NY and DACS, London 2020.

Copyright © Anthony Browne 1981
HANSEL AND GRETEL by Anthony Browne
Reproduced by permission of Walker Books Ltd, London SE11 5HJ
www.walker.co.uk

Copyright © 2004 Anthony Browne
INTO THE FOREST by Anthony Browne
Reproduced by permission of Walker Books Ltd, London SE11 5HJ
www.walker.co.uk

I am most grateful for personal permission to use material given by: John Beebe, Donald Cupitt, John Hill, Murray Stein, and David Tacey.

List of Illustrations

Fig. 1. Giacometti, *Four Figures*.
(Tate Modern Gallery, London) 31

Fig. 2. Robert Therrien, *Table and Four Chairs*.
(Tate Modern Gallery, London) 32

Fig. 3. *Alice in Wonderland*.
(Original Illustrations by John Tenniel) 32

Fig. 4. *Gulliver in Lilliput*.
(Arthur Rackham) 33

Fig. 5. Maurizio Cattelan, *Him* 34

Fig. 6. Large basket on hills 35

Fig. 7. Quarles, *Emblems*, Invocation. Bk. 1 53

Fig. 8. Quarles, *Emblems*, Desire. Bk. 3 54

Fig. 9. Salvador Dalí, *Christ of St. John of the Cross*.
(Glasgow Art Gallery) 59

Fig. 10. *King Solomon's Mines* 67

Fig. 11. St. John of the Cross, *Ascent of Mount Carmel* 68

Fig. 12. Dream gate and meadow 101

Fig. 13. Dream horizon 102

Fig. 14. Dream prison bars 131

Fig. 15. Anthony Browne, *Into the Woods*.
(Cover of book with that title) 148

Fig. 16. Anthony Browne, *Hansel and Gretel.*
(Looking Back) 150

Fig. 17. Anthony Browne, *Hansel and Gretel.*
(Alone in the Forest) 153

Fig. 18. Anthony Browne, *Hansel and Gretel.*
(Return to Father) 156

Fig. 19. Quarles, *Emblems,* Bk. 5 176

Fig. 20. *The Virgin and Child* (*Madonna with the Iris*).
Workshop of Albrecht Durer. 1471–1528.
(National Gallery, London) 184

Fig. 21. Joan Marr, *Turning Away* 185

Prelude

At home *in* the language of the soul. At home in. To be *at*, is to be situated. The force of at home lies not only in the substantive home, with its manifold sensible and symbolic associations. *At* gives rest there. Similarly, *in* the language of the soul. *In* also situates, offers containment, but not exclusively in material space, but also in an abstract, imaginal reality. Yet how often do we linger with these overlooked, minimal but productive atoms of our habitual speech, in whichever language we feel at home in, or dare to move out into? Moving *out into* is motion accomplished, not only in the verb, move, but *out into* actively transports us from here to an elsewhere. How might we start to unpack from here to elsewhere?

In his book *At Home in the World*,[1] John Hill reminds us of a report that "Three Irishmen came to King Alfred in a boat without any oars from Ireland, whence they had stolen away because they desired, for the love of God, to be in a state of pilgrimage—they reckoned not where/whither."[2] We find these words, *whence* and *whither*, in numberless variant dialectal forms in the corpus of early English. An Anglo-Saxon biblical translation of John 3:8 says of the wind: "*Đu nast hwanon he cymþ ne hwyder he gæþ.*" Tyndale's translation of 1535 translates this: "The wind bloweth where he listeth, and thou hearest his sound: but canst not tell whence he cometh and whither he goeth."[3]

Luther renders the passage: "*Der Wind bläst, wo er will, und du hörst sein Sausen wohl; aber du weißt nicht, woher er kommt und wohin er fährt.*"[4] Both translators, Tyndale and Luther, affected significantly the development of their respective languages. Those passages of scripture that figure most vividly in our folk mind come to us from Tyndale through the King James Bible. In my experience of English-speaking analysands, even those who own no Christian affinity, find themselves using such phrases and images in dream report and conversation, especially when emotion is intense. The mysterious whence and whither of the wind is a case in point. The Anglo-Saxon words used are embedded in the Anglo-Germanic-Scandinavian soul.[5] I could engage *thence*, *hither*, and *thither* in the same way, and so with many other words that will play fugally through this study. Although *whence* and *whither*, as orientational adverbials, are archaic, they are still vital to cultural forms of thought, and still habitually used in modern retellings of fairytales. I am interested in the implications and amplifications of the stretch between them and the adverbials they spawn. Although they have primary physical momentum, they also reach out to a metaphysical dimension, as we hear in biblical texts echoing through Western languages.

Hill comments that setting off "without sail or rudder, carried only by wind and wave" is typical of Irish saint or hero embarking on the journey of faith.[6] Despite our high-tech navigational equipment, despite all our therapy, we do not actually fare much better. Even when we know where we intend to go, we cannot always know *where* we will end up. We cannot even be sure of *what* we seek. Describing his African travels, Jung formulates this shrewdly. He both did and did not have a *whither*, though his sense of a fearful *whence* was a "Europe and its complex of problems," from which he admitted a "secret purpose of escaping." But he discovered his whither, both in physical and psychic terms, only at the end of his journey.

> Thus the journey from the heart of Africa to Egypt became, for me, a kind of drama of the birth of light. That drama was intimately connected with my psychology....I had not known in advance what Africa would give me; but here lay the satisfying answer, the fulfilling experience. It was worth more than any ethnological yield would have been....I had wanted to find out how Africa would affect me, and I had found out.[7]

All fiction, all life, moves between expectation and surprise; the fulfillment of our anticipation, or a refusal of it, though both might afford transformation. In reality, the individuation experience usually thwarts expectation and prescription.

The overarching archetypal background to these words for source and destination is, of course, the passage from birth to death, the indelible and universal whence and whither that has been imaged by English poets and religious writers in the rhyming womb/tomb collocation. This transit to mortality, Freud urged, should be confronted and integrated as foundation for therapy.

Such vocabulary is the stuff of what follows. I am fascinated by such supposedly innocent lexis, the grammatical particles (in the past some have said *mere* grammatical particles) that are the bread and butter of our speech. *Whence* and *whither*, archaic paradigm of *before* and *after*, *where from* and *where to*, introduce spatial and temporal stretch: time tension, space tension, affective and mental tension, physical and psychic tension. Then *yonder* lies *beyond whither*. Such words seduce psychological interest.

Jungians such as Margaret Wilkinson have applied neuroscientific research to therapeutic praxis, documenting vicissitudes and victories in psyche's developing experience of language making. What has central importance here is the necessary "crossing-over" between right and left hemispheres of the brain and the relationship between these in remembering and integrating experience, perhaps even healing past trauma. Such discourse depends on these minor members, *over* and *between*, activating neural operations, which rely on metaphor and narrative. The language I am tracking provides the links that make narrative coherent and supplies that crucial *as-if* link without which metaphor, and Jung's psychological method, cannot be described.[8]

Metaphor is a means of imaging the invisible; story is a means of organizing and embodying experience. By analogy with the wind making its energy known by its effects, I see the effect of the language I'm exploring. One cannot see an adverb, a preposition, or a conjunction in the way one sees a noun such as tree, but one can feel their syntactic effects. We might conceive of them as transitive nerve impulses, synapses that carry feeling and actively direct meaning.[9] In similar ways, psyche is pulled by such movement through narrative, as I will explore particularly in the chapter on fairytales. We live inside metaphors, rather than simply using them to make sense of our perceptions, and paradigms of orientation are built into our language unconsciously and subliminally.

At, in, whence (where from), *whither* (where to), as adverbs, prepositions, interrogatives, are all closed-class words; they do not inflect.[10] They are fixed in one shape, though linguistic habit constantly defies this law, as indeed I will do when I speak of "whithering"—creating a noun to meet expressive need. From here to elsewhere, whence to whither. That is where I shall wander in what follows. I feel about such minutiae of words, each speck of utterance, rather as Darwin felt about the earthworm, that "tiny unsung creature...which transformed the land."[11]

My passion is poetry and my delight in language is poetic. For me, as for Seamus Heaney, the dictionary is invigorating. The poet remembers discovering his *Wörterbuch* as a boy and experiencing its word-hoard as "Haunting granaries of words like breasts."[12] Like him, I feel that words have fed me. I am sustained by daily lexical bread. How different an all-too-typical current experience recorded by Henri Nouwen:

> Wherever we go we are surrounded by words....It has not always been this way. There was a time...without radios and televisions, stop signs, yield signs, merge signs, bumper stickers,...without the advertisements which now cover whole cities with words.
>
> Recently, I was driving through Los Angeles, and suddenly I had the strange sensation of driving through a huge dictionary. Wherever I looked there were words...they said, "Use me, take me, buy me, drink me, smell me, touch me...." In such a world, who can maintain respect for words?
>
> ...[T]heir limitless multiplication has made us lose confidence in words and caused us to think, more often than not, "They are just words."
>
> Teachers speak to students for six, twelve, eighteen, sometimes twenty-four years. But the students often emerge from the experience with the feeling, "They were just words."...Politicians, business men, ayatollahs, and popes give speeches and make statements...but those who listen say: "They are just words."[13]

Such linguistic inflation is soul-deadening. We protest against it, as did students from the University of Frankfurt in 1968, rebelling against the dictates of the patriarchal academy with their banner, "No more quotations!" Our culture has been here before, breaking out of servitude to classical learning, disputing the hegemony of the word. And yet language is there for us, faithfully nourishing our communication, our self-discovery and revelation. Who can champion that lost respect for words? In our work as analysts and in our own living experience of psyche, we need to return to the poets to refresh "the thoughts of our hearts." We need to restore the poet within to revitalize the speech of our souls and the language of our psychologies.

In his paper "On the Formation of Mould," Darwin deals with essential phenomena that have been overlooked because they cannot be seen. He takes advantage of the pun on being "overlooked"—looked at too much, too often—which can result in blindness. Adam Phillips contends that like Freud, Darwin regards those things that can be seen as the result of hidden process; "the ground is as it is because something is happening underground; what is visible is, as it were, the end of a story."[14] Phillips explores Darwin's desire to justify the ways of worms to man. I have the presumptuous desire to do the same for the particles and subterranean movements of our language. I want to stimulate awareness of what happens underground in a sentence, rhythms activated by the overlooked words that we do not heed for their dictionary content, seeing archetypal forces at work *beneath* and *behind* them.

Perhaps I should justify writing this study in English. It is my native language, but it is peculiarly suited for such a project. Henry Hitchings suggests that "English has become, some say, the world's second first language."[15] England and its bastard language have been invaded and penetrated by Romans, Scandinavians, and French, and because of its colonial history, it has also been fertilized by people from its far-flung ex-colonies, so becoming the "world's auxiliary tongue."[16] George Steiner documents the human desire for a mono-language. It would seem that English is being pressed insidiously to that task through the invention of "globish," a reduction of English to a business model in which financial and commercial interests traffic in things, the language of consumerism. Globish is a "merely marketing language," a "de-caffeination of English" not welcomed by native speakers.[17] It is documented that certain Korean parents, ambitious for their children's success in international markets, have surgery performed on their children's tongues to enable them to pronounce English. This is meant to ensure international success and presumably world concord! English for business is also business for English, as Hitchings wryly observes. Yet in the sixteenth century when vernacular languages made their début, it was lamented that "to write in English is to write in sand." Latin then surpassed any vernacular tongue. In some ecclesiastical quarters today, it is still felt that God inhabits Latin *lux* in ways he cannot inhabit native "light." English stands in a particularly fruitful relationship to other tongues, to which I will occasionally refer.

My love of language embraces all language and I acknowledge that noun, verb, and adjective—those open-class words—excite, incite, and energize symbolic narrative in all expressions of psyche. But these open-class or full-words have always stolen the limelight. It is quite clear from English grammars through the centuries that substantives were always given priority.[18] A grammarian such as John Horne Tooke rejected the multiple parts of speech, arguing that nouns and verbs alone should be sufficient, since language begins in the material world. He had no tolerance for prolixity and wished that women would not verbalize their feelings at all, just purr! How much faster and efficient communication would then be. Tooke's work belongs in the tradition of the *res et verba* debate. This discourse about the relationship of the word to the thing it signifies goes back to classical rhetoric and continues to excite interest, as twentieth-century semiotics affirmed.

David Tacey takes primitive nominalism to task, referring to Nietzsche's "word magic" in his castigation of the way in which certain Jung-related projects (such as some twentieth-century men's movements) create nonce-words to perform a kind of linguistic magic. One word he berates is *Fatherson*, but much Jungian terminology has been abused in similar ways, when neologisms seem "elevated to the status of archetype" and as such cast spells over thought and feeling.[19] Substantives are particularly prone to this kind of abuse. Jung is intensely aware of this danger and was always in touch with what psyche gains and what psyche loses in all traffic between soul and culture.

> Man's advance towards the Logos was a great achievement, but he must pay for it with a loss of instinct and loss of reality to the degree that he remains in primitive dependence on mere words. Because words are substitutes for things, which of course they cannot be in reality, they take on intensified forms, because eccentric, outlandish, stupendous words swell up into what schizophrenic patients call "power words". A primitive word-magic develops, and one is inordinately impressed by it, because anything out of the ordinary is felt to be especially profound and significant.[20]

We must not confuse the transactional force of particular words with this phenomenon of the power word. The absurdity of Tooke's position is deftly satirized in Jonathan Swift's account of *Gulliver's Travels*. In Laguda, Gulliver is guided round the School of Languages. These sensible people

> shorten discourse by cutting polysyllables into one, and leaving out verbs and participles, because in reality all things imaginable are but nouns.
>
> The other was a scheme for entirely abolishing all words whatsoever, and this was urged as a great advantage in point of health as well as brevity. For it is plain that every word we speak is in some degree a diminution of our lungs by corrosion, and consequently contributes to the shortening of our lives. An expedient was therefore offered that, since words are only names for things, it would be more convenient for all men to carry about them such things as were necessary to express the particular business they are to discourse on…many of the most learned and wise adhere to the new scheme of expressing themselves by things, which hath only this inconvenience attending it, that if a man's business be very great and of various kinds he must be obliged in proportion to carry a great bundle of things upon his back, unless he could afford one or two strong servants to attend him.
>
> Another great advantage proposed by this invention was that it would serve as a universal language to be understood in all civilized nations, whose goods and utensils are generally of the same kind.[21]

I fear that some symbol dictionaries, and the misunderstandings they might sometimes inadvertently fuel, can produce something of the same tyranny, seducing that kind of attitude in concretizing minds as they range over such evocative images, visual and verbal, of things and processes, palpable and embodied.[22] These images supply the content of our dreaming and imagining, but the dream offers even more, dynamically. In comparison, the auxiliaries and conjunctions of my study might seem very dull. But there is a danger that our work can become too substantive. A. E. Bennet recalls Jung voicing similar concerns about Freud's conception of the symbol, which he saw as limitedly semiotic. Jung's own view was that the symbol represented something known but not consciously recognized, "observable in its effects" but not "capable of definition." He thought that Freud saw in the symbol a "material significance," as though it actually referred to "actual objects or persons," which might exclude the immaterial, abstract aspect. He therefore judged Freud's symbol to be "merely a substitute for the real thing."[23]

When analysands use the sandtray (which can be completely speech-and-word-less), I have sometimes had a sense of pure substantiality, when sandplay can feel as though the objects provided are themselves directive. I remember a gifted analysand working wordlessly with the sandtray, becoming aroused by a negative complex that she needed to embody. "You have nothing ugly in this room!" she exclaimed, then found a large paper clip, twisted it into a contorted shape, and with some relief isolated it on an island created in the sand. There was no word for such a thing. But once objects are found and placed in a sandtray, relationships between them can be made conscious and perhaps verbalized.

Language is at the heart of our lives, and it can also be the life of our hearts. In theology and psychotherapies, the primacy of the word has been accepted with accompanying image. The relationship between word and image has been explored and contested. In the Jungian world, we are now productively transgressive, speaking, for example, of the "acoustic image."[24] Sound, word, and talk remain essential. Jung himself was emphatic about the kind of language he must use. It was necessarily equivocal, he insisted, when vindicating himself from Martin Buber's charge of ingenious ambiguity.

> The language I speak must be ambiguous, must have two meanings, in order to do justice to the dual aspect of our psychic nature. I strive quite consciously and deliberately for ambiguity of expression, because it is superior to unequivocalness and reflects the nature of life....I purposely allow all overtones and undertones to be heard, partly because they are there *anyway*, and partly because they give a fuller picture of reality.[25]

I cannot resist drawing attention to the *anyway* (*jedenfalls*) of the final sentence here, through which Jung so typically accedes to the just-so reality of psychic experience. The style that Jung thought essential would be considered anathema in typical rational scientific writing. Jung was always anxious that his work be translated by a native German speaker, preferably someone familiar with his own local speech. He was keenly aware of how seriously it could be misconstrued through mistranslation, and so needed sensitivity to style and nuance.[26]

The aims and ideals of early scientific writing were introduced in the English-speaking world in the seventeenth century. A linguistic crusade against the poetic excesses of "conceited" writing culminated in the formulation of an ideal "plain style." In literature, these ideals were allied to a neoclassical revival, manifest in Ben Jonson's declaration, "Pure and neat language I love, yet plain and customary." This style became the vogue of pulpit as well as other prose forms.[27] Jonson saw language as "the instrument of society," so clarity of discourse was the paramount value. The urgent need for this stylistic revolution by "sober and judicious men" was laid out zealously in Thomas Spratt's *History of the Royal Society*. These idealistic scientists were mandated to "bring knowledge back again to our very senses...bringing all things as near the Mathematical plainness as they can," in reaction against the florid style previously courted, which they did not think could serve the needs of the enlightened scientific mind.[28]

Playing with the language of Jungian psychological discourse illuminated the dilemma we have in identifying our practice as science or art. It is both, of course, but it is perhaps more subject than other psychologies to a kind of dualism. There must be significant difference between our professional, collegial discourse and our speech in the private *temenos* of therapeutic space. We need to be fluent in the idiolect of each. We might conceive of this as an application, an expansion, of

Saussure's distinction between *langue* and *parole*, characterized by van Lier as "the unruly side" (*parole*) and "the quiet side" (*langue*). The latter is more biddable and accessible to investigation. This is what I expected when I began. But hours at the word processor made such easy distinctions inauthentic. Our house-trained, more scientific Jungian meta-language could prove almost as feral as the talk at the soul face. A paradigm of two languages is useful, but because in the end they serve the same psychic grammar, they will converge and contaminate each other. We practice bilingually, depending on whether we are inside or outside of the live analytical experience. In the latter, we might talk about, we might theorize about the experience. But even in our discourse *about* psyche we are still *in* psyche, and even as we theorize we fantasize. Perhaps even our scientific language is fantasy; and we do not begrudge such a *perhaps*. We thrive on it.

This is not and could not be an exhaustive study. It is extremely personal, charged by whatever language was constellated at time of writing. It could have gone in very different directions. Writing has been problematical because it was difficult to know just how to organize the ideas, since there were so many little pieces to gather together. Three images kept coming to mind. One was that I was trying to catch rain, unsure where to put the rain barrel to collect each drop. And I felt as though I was threading beads on a string, and from time to time had to free them all and re-thread them in different arrangements of shape and color. Sometimes it felt like standing on the edge of the ocean with wave after wave lapping on the shore, wanting to value each one. I was always aware of Steiner's warning that whereas men of old read the stars, the educated person today reads books about astronomy![29] Our analytical training, when most efficacious, forms rather than trains us to do both. To read the stars and write about them.

Many things contributed to the conception of this work. I was haunted by an elusive memory of a novel read in the mid-nineties by a novelist I didn't then know. Something had stayed vivid; something was still reverberating in my imagination. My mind had been stirred by a single word I had stored, an explosive word, repeated and in context, soul-shivering. It was no more than a verbal auxiliary with a subjunctive and conditional errand. It was the word *would*. I remembered and reread Ian McEwan's novel about a man

PRELUDE   11

whose small daughter was kidnapped while shopping with him. After her loss, he remained, though "barely consciously, on the watch for a five-year-old girl."

> It was not principally a search, though it had once been an obsessive hunt.... Two years on, only vestiges of that remained; now it was a longing, dry hunger. There was a biological clock, dispassionate in its unstoppability, which let his daughter go on growing, extended and complicated her simple vocabulary, made her stronger, her movements surer. The clock, sinewy like a heart, kept faith with an unceasing conditional; she *would be* drawing, she *would be* starting to read, she *would be* losing a milk tooth. She *would be* familiar, taken for granted. It seemed as though the proliferating instances might wear down this conditional, the frail, semi-opaque screen, whose fine tissues of time and chance separated her from him; she is home from school and tired, her tooth is under the pillow, she is looking for her daddy.
>
> Any five-year-old-girl—though boys would do—gave substance to her continued existence.[30]

Those *would*s disconcerted me and bore in me a respect for the psychological potency of auxiliaries, alerting me to the distance between *could* and *would* in praxis. All of the heart's anguish was in them. It is language at the soul face.

A major frustration is that apart from the lack of space in a book such as this, I do not have the facility with other languages to work in and within their literatures. I do know that whatever literature I read in German and French, even Latin (helped by translations), I find there what I observe in English. The same paradigms are at work. This kind of study could be done with any Indo-European language, and I trust that readers will constantly translate my perceptions about English usage into their own tongue. For example, I ask you for a moment to linger imaginatively with French particles, *loin d'ici, jamais, peut-être, car, où, Ô toi que, ô toi qui*. And then experience them in a poignant lyric from Baudelaire's *Les Fleurs du Mal*.[31] Or the closed-class words, *Du, willst, die, nicht, anders, dich, als, so, mit, dieser*. Then respond to what they accomplish in a Rilke poem.[32] We cannot write or speak without such diction; these are minimal, workaholic words, never at rest, inadvertently and humbly assisting the archetypal flow of thought and imagining. But with amplitude to serve psyche.

My illustrations seem random. I could find my material anywhere and everywhere. My choice is necessarily idiosyncratic. Yet in such language we are always familiarly at home. Being at home in language, one experiences oneself and perhaps oneSelf on the road, the *Wanderwegen* of the soul, moved by syntactic motion and adverbial dynamics, responding to the push and pull of prepositions and the resting places or disruptions of pronouns with their surprising networks and antagonisms. I will play freely with such words and consider their dynamics in the discourse of analytical psychology, dream record, fairytale, and myth.

On completing the book, I had a dream that at first disturbed and then comforted me:

> I am bringing something for Murray. A bunch of lovely, very tiny silver spoons. I'm not sure why he wants them but it feels important. As I hand them to him, I realize that one of them is missing, and in its place, there's a bent spoon that is designed to sit on the side of a marmalade pot, with a curve at the end to hook on the side. I go off to find the missing spoon.[33]

The dream made me look rather differently at Eliot's "Lovesong," where his antihero, Prufrock, laments about his seemingly insignificant life.

> I have known them all already, known them all—
> Have known the evenings, mornings, afternoons,
> I have measured out my life with coffee spoons;[34]

I had to ask: Is this study naively banal (my fear) or am I bringing moribund coffee spoons to new life, revaluing the seemingly trivial, the unvalued workwords, that have even been classified as "empty"? The dream spoons are made of silver. Again this reminds me of Darwin's project, his "undogmatic shuffling of the hierarchies to see earthworms…as maintaining the earth, sustaining fertility." "Never say higher or lower"…Darwin jotted in the margins of a book."[35]

I hope by this study to make readers more sensitive to language, that we might read and listen more keenly to and for psyche in professional reflection and in analytical encounter.

CHAPTER ONE

Whence and Whither

Thoughts, whither have ye led me? with what sweet
Compulsion thus transported to forget
What hither brought us?[1]
—John Milton, *Paradise Lost*

When embarking on a new project, like Milton's fallen angel, we ponder the questions: where does this come from, where does it want to go, what is it for? This whence and whithering will figure prominently in this very personal book. Similarly, I have long been haunted by the archaic word *yonder*.[2] Perhaps one reason for this lies in James Hillman's notion of the soul's code: *yonder* has been in me *in nuce* since childhood. *Yonder* has hounded and urged me in sleep as in waking, through my experiences of poetry, theology, and psychology, and in my experience of lived life, even as a child alone in a field of grass that felt endless. Auden identified the poet as one who hangs around words listening to them talk, a relationship not only between the word and the poet, but *between* word and word. I have spent my life hanging around words and this book is one result of an increasingly conscious loitering that has come to strange fruition in analytical work. I want to explore how the commonest words communicate with each other, coming together to say new things, say old things more intensely. I want to attend to the way we use words in our analytical psychology, in our *praxis* as in our more technical discourse and in our imagining.[3] I have been caught in dyadic *here/there* energies played by religious and philosophical writers. A lifetime's experience of and with language has caused me to engage with it rather differently in my analytical work. Throughout these pages, I modulate between the language spoken and heard in my practice room and the words of the poets; words in praxis and the words about our praxis.

One of the things that has happened to and for me is that certain words that *hitherto* have been generally dis- or mis-regarded have become richly charged, insisting that their energies be recognized in new ways, or at least with more consciousness. I might adapt Heaney's comment about his discovery of prolific mint growing unnoticed in his garden that "spelled promise / And newness in the backyard of our life."[4] I would like to spell out the same promise and newness from the backyards of our speech. The words referred to above have been working very hard without acknowledgment, a linguistic underclass, words that I first became aware of as form-words (more recently called function-words) in contrast to the more celebrated full-words of grammatical taxonomies.[5] Poets have worked these humbler lexical items hard, sometimes perhaps unintentionally. (Tune in here to the ambience of *perhaps*, a very Jungian qualifier.) The same poetic exploitation of verbal simplicities might also be tracked in dreams. Hitherto in our dream work we have, like most analysts before us, concentrated on nominal, adjectival, and verbal forms. I do not diminish in any way the significance of such lexis; these full-words carry enormous power. In important ways, they carry us. Some would argue that we cannot think without them. They usually convey the symbolic content of dreams and fantasy. This aspect of lexical experience is splendidly illuminated in Paul Kugler's *The Alchemy of Discourse*.[6] He listens in to psyche's histories, etymologies, the memories that inhabit words, attending to archetypal containment within them. In most lexical studies, precedence is given to nouns, super-valuing the substantive. Even this name confirms that the noun is more substantial than other parts of speech.[7]

I share the poet's excitement with these essences, feeling the awe Heaney felt as he remembered once entering the worshipping community through sharing the words of the Roman Catholic Missal:

> And we lifted our eyes to the nouns.
> Altar-stone was dawn and monstrance noon,
> The rubric itself a bloodshot sunset.[8]

Back in those holy days, the liturgy fed the poet's expanding soul and housed it in language. His grammatical reflection is apt for my purposes, especially when he remembers the boy feeling involved in grammatical flux.

> Intransitivity we would assist,
> Confess, receive. The verbs
> Assumed us. We adored.[9]

Such was the poet's containment in the word become Word, and Word became words. Heaney needed in some humble way to feel alive in dialectical exchange. It is transitivity that I am particularly moved by, being caught up in the inner and outer activities of speech. While acknowledging the privileged status of nouns that so often carry symbolic content, I will be concerned with more functional forms, for here I see, in perhaps new ways for Jungians, what Steiner aptly described as the "field of relevant force and intimation in which words conduct their complex lives."[10] An insight that would have appealed to Jung.

Jung did not include one single form-word, not one mere linguistic particle, in his word list for the Word Association Experiment. In 400 stimulus words, there were no prepositions, for example, but 231 nouns, 69 adjectives, 82 verbs, 18 adverbs, and numerals. The only adverbs are formed from significant nouns, e.g., friendly.[11] There are still no form-words in our standard word list and the closed forms of numerals have disappeared. This represents the assumption that such particles need to be in relationship with other words in order to create meaning, implying that they cannot stand alone. Jung insists that "each complex strives to live itself out unimpeded,"[12] and as I will argue, there is archetypal imperative, archetypal intentionality, in the kinesthetic energies of unobtrusive form-words. One might feel the essence of this at a sacred moment in the Eucharistic doxology, when the presence of Christ is invoked through three prepositions—*per* ipsum et *cum* ipso et *in ipso* (through Him, with Him, in Him)—proclaiming the inherence of Christ in the mystery.[13]

I invoke here the classical *topos* of *multo in parvo* (much in little, great in small), an apologia for the brevity of sonnet or lyric. This is also an archetypal modality, manifest in our experience and fantasy. It is especially relevant to literary expression, even at the level of punctuation in visual script. What a load the mere dash can carry in graphic record, the life of Jung contracted to 1875–1961. There is boundless energy in all punctuation, especially exclamations and question marks in written texts, their impact and purpose replaced by vocal and gestural equivalents in spoken communication. For the Hebraic scribe, the single letter carries the meaning, for "every *aleph* has in it something of the breath of God."[14] The transcription of text was of paramount importance in the tradition of the Kabbala, where one single error required that a manuscript be removed. In the tiny graphic form of a letter, "manifold energies of meaning are incised."[15]

I enter my exploration through lyrics by Carol Ann Duffy, first celebrating some "big" words through meta-lexical play.[16] In a poem entitled "Caul," she reflects on the folk luck she was born with:

> No, I don't remember the thing itself.
> I remember the word.
> Amnion, inner membrane, *caul.*
> I'll never be drowned.[17]

Memory of her actual biological entry into life is lost as felt experience, but since infancy, talk of it enforces it in consciousness as potent substitute, perhaps through maternal speech. The word "caul" with its aura of emotion has power to "call" her to her story. The final stanza confirms the psycho-lexical momentum:

> The light of a candle seen in a caul
> eased from my crown that day,
> when all but this living noun
> was taken away.

The word endures. Our analytical work is often arrested by such "living nouns," which carry the symbolic load most obviously. In "Away and See," Duffy continues to exult in the power of words to signify and celebrate experience:

WHENCE AND WHITHER

> Away and see the things that words give a name to, the flight
> of syllables, wingspan stretching a noun. Test words
> wherever they live; listen and touch and smell, believe.
> Spell them with love.[18]

Words nourish imagination. While listening to water flowing, her sensitivity to the diverting work of words inspires the lyric, "River":

> At the turn of the river the language changes,
> a different babble, even a different name
> for the same river. Water crosses the border,
> translates itself, but words stumble, fall back…[19]

Human language lacks the river's fluidity if we "nail words to a tree," fixing the flowing forms, making them mean too rigidly. G. K. Chesterton also speaks of such arrest, lamenting the "things that are always misunderstood, because they have been too often explained."[20] This seduction into explanation can mar analytical praxis. It is wiser to adopt Wolfgang Giegerich's valuing of "passion kindled about what is in the ununderstood," his urge to "harbor the *un*understood," "carrying the ununderstood to full term."[21]

Alice fills her Wonderland with noisy delight in inflated diction, those "nice grand words to say."[22] While delighting in those sounds of words, Duffy is more profoundly engaged. But she would not admit any minimizing of the significance of "merely" phonetic qualities.[23] Clang associations were at first considered to be just signs of fatigue, but later they were thought to result from ego's more significant lack of attention. In ordinary speech, sound is vitally suggestive and even in dream life we can benefit from phonetic play. An analysand began a session reporting a quarrel with a partner during which charges of "collusion" were made. The dream that followed that episode concerned a road accident, a "collision." Reflection on the dream threw helpful light on relationship issues, through the chiming of collision and collusion. Soundplay usually has psychological import. Nouns, verbs, and adjectives have manifest vitality more easily valued in them than in what I will continue to call form-words. But the more prominent nominals have limitations, too. It is a well-aired grievance among Jungians that we have a tendency to reify through nominalization. The same problem teases theological and philosophical discourse. In reaction, some theologians insist that "God is not a noun,"[24] just as analysts insist on the verbal essence of psyche and consciousness, insisting that archetypes are verbs, not nouns. But even those who resist in theory continually write and speak, against their better judgment, of *the* unconscious, *the* psyche.

Poets have always transgressed boundaries between parts of speech. Such creative license offended Enlightenment proprieties, one eighteenth-century critic scorning Shakespeare's habit of "verbing it with nouns."[25] Examples are numberless, as when Pompey speaks of "Julius Caesar, / Who at Philippi the good Brutus *ghosted.*"[26] His usual grammatical promiscuity is exercised in Lady Macbeth's anguished self-questioning:

> Will all great Neptune's ocean wash this blood
> Clean from my hand? No; this my hand will rather
> The multitudinous seas incarnadine,
> Making the green one red.[27]

Such linguistic morphing is of great interest to us in our analytical communications, making one part of speech into another. *Making into.* The process is native to our language habits. Suicide used as verb, fun as epithet are typically integrated into contemporary grammars that describe what we actually say, rather than prescribe what we ought to say.

Paul Coltman shares my enthusiasm for unassuming, industrious form-words, celebrating them in a short lyric starkly entitled, "but."

> The other day while I was writing
> a 'but' scuttled across the page
> and sat down at the end of the line.
> I was surprised. I had grown accustomed
> to certain temperamental words
> flaunting their personalities.
> ('Thunder' has rumbled reluctant
> ever since it was noticed by Milton;
> 'silks' are spoiled and rustle self-consciously;
> 'cuckoo' is vulgar, of course, a nuisance;
> 'cherub', fat with spiritual flesh,
> sits comfortably on its little round bottom;
> and you have to give consideration
> to words such as 'turquoise' and 'diadem'—

> they are aristocrats, so to speak.)
> But if 'if' and 'and' and 'for' and 'by'—
> the workers—began to claim privileges
> it would be nothing short of revolution.
> Imagine 'or' or 'now' or 'so',
> an exigent 'the', a dominant 'and',
> but it is simply impossible, absurd,
> but suppose they did. Absurd, but.[28]

The poem is dominated by monosyllabic form-words typically cognate with Germanic languages. I suggest that even the little words, the workers, have personality to flaunt!

In a less whimsical vein, Dostoevsky plumbs the potential depths of a French *but* in his Russian novel, *Devils*, where Mrs. Stavrogin challenges Verkhovensky's *yes but* with the spirited affirmation, "There's no *mais* about it, no *mais* at all!"[29] So much of the spiritual undercurrent of this novel inheres in this *but*. There is similar charging of the unchanging affirmative *yes* in Derek Walcott's poem when he hears "yellow butterflies rising on the road to Valencia / stuttering "yes" to the resurrection; "yes, yes is our answer."[30] In typical symbolic reflection, we might be drawn first to the metamorphosing butterfly; but soul's energy here lies equally in *yes*, charging a sense of rising from pupa's deathlike incubation. But *yes* carries this, too, the thrust to affirm the individuation process.

We usually associate English monosyllabic diction with its Germanic roots and our polysyllabic word-hoard with the Romance languages. But it is not merely a matter of monosyllabic form. Certain native compounds can become logically or temporally complex, as in *heretofore* or *nevertheless* (German *nichtsdestoweniger*), the latter capable of carrying huge psychic loads. German goes on budding even more prolifically, augmenting ideas continuously through unstoppable compounding. Anglo-Saxon diction feels like the bread and butter of English speech, especially our informal, subjective conversation. Such diction is eschewed in scientific discourse, which favors a more neutralized terminology and prefers word building from Latin and Greek particles in the formation of neologisms, as new discoveries call on the Adam in us to name them. Core words for essences and things have long been imported into English and still most commonly affixes are commandeered from other languages, especially dead ones that cannot resist. In this way, they can be roused to new life in new contexts, working just as hard in exile as in their original home culture. In the following chapters, I will be attending to such morphology through the energy of affixes, such as *sub-* and *trans-*, acknowledging their participation in psychoanalytic discourse.

I do not hesitate to cleave to the poets, affirming Freud's remark about the preeminence of the artist's communication. "In the field of symptomatic acts, too, psychoanalytic observation must concede priority to imaginative writers. It can only repeat what they have said long ago."[31] The poet allows all words equally to contribute multiple possibilities. Consider e e cummings, who experimented so ruthlessly to democratize language. Every word must work equally hard; none should grab the floor of the poem by capitalization, which inevitably, at least in English, accords unearned value. Most of cummings's lyrics demonstrate his revolution in action, with an unusually high count of form-words, all such humble particles made to pioneer fresh nuance. He exploits the adjective "pretty" and the qualifier "pretty" to create a newly conceived sociological location, a "pretty how town," where the amorphous energy of *how*, in clear affiliation to anyhow, determines its quality:

> anyone lived in a pretty how town
> (with up so floating many bells down)
> spring summer autumn winter
> he sang his didn't he danced his did.[32]

Much of cummings's poetry redeems the neglected, recharging words like *up/down* and verb particles like *did/didn't* to give life to novel perceptions.

At moments of maximum crisis, Shakespeare also pressures monosyllables and form-words to generate tension, often in contemplation or imminent experience of death's mystery, as in Hamlet's agonizingly multilayered, minimalist questioning, "To be or not to be." *That* follows, as summation of all that the dilemma involves. *That* is the question. Or Othello's self-communing, where Shakespeare exploits the intensely ambivalent phrasal verb, *put out*. Othello agonizes, "Put out the light, and then put out the light." The only two full-words in this monosyllabic pentameter are "put" and "light," light glowing with symbolic implication. The other words are "mere" particles.[33] And yet this minimal line expresses the murderer's torment, as he weighs the consequence of his action, the energy of *put* absorbed into *out*.

Although form-words are uninflected and do not change their shape, they do change direction. This is a characteristic I will be tracking; they carry energy and purpose, channeling psychological, often unconscious, motivations wherever they need to flow. Often inadvertently, they voice the determination of the complex. Psyche's language is sometimes more prepositional than propositional.

In what follows, I will hang round the actual words of analytic exchange and hear words talking to each other, marking the unremarked and the unremarkable. I will not detract from Duffy's reveling in words that carry memory and the charge of personal destiny (grand words like caul) that can excite records of psychic experience. However, such naming can close off, enclose, or encase thought, arresting ideas as too "said." The process of building new nominals can also be breathtaking, as when poets exploit the piling of affixes, speaking of grief being wound up "into a mysteriousness" and his mood as one of "repining restlessness." Such abstracting does not reify as it might in nonpoetic usage, but releases words into endless possibility.[34]

All communication is psychological action and a proper domain of psychology, unequivocally in communications within analysis. Over a hundred years ago, William James made illuminating remarks about language, paying due reverence to particles, claiming that we

> ought to say a feeling of and, and a feeling of if, a feeling of but, and a feeling of by, quite as easily as we say a feeling of blue, or a feeling of cold. Yet we do not: so inveterate has our habit become of recognizing the existence of the substantive parts alone, that language almost refuses to lend itself to any other use.[35]

For too long we have privileged "the substantive parts alone." I hope in some small way to rectify this oversight, so that we might feel *and*, smell *if*, and taste *whither*.

In the next chapter, I address the language that authentically embodies psyche, giving attention to words serving our whence and whithering, acknowledging especially the energy asserted through prepositions, adverbials, conjunctions, and ubiquitous compounding.

Other chapters will observe psyche making such diction express the unconscious world through dream, analytical discourse, and therapeutic experience at the soul face. Later chapters will track the attempts of the same language to speak of the psychological, biological, and spiritual task of individuation, through myth and fairytale.

I will use a perhaps irritating convention in order to draw attention to a central point. I will italicize key function-words to set them apart, and in order to accentuate their structure, I will hyphenate compounds, where pre-positionals and ad-verbials are used to form significant lexical structures, and where affixes are used to build fresh constructions, to accentuate their presence. Many of these, perhaps most, are now scarcely recognized as compounds, so thoroughly grafted together have they become, and so integrated into our lexicon. I will do this with native and non-native verbal particles alike.

CHAPTER TWO

Native Rhetoric of Psyche[1]

> Every definite image in the mind is steeped and dyed in the free water that flows round it. With it goes the sense of its relations, near and remote, the dying echo of whence it came to us, the dawning sense of whither it is to lead. Just as the echo of the whence, the sense of the starting point of our thought, is probably due to the dying excitement of processes but a moment since vividly aroused; so the sense of the whither, the foretaste of the terminus, must be due to the waxing excitement of tracts or processes whose psychical correlative will a moment hence be the vividly present feature of our thought.[2]
> —William James, *Psychology: A Briefer Course*

Whence, hence, and *whither* are directional pointers. This study examines psychic trajectories, positing that there are archetypes of direction inherent in all life forms and experiences, and specifically for our purposes, in what Jung formulates as the individuation process. Inevitably this is reflected and enacted in our language when we communicate such concerns. Preoccupation with direction will constantly involve us in discussions of energy. One might say that the economics and husbandry of energy is a most vital issue for all psychologies, especially that of Jung. His mature paper "On the Nature of the Psyche" is absorbed by the properties of psychic energy, manifest in the activity of the complexes. Activity is energy aroused.

Describing the writing of *Answer to Job*, Jung confessed that he was "gripped *by* the urgency and difficulty of the problem and was unable to throw *it off*."[3] Perhaps all of his complex psychology lies in these few words. One might wonder what his "it" is. Does *it* refer to the urgency, the difficulty of the problem, the issue itself, or all three? So much is enclosed in this voluminous *it*. I envy Jung the profundity of his project, the grand narrative of Job and the problem of evil. I, however, am merely gripped by little words. What dignifies my own experience is the conviction, Jung's and mine, that psychology is a field of experience, not a philosophical theory.[4] So in this field of charged linguistic and poetic experience, what archetypal energies are constellated? How does Psyche speak? If the image is the unit of psychic communication, what kind of imagery is insinuated through prepositional, adverbial, and merely functional lexical presences? Are there archetypes of direction that are more difficult to image or express symbolically? Do we need sometimes to re-focus from symbol, as nominal form, to the symbolic as relationship?

Poets articulate our experience. So Heaney, that poet of underground process, while prosaically eating oysters, is roused to realize his eating, his politics, and his saying as one act of consciousness:

> I ate the day
> Deliberately, that its tang
> Might quicken me into verb, pure verb.[5]

Whether we know it or not, language quickens us in life and praxis. Words take hold of us, as does much other nonverbal communication that we might want or need to make conscious. I hope to nurture that greater consciousness of words enacting psyche.

I employ here the Greek idea of the *daimon*, in the sense Plato gave to it in his report of Socrates' dialogue with Diotima in the *Symposium*. Socrates is exploring the nature of love as experienced by human creatures whose being is halfway-*between* beast and god. This in-between state he commends in many affairs of mind and heart, especially his own special concern with that "condition halfway between knowledge and ignorance." Love's nature is also to be in this halfway-between place, between the beautiful/good and the ugly/bad. It is a "both/and" place where psyche is at home. Despite Socrates' protest that Eros is a great god, nevertheless he is "something between the two." What follows in Diotima's definition is crucial.

> "What can Love be then?" I said; "A mortal?" "Far from it." "Well what?" "As in my previous examples, he is half-way between mortal and immortal." "What sort of being is he then, Diotima?" "He is a great spirit (*daimon*), Socrates; everything that is of the nature of a spirit is half-god and half-man." "And what is the function of such a being?" "To interpret and convey messages to the gods from men and to men from the gods, prayers and sacrifices from the one, commands and rewards from the other. Being of an intermediate nature, a spirit bridges gaps between them, and prevents the universe from falling into two separate halves....God does not deal directly with man; it is by means of spirits that all the intercourse and communication of gods with men, both in waking life and in sleep, is carried on....Spirits are many in number and of many kinds, and one of them is Love."[6]

This Eros is undeniably a go-*between*. Hence his agency in relating people. This daimonic energy *between* I want to engage, that of Eros being just one kind among many. There is also perhaps a syntactic daimon in our grammar, exerting influence, pointing, guiding, behaving as moving parts in the sentence engine.

I will use Gerard Manley Hopkins's dialogue poem "The Leaden Echo and the Golden Echo" as one poetic matrix for my reflections. (See full text in the Appendix.) I linger with it because it illustrates the energies I want to constellate, the energy fields I want to enter. In poetry, rhythm is a means of propulsion, either urging ideas forward or slowing them down for reflection. This poem thrusts forward breathlessly from the start in its attempt to search out, get hold of, and preserve life's transient beauty. Such is the hopeless desire of the Leaden Echo.

> How to kéep—is there ány any, is there none such,
>   nowhere known some, bow or brooch or braid or
>   brace, láce, latch or catch or key to keep
> Back beauty, keep it, beauty, beauty, beauty, ...from
>   vanishing away?[7]

In these three run-on lines, there are 22 form-words and only 11 full-words, two of them repeated (keep and beauty); and there is much repetition in sense and sound. Alliterating *b*'s and assonantal vowel movement throw a trajectory through fettering words to the capture of beauty in *bow, brooch, braid, brace, lace, latch, catch,* and *key*. In this catalogue, coordinating conjunctions are limited, the dense list evoking profuse material densities and the simultaneity of things associated by *or*. There are only two verbs, a past form and a present participle, *known* and *vanishing*. The hard "k" sound progressing from "keep" through "catch" to "key" might evoke desperation of almost violent gesture in this impossible grasping-at beauty. Such striving meets the impenetrable wall of resistance asserted through *back*, placed dominantly in the front position of the run-on line. Through *back*, all our yearning to hold on to youth, not to let go, is almost aggressively asserted. But Hopkins makes beauty resistant to verbal assault and it evaporates as it must, vanishing-*away*. Such heavy acquisitive yearning is thwarted, ending in leaden despair:

> So be beginning, be beginning to despair.
> O there's none; no no no there's none:
> Be beginning to despair, to despair,
> Despair, despair, despair, despair.

There is no nominal place, no Paradise, no definable location where beauty can be captured (kept); there is "none such, nowhere known some" or any means to imprison it. Here again a predominance of form-words, 14 of them, climaxing in the annihilating line, "there's none; no no no there's none." The verbal participle "beginning" is repeated three times. "Despair" used as verb and noun is repeated seven times, fading away into deathly hopelessness. The sudden interruption of the Golden Echo is a stirringly simple responsive echo in lexical kind: "Spare!/There ís one, yes I have one (Hush there!)/Only not within seeing of the sun." Its certainty of voice is modified only by the qualifying *only*. Lead is answered by alchemical gold,

> Somewhere elsewhere there is ah well where! one,
> Oné. Yes I can tell such a key, I do know such a place, …

An astonishing rhetorical line: "Somewhere elsewhere there is ah well where! one," But this place is not named Paradise, it is an *elsewhere* that is *yonder*. It can have no other name. The Golden Echo's vision of, and faith in, that *elsewhere* builds to the final climax:

> Where the thing we freely fórfeit is kept with fonder a care,
> Fonder a care kept than we could have kept it, kept
> Far with fonder a care (and we, we should have lost it) finer, fonder
> A care kept.—Where kept? Do but tell us where kept, where.—
> Yonder.—What high as that! We follow, now we follow—
>   Yonder, yes yonder, yonder,
> Yonder.

Here are 54 form-words in the service of only nine different full-words. A potent vocabulary invoking *somewhere, elsewhere,* and back of *yonder*, each becoming symbolically charged. How can such a minimalist word-hoard generate such haunting perception? This is a crass way to analyze poetry, but very illuminating!

The impact of Hopkins's *back* sensitized me to its potency. At the beginning of an analysis a woman cried out in distress, "I want it back. I want it all back." This abrupt monosyllable was highly charged with her pain and her basic psychological predicament. She could not let go of resentment that prevented her from engaging with life following a betrayal. Much time was spent unpacking exactly what *it* was that she was demanding *back*. And how could she get it back, and how might this *back* be experienced? This one word immured the blockage.

Reflecting on Jung's claim that "the concept of libido in psychology has functionally the same significance as the concept of energy in physics," Tacey describes things being "dissolved into energies."[8] My subject is language libido, even its physics. *Back* arrests energy and *yonder* releases it.[9] The fact that in the course of physical life we have to turn back suggests that our natural orientation is forward, no doubt because our eyes are at the front of our heads. But we are drawn backward, too, and have to accommodate such a re-orientation with a special gesture of body and mind. We might say that our inclination forward establishes the ground plan for individuation; we are pulled *yonder*, experiencing ourselves as being some distance away, but in the visual field. An archaic word, *yonder* carries a special load when used in the twenty-first century. It derives from *yon/yond* used as demonstrative, adverb, and pronoun. In the past, it was capable of expansion in the obsolete *yondermost* or *yonmest. Yonder* could go further.

Our postmodern *yonder* has surpassed any previous *yondermost*. In their exploration of orientational metaphors, George Lakoff and Mark Johnson discuss the blatant significance of "the fact that we have bodies of the sort we have and that they function as they do in our physical environment," that is, we stand upright.[10] Our primary orientations are inevitably up/down, side to side, back/front. These literal spacializations create metaphoric networks in the imagination and permeate our core cultures and dreams. Near/far, center/periphery provoke vital elaborations of our experience living, thinking, and imagining within our particular bodies. If like the serpent we were doomed upon our bellies groveling to go, our cultures would be very different. It is fascinating to see how these literal physical realities permeate the analogical mind. This is psyche's natural terrain and therefore the stuff of dreams.

Such have been the shifts and expansions of our science and our knowledge of the universe that we have made past yonders obsolete by our current experiences of *beyond*, now needing to move into a field of *even-beyonder, beyond-yonder*; size and scale pursued and experienced in both directions, atomic, subatomic, as well as reaching out beyond the supernova realm. Measurement has had to shift with the discovery of new horizons, light years bewildering our sense of distance and time. When the seventeenth-century poet contemplated his yonder, the sublime was located "beyond the utmost stars and poles." Herbert was agonizing over the predicament of time and sought release from it.[11] He was dismayed by the distances in time and space that might "detain me from my God." In "Prayer," he experiences prayer as a means of touching this kind of inner space, transporting the soul into "*something* understood." His tight sonnet is a catalogue of appositional definitions of prayer. (See full text in the Appendix.) "Something understood" is the climax of the last line, which has vast potentiality far exceeding preceding evocative substantives such as "land of spices." *Something* invites a sense of the trusted unknown of soul territory, beyond the capacity of all the previous metaphoric nominal compounds to articulate. *Something*: a work-a-day and wake-a-day word becomes capacious and pleromatic. How often analysands reach that point of inexpressibility when they invoke the crucial "it's just *something*…"— conceptually, imagistically, they cannot yet go further. But how cramped Herbert's vision of vastness might now feel when we look with awe at the other side of the moon, and have seen our planet from interstellar space. How psyche adjusts to such proportional shifts is of daily concern in our praxis, for this astonishing perspective touches every area of our lives. This is brought home vividly by a book of aerial photographs that has impressed many analysands.[12] In *La Terre Vue du Ciel*, textured images of garbage sites in Mexico are transformed by distance to a harlequin quilt of great beauty. Or a shanty town in Africa is transmuted through perspective into a gloriously patterned composition. Our gift or our curse is to shift from Herbert's "*au* ciel" to our new vantage point, "*du* ciel."

Such a view *from above* affects us relationally in our personal lives; we are bewildered and overwhelmed *down here* by the sheer scale of human population. There was a time when people were aware only of *how many* lived in their village. The drive to enumerate affected them as much as it does us, but we now know the population figures for every-where on the planet at the touch of a button. We have government offices devoted to counting. This phenomenon is not new. The census that took Mary and Joseph to Bethlehem is probably a back-formation of history, but first-century records do indicate that such practices were customary.[13] "How many people?" is a question we seem driven to ask. An analysand who did an inventory of the people he had dreamed about had to limit it to the last six months, since there were so many. How many? So many! This is the vernacular of man-the-counter. Given that each person we dream about represents a part of ourselves, we do well to get to know as intimately as possible as many as we can of our inner community. J. W. T. Redfearn reminds us of this multitude in *My Self, My Many Selves*.[14] Contemporary expansions of scale bewilder. Just how many people does each of us know as we travel around the world creating new connections? My e-mail address book is no reflection of the actual contacts I have, yet alone persons I read about and see on world news. The latter are virtual people but intimately confronting and constant dream figures. These various and ever-expanding networks mirror contemporary life, the impact of their acceleration and intensity documented in sociological studies like Daniel Bell's *The Cultural Contradictions of Capitalism*. Since that publication, social horizons have expanded even further.[15] These are fresh yonders to be integrated by the contemporary psyche. We are caught in the need to hold on to the personal, while being drawn or driven forward to the global. Like Jung, we are all revolutionary conservatives, or conservative revolutionaries. We change ineluctably even at the cellular level, and we do so either consciously or unconsciously. The parameters of macro-micro and macro-nano experience are especially challenging, a particular kind of stretch from *here* to *there*.

The tensions in *from-to* perspectives, between little and big, are played with special impact in the visual arts. A recent exhibition was devoted to a manipulation of scale.[16] A surprisingly small sculptural piece by Alberto Giacometti presented four stark, elongated figures in formation. Even though they were physically only a few inches high, they were experienced as tall, distant, and threatening in a psychological yonder in empty space. (Fig. 1) Giacometti related this to sitting in a Paris brothel with four naked women standing at the far end of the room. "The distance that separated us…the polished floor seemed insurmountable in spite of my desire to cross it, and impressed me as much as the women."[17] His figures illuminate subjective experience of size. At the other end of the scale was Robert Therrien's a massive installation, *Table and Four Chairs*. (Fig. 2) As viewers walk round and underneath these oversized familiar forms, they feel physically, perhaps emotionally, diminished or excited by a challenging fresh perspective. The experience is mirrored in many previous literary works, like Alice's size-distorting experiences down her rabbit hole, or Gulliver's in Lilliput and Brobdingnag, where he is physically inflated or be-littled in relation to the people and objects around him. (Fig. 3 and 4)[18] These visual images throw light on the distortions in perception caused by our complexes.

Many paintings record similar distortions, where the spatial serves the psychological and illuminates analytical psychology's concern with the inner imago as opposed to the outer image. René Magritte accomplishes the same macro-micro disturbances in *The Spirit of Geometry*, exchanging the heads of mother and infant, shrinking one and enlarging the other, creating an uncanny inversion. These imaginary representations of inner reality play the macro-micro psychological paradigm in ways that support Donald Winnicott's

Figure 1. Giacometti, *Four Figures*. (Tate Modern Gallery, London)

observations of mother-baby dynamics, or Jung's attention to experiences of inner parental imagos. They might all be experienced as elaborations of *from-to* dynamics. This word, dynamic, is central to my reflections. Dynamic, as noun or as adjective, derives from Greek δύναμις, the producing of strength, power, motion, the opposite of

Figure 2. Robert Therrien, *Table and Four Chairs*. (Tate Modern Gallery, London)

Figure 3. *Alice in Wonderland*. (Original Illustrations by John Tenniel)

Figure 4. *Gulliver in Lilliput.* (Arthur Rackham)

Figure 5. Fig. 5. Maurizio Cattelan, *Him*

stasis; a force varying in intensity from the scarcely perceptible to the explosion of dynamite. I see it as relevant to linguistic as it is to physical contexts.

NATIVE RHETORIC OF PSYCHE

Maurizio Cattelan presents Hitler reduced to visual insignificance, a puny figure in echoing space and diminished further by the sculpture's bare pronoun title, *Him*. (Fig. 5) Belittled by perspective, the monster is further minimized by the anonymous pronoun, his name denied. This often happens when analysands refuse to name undesirable figures until s/he can be encountered in the safety of therapeutic *temenos*. Cattelan intended that his figure be approached from behind, where he appears as a small boy kneeling. Only from in front does one see the head of Hitler on a boy's body. The verbal-icon composite here accomplishes the judgment of Hannah Arendt that the Nazi criminal was dangerously "banal," "terribly and terrifyingly ordinary."[19]

Our spatial orientation perhaps responds more immediately to size than to any other formal aspect. The first method of portraying importance is through magnitude, as we see in children's drawings where big things are important, small are not. This same register of scale is operative in analysands' drawings that use a primitive sense of proportion, especially when they arise from raw unconscious experience. (Fig. 6) I use the words "primitive" and "raw" cautiously;

Figure 6. Large basket on hills.

this is the vocabulary of a sophisticated adult Ego, educated in the laws of perspective. The use of scale represents the emotional charge of people or things, an intelligent if obvious means of *fore*-grounding and *back*-grounding, both invaluable indicators of psychic strength, the performance of the complex. Jung suggested that

> this liking for diminutives on the one hand and superlatives—giants, etc.—on the other is connected with the queer uncertainty of spatial and temporal relations in the unconscious. Man's sense of proportion, his rational conception of big and small, is distinctly anthropomorphic, and loses its validity not only in the realm of physical phenomena…. That the greatest effects come from smallest causes has become patently clear not only in physics but in the field of psychological research as well. How often in the critical moments of life everything hangs on what appears to be a mere nothing![20]

The grammatical form of the comparative, adding *–er* to word stems, and the superlative form, adding *–est*, are elementary ways of adjusting magnitude to reflect value. The comparative anticipates an expressed or silent *than*, which creates proportional relationship—a scarcely perceptible linguistic move that achieves much in establishing paradigms of value. It is often used in dream commentary where unconscious imagining negotiates conscious experience. "She is so much bigger than that in real life," analysands say. Dreams magnify or contract in order to deconstruct archetypal inflations or deflations at the core of a complex. Often, the child's experience of size that shaped personal complexes will dissipate with the assistance of dreams, when the adult can recognize proportions of true reality. "It's amazing…he is so much smaller than I remember." This is the dream's work of compensation.

The adult seeming big to a child, the child seeming small to the adult, affects how each has been perceived, conceptualized, and activated in the creation of the inner imago. Such scale is contested by the phenomenon of *l'enfant divin*. In many cultures, there are myths about this special creature, the paradox of "smaller than small, greater than great" often quoted by Jung.[21] He reminds us of the absolute value of the child in his essay on that archetype, absolute because the child symbolizes "the most ineluctable urge in every being, namely the urge to realize itself….an incarnation of *the inability to do otherwise*."[22] He stresses the importance of the child figure in dreams for that reason, which so often counters the response of neurotic adults, who resent and reject the appearance of their own inward child as embarrassingly child-ish. The task of converting that insidious affix *-ish* to the acceptable *-like* is often very distressing. The child represents futurity, the potential for what might develop. The momentousness of the infant is realized in the West's familiar Bethlehem story, elaborated crisply in Richard Crashaw's salutation to the newborn:

> Heaven in earth! and God in man!
> Great little one, whose all-embracing birth
> Lifts earth to Heaven, stoops Heaven to earth![23]

Such stooping and lifting enforces the scale, from big (God) to little (baby) united in this epiphany. Wordsworth also restores potency to the diminished child in his famous "Ode," where he embraces the lost but valued child in himself, remembering him not so much in *temps perdu* as in *temps retrouvé*.

> Thou, whose exterior semblance doth belie
>   Thy Soul's immensity;
> Thou best Philosopher, who yet dost keep
> Thy heritage, thou Eye among the blind…[24]

In less extravagant ways, in analysis we restore the child to his/her appropriate psychic, symbolic, dimensions—a restorative *from-to*. This is particularly important in work with adults whose sense of self was distorted in childhood and who grow up feeling diminished.

Distortions of size, measure, perspective can be echoed in temporal terms, as in Wordsworth's opening lines from "Tintern Abbey": "Five years have past; five summers, with the length/Of five long winters!"[25] The emotional cathexis to past events distorts experience of time, which can distance the past beyond recall, while the eruption of that past can have the shattering immediacy of yesterday. What Jung describes as the "uncertainty of spatial and temporal relations in the unconscious" is constantly manifest in analytical experience. A full analytical hour can seem like ten minutes, or it can feel interminable, as can the interval between sessions when transference is intensely constellated.

In all this, we are playing the macro-micro axis. At home in the Greek language, and work as adjectives, large (μακρος) and small (μίκρος). They have proved so useful that they have developed subsequent life as prefixes in many languages, becoming stable forms, agents of instant aggrandizement or diminution. Mega- (μεγα) behaves in a similar way, size now measured in amount. How big? How much? These are some of the first questions we ask and as the big picture expands, small things look even smaller. This is a crucial development in psychotherapy, where psychic data is shaped by complexes. These questions are vital because since size is comparative, it governs our sense of the value or significance of our place in the world.

At what cost? is one of the most insidious questions we soon (too soon) add to our repertoire. How quickly man the counter is called into being. In some classrooms in the United States some teachers have suggested that in order to motivate children to learn to count, numbers should be preceded by the dollar sign! In relation to our current cultural condition, Theodore Roszak reflects on what he calls the "mystique of quantity." The magnitude we now have to contend with feels infinite and, as he insists, "infinite is not simply very big; it is *meaninglessly* big, an immensity that seems to devour every value and virtue within it."[26] In a very different mood, Bell speaks of the human being as a "self-infinitizing creature who is impelled to search for the beyond."[27] This creature is typically the questing soul that comes into analysis, often successful in negotiating the earlier stages of life that have required Ego's well-honed skills, but is now compelled to traffic with psyche's Self, feeling the urgent magnitude of dynamics that bewilder. In the past, such demands could be met through religious practice, but many secular people now feel ill-equipped to respond to such spiritual pressures. It would seem that psyche can tune in to the infinite, but the Ego, the constructor and mediator of meaning, can founder on the meaninglessness of scale. In most analyses, some anchoring of the infinite in human meaningfulness seems to be accomplished through symbolization.

In the twentieth century, we moved from a less formidable *yonder* of the past to a vaster cosmic yonder; but twenty-first-century horizons expand even *beyond-yonder,* a psychologically unnerving scale. Going beyond is an incremental rhythm innate to human experience in many forms. We have certainly not been unaware of it for a century or so in works with which Jungians are very familiar, such as Nietzsche's *Beyond*

Good and Evil and Freud's *Beyond the Pleasure Principle*.[28] Both were paradigm shifting for the thinkers themselves and for the intellectual world that received or reacted against them. They reached beyond previous convictions in time, scope, and range of thought. These are different registers of *beyond*.

In one common usage, *beyond* has slipped from the spatial to the temporal and carries us into another dimension of human experience. In any beyond we ex-ceed what came before. (How tirelessly industrious that prefix, *-ex*.) As human creatures, we yearn for that beyond and every culture tries to formulate what it might be. Some critics suggest that we live in an era of "Beyondness" and our composers create music evoking the "beyondness of things," while theologians speak of an awareness of "beyondness at the heart of things," a perennial awareness of "the transcendent—that which is greater and other than we are, and just out of reach. It is what artists try to capture; it is what causes many scientists exploring the mystery of inter-stellar space or the human genome to speak of their sense of wonder."[29]

The beyond that Jung dared explore is the obscure and hidden space of depth psychology. We hear the rhetoric of this *beyond* most urgently in his *Red Book*. Many readers have the advantage of hearing his prepositional and adverbial play in German, his *diesseits, jenseits, zwar, besondere*, workaday particles charged with fresh purpose. In the English translation, we respond to that same exertion of function words, compelling downward:

> It is as agonizing as a sleepless night to fulfill the beyond from the here and now, namely, the other and the opposing within myself. It sneaks up like a fever, like a poisonous fog. And when your senses are excited and stretched to the utmost, the daimonic comes as something so insipid and worn out, so mild and stale, that it makes you sick. Here you would gladly stop feeling across to your beyond. Startled and disgusted you long for the supernal beauties of your visible world. You spit out and curse everything that lies beyond your lovely world, since you know that it is the disgust, scum, refuse of the human animal who snuffs himself in dark places, creeps along sidewalks, sniffs out every blessèd angle, and from the cradle to the grave enjoys only what has already been on everyone's lips.

> But here you may not stop—do not place your disgust between your here-and-now and your beyond. The way to your beyond leads through Hell and in fact through your own particular Hell....
>
> How can it be otherwise?[30]

Jung's use of *beyond* here has the intensity and frequency of a complex, now functioning also as a noun. He insists that the beyond has to be "fulfilled," demanding interrogation and full surrender. Each such beyond is unique, as is each hell, our own particular *zwar* and *besondere*. Always *beyond* stands in relation to *here-and-now*.

Lakoff and Johnson point out the obvious but arresting reality that time is habitually represented through moving object metaphors: the time will come, the time for action has arrived, before us is a great opportunity and we don't want it to pass us by, and so on. By virtue of this fact, "time receives a front-back orientation facing in the direction of motion, just as any moving object would. Thus future is facing toward us as it moves toward us."[31] "I will meet the future head-on." "I can't face the future" is often the lament at the outset of analysis. Simultaneously, time can pursue from behind, driving us forward as in Andrew Marvell's notorious image of time at his back, its "winged chariot hurrying near."[32] Especially in times of anxiety and uncertainty, both personal and cultural, we have a sense of having experienced the best of times, and only worse are to come. This seems to be particularly true in the current global crisis, intensified by accelerating rates of change. We have come face to face with that *beyond-yonder*. It would seem in academic discourse, now filtering down to popular debate, that the *post-* phenomenon is shifting again.

The Latin affixes that have proved so important to conceptual formulations might now be losing their charge. We live in an age often designated as *after*. Our native *after* is returning, particularly in discourse that pushes us to the edge of our old thinking. For example, Miroslav Volf implies that *post-* has become too academic and objective.[33] The collocation *post*-Holocaust has provoked us in the past, but can now be a means of distancing. *After*-Auschwitz hurts more, brings it home more nearly. It is not just, not only, time since; *after*-Auschwitz is a condition of soul that we must all encounter personally and in our praxis, witnessing psyche struggling to accommodate holocaust terror beyond integration, which pushes our humanity to limits we have not been compelled to face *before*. Steiner actually speaks of a "grammar of the death camps" that compels our civilization into this *after* world.[34] Similarly, the Latin prefix, *contra*, has ceased to generate the force we need, which is now offered by native *against*. So we take these fragments of speech out of the academy and re-house them in the heart.

This struck me forcibly when reading the ambiguously titled *Life. after. Theory*, whose preface immediately enquires, "What are we 'after'?"[35] Are we after theory, or after theory? *After* in temporal terms, or *after* in pursuit of desire? The ensuing essays say yes to both questions. For a few decades, we have been after theory, wanting it, going after it in every grove of academe, truly, madly, deeply. Theory had serious scientific credibility. Now for many the well feels dry. Most of the postmodernist writers in this collection of papers have become post-postmodernists. In every discipline, we are now after theory. This seems a bathetic temporal use of *after*, at least when we consider the possibilities in other dimensions.

Other encounters with *after* call out through our music, for me especially as in choral polyphony such as Palestrina's motet *Sicut cervus desiderat ad fontes aquarum*. Most English translations of this psalm retain the prepositional verb pant *after*. "As the hart panteth after the water brook, so panteth my soul after thee, O God." Palestrina's music evokes the straining of the *"ad fontes," ad* a preposition in Latin that urges toward, with a sense of being drawn to what lies ahead. Luther's psalm empowers *nach* with the same directional straining.[36]

Jung's use of *nach* in his *Red Book* is typically in the context of longing, the pull of the soul along with the body. He is drawn-down-toward the depths of soul, *nach der tiefe*,[37] and even as he hangs on his cross, he cries out, "I am weary, weary not only of hanging but of struggling after the immeasurable."[38] Similarly, he later experiences an inchoate "longing after the immeasurable."[39] Jung's *hinauf* and *entgeg* enforce the same motion of soul. In his encounter with Ammonius, he lunges from past to present, through a charged *towards*, gaining perspective on his experience: "exultant longing tears me towards the zenith."[40] The language of this most intimate work is astoundingly kinesthetic, exploiting prepositional dynamics. He responded to this energy, we do not know how consciously, in inscribing the famous dictum, *vocatus atque non vocatus, deus ad-erit.* God will come, but with the sense of come-*toward*, perhaps even come-*after*. Many times I have accompanied analysands struggling with that unknown that draws them, articulated only in a perplexed "I just don't know what I'm *after*, it's just something that won't go away." A comment in Frank Kermode's essay "Value after Theory" resonates with this. He says, "Translucent theories, like lightly frosted, tinted or misty windows, never let us forget that we are looking from somewhere to somewhere else, and that there is something between us and what we gaze upon, or what gazes upon us."[41] How easy to overlook such sentences that need so much unpacking, of its *somewhere else*, *something between*, as well as the gazing *upon*. In our work, we also must allow theory to be transparent, seeing through it, not resting the eye upon it.

The title and concepts of *Life. after. theory* can evoke another *after*, an after that is fundamentally temporal, as in after-noon, but much more. The hegemony of theory in the universities has itself now been largely deconstructed or dismissed; in that sense, theory as pre-eminent way is passé. It is perhaps Jung's spirited insistence on the living psyche that prevented analytical psychology from falling into the same narrow circuit. Our *theoria* flourishes, but not at the expense of *praxis*. The academy fares less well. Steiner observes pungently that in humane letters, theory is often intuition grown impatient.[42] There is a more aching sense of *after* abroad in our culture, reflected on by this group of once *avant garde* theorists. There is also the nostalgic *after* of a reactionary such as Theodore Dalrymple in his often profound if disturbing set of essays, *Our Culture, What's Left of It*, or Richard Holloway's *What Is Left of Christianity*.[43] More recently, a Christian agnostic reflects on the spiritual culture *After Atheism*.[44] A recurrent theme of Steiner's writing is that we are a civilization not only in danger of living *after* the book, but even more heinously, living *after* the word.[45] This is reflected in two titles pondering the fate of the word, a fascinating stretch from Marshall McLuhan's *Gutenberg Galaxy* to Sven Birkerts's *Gutenberg Elegies*. There are numberless texts that lament the passing of what was greatly valued in our culture, dooming us to live with an emptied *after*-world. It is the fate of analytical psychology to be *after* Jung. Sonu Shamdasani ends his incisive *Jung Stripped Bare* with "life after biography"![46] Ways of living after Jung need to be found now living with him is past. And we all inhabit a new world after and beyond a defunct patriarchy that we must individuate into collective reality. A common task in therapy is the renewal of the paternal.

Innocent particles functioning as affixes can hijack language and culture! Marilynne Robinson addresses the *neo* phenomenon of so much academic chatter, speaking of all the revisers of the revisions of revisions of seminal thinkers who typically announce

> with the prefix "neo-" their claim on the world's attention, and at the same time their undiminished fealty to the school from which they might otherwise be seen to depart. The prefix "post-" signifies, of course, that they have crossed some sort of threshold, and can therefore make some new claim on the world's attention.[47]

It behooves us as therapists in the intellectual tradition of Jung to be alert to these cultural shifts and slips, many of them hinting at the presence of Hermes, that mischievous and profound agent of communication. He is active in the living *after*. We would do well to ponder personal implications of living *after* analysis.

At the popular level, the dimension of *after* is sometimes lived out in a contemporary *topos* of "grumpy old men," an extension of the dystopia tradition that laments living in a flawed world that has lost its way by abandoning a utopian past. Universal myths of degeneration from a golden age to an age of iron remind us that this sense of loss of all that was good is archetypal, and lives in tension with the equally powerful evolutionary myths with their gospel that we are progressing toward an age more golden than the first.[48] Our current dystopic cynicism may be, in part, reaction against that myth of progress that derived from enlightenment optimism about the glory of man released from irrational and nonscientific thinking. The twentieth century, a century of the savagest wars, has rid us of such illusions about human progress. But human history has always had to wrestle with this sense of living *after*, imaged so variously by artist and dreamer. Psychologically we all live *after* paradise, temporally and in terms of our terrible desire. This is the primordial suffering of all who must to leave the walled garden of foetal life and subsequent childhood, as our case histories document.[49]

Steiner explores our imaginative and linguistic capacity to deal with this temporal *after*. He celebrates the "radiant scandal of our investments in tomorrow, and in after tomorrow." The evolution of our grammars should fill us with wonder at the "subjunctives, optatives, counter-factual conditionals and…the futurities of the verb…that has defined and safeguarded our humanity." He continues,

> It is because we can tell stories, fictive or mathematical-cosmological, about a universe a billion years hence; it is because we can…discuss, conceptualize the Monday morning after our cremation; it is because 'if'-sentences…can, spoken at will, deny, reconstruct, alter past, present and future mapping *otherwise* the determinants of pragmatic reality, that existence continues to be worth experiencing.[50]

These are large and justifiable claims and Jung's teleological bias would affirm their psychological wisdom. We struggle with language to capture thought, exploiting the potencies of our humblest word-forms. What full nominals would be able to do the work of *otherwise* in the quotation above? Mapping *otherwise* might be seen as a paradigm for transformative analyses; it is a psychic project that the depressed soul cannot entertain, imagining *otherwise*.

Many myths depict life after their culture's particular flood, as do many contemporary novels and films, fantasying living *after* holocaust, survival in a *post*-holocaust world. I refer here not only to the Jewish Shoah, but also the fearful imagining of global *post*-nuclear holocaust, with Hiroshima as but a *fore*-taste. Or the planet's and humanity's annihilation after the total exhaustion of natural resources and the destruction of all life. We saw something of such catastrophic fear in the recent Japanese tsunami and nuclear reactor damage. These are traumatic and traumatizing afters that are brought into analytical therapy every day, penetrating even children's bookshelves.[51] They present a register of unimaginable horror in many distressed souls and this is not limited to Jewish people. The concentration camp has become a primary symbol of ultimate betrayal and cruelty *beyond* which we cannot conceive. Increasingly, this is the terror anticipated *after* global warming. In the late twentieth century we added to our lexicon the term "paradigm shift," coined by Thomas Kuhn to designate the radical change in dominant assumptions, originally in scientific thought, but later used to indicate a radical shift in any system of thought. It is claimed that the Holocaust created such an apocalyptic occasion; *before* and *after* it, humanity was different. The same sense of before and a radical after once heralded our Western time frame, moving us from BC to AD. This collective truth pertains also to personal histories, especially those involving trauma, as our daily work with adults abused as children affirms. They live *post*-abuse, *after*-trauma, and this shapes their psychic organization. Other traumata must be lived after in the same way. Recent communications from earthquake survivors in New Zealand and Japan demonstrate that already, within months, life is being apprehended as before or after the quake. And 9/11 has become a first-world watershed of terrorist terrors. America lives vividly after "The Twin Towers," collectively and personally.

We might all reflect on the question, What do we live after?—either in terms of our desire, or in relation to traumatic events that bisect our life before and after. Or even joyful, transcendent experiences that change our sense of lived life in time and space to a pre- and post-life. Religious conversion records typically use this kind of language. As John Newton exclaims at the work of Amazing Grace, "I once was blind but now I can see, I once was lost but now am found." *Once—but now*: such massive load these particles can carry. We cannot reflect without such time adverbials to frame thought.

We are not dealing here with symbols per se, but with modes of experiencing and formulating archetypal modalities in which psyche is at home, an unexpected aspect of what Hillman has called the rhetoric of an archetype, perhaps that of transformation or simply change. The energic field of *between* has similar valence, as much ambivalence/polyvalence as *beyond* or *after*. *Between* and *yonder* can be used as preposition or adverb, which gives them opportunity for diverse dynamic operation in linguistic and psychic syntax. In its earliest Anglo-Saxon usage, *between* implied some disposition of two-ness, as in peace between two friends (*friþ freondum bi tweon*). Later, its scope extended beyond just two, the field of interaction widening to an unspecified number, fulfilling the remit of a related form-word, *among*, which designates position simply in the midst. *Between* is always intermediate and inter-mediating, establishing a relational transaction. It posits tension. Even in the post-Christian world, the position of crucifixion is fixed *between* two offenders, the innocent *between* the guilty. A very non-Christian analysand once insisted that he knew this symbolic soul station from within, that is, the innocent hanging between the guilty; "crucial" was his own word. This sensitizes us to the psychic phenomenon of *between* as figure of psyche's mapping.

I want to reflect on wider cultural sites, especially our symbolic situation *after* Babel, the title of Steiner's wide-ranging study of man-as-language-creature.[52] He first evokes our multilingual predicament: "We do not speak one language, nor half a dozen, nor twenty or thirty. Four to five thousand languages are thought to be in current use."[53] While he may not be able to explain, he does richly exploit the possibilities offered civilization by "this crazy quilt," this "destructive prodigality."[54] And he is also able to demonstrate its creative potential in mobilizing human beings to close the distances *between* them. He reflects on the universal desire and effort to create a mono-language to facilitate communication between endlessly diverse peoples, differentiated by geography, climate, and most notoriously, alien speech. In psychic depths beyond recall, there is a yearning for the speech *before* Babel, the Adamic vernacular of mythologies of origin where the first naming happened. This mythopoeic idea of primary language is profoundly attractive and in many idiosyncratic ways can be constellated in analysis. Steiner suggests that

> the Adamic vernacular not only enabled all men to understand one another....It bodied forth, to a greater or lesser degree, the original Logos, the act of immediate calling into being whereby God had literally spoken the "world." The vulgate of Eden contained, though perhaps in muted key, a divine syntax—powers of statement and designation analogous to God's own diction, in which the mere naming of a thing was the necessary and sufficient cause of its leap into reality.[55]

The desire and search for this universally accessible language is a reaction "against the privacies of individual usage and the disorder of Babel." The attempt to create bridges between privacies is clearly an enactment of psychotherapy, which acknowledges both the "disaster" of Babel and the paradoxical opportunities it gave humankind for prolific individualities. We might see Babel as initiating a new kind of *between*, creating division and antipathy, but also making relationship a necessary, conscious labor, privileging com-munication *between* in order to close the gap *between*. Hence the crucial importance of translation, at various levels, inter-preting between privacies. At a macro level, this is the work of the United Nations and a multiplicity of global networks. It is also a social necessity, inter-preting at micro levels between smaller communities and between persons. Even in our intrapsychic life, it also invites interaction between splinter personalities. In fascinatingly contra-puntal ways, the archetypal urge to com-municate is answered by a continuous process of language creation, initiating a private speech to include the elect and exclude the other. Even within a coherent language group, we have to contend not only with dia-lectal speech, but also the lingo of teenagers, the meta-languages of academic disciplines and other interest groups. In such ways, we continue to delineate those who are *in*, and those who are *out*, insiders and outsiders. The specialized language of computers is illustrative. Just as the first print technology supplied vocabulary for metaphor known only to the cognoscenti, so now our sci-fi word-processing culture, and even our dreams, speak in terms of crashes, webs (not made by spiders though deriving from them), screens, and the like, mirroring and exploiting metaphors of our conscious applications. These constitute generational dialects, creating new gaps *between*. But at the same time, that very web closes larger-scale betweens, making possible transfers of information, reminiscences, or even money, *between* continents by day and night. The in-sider/outsider paradigm is constantly activated in troubled lives. It is on this axis that relationships between individuals, their families, and the collective are played out. It is a field necessarily entered in therapy, complicated and enriched through transference.

I agree with Steiner that "any model of communication is at the same time a model of trans-lation, of a vertical or horizontal transfer of significance." Meaning goes out from one language to another, building a "common architecture" of human speech.[56] Language thus both creates and dissolves otherness. We know this only too well in the trials and errors of analytical exchange. Our task is facilitated and transformed by our engagement with symbolic material, for cultures relate dia-logically through and with their universally resonant symbols. We attest to a psychic law behind the cultural structure of analogies in different cultures. Susan Rowland strongly affirms the symbol's mediation between cultures, elaborating the process through Mikhail Bakhtin's ideas of the centri-petal and centri-fugal tensions at work in the psyche.[57]

Between both opens and closes gaps between people; and we might say that *across* is equally active in adjusting those spaces. This is the work of trans-lation, from one language to another and in any number of other ways relevant to psychology's tasks. We are constantly translating; one might say that we live in a state of trans-lation, even intra-psychically, as well as inter-psychically. As we record our dreams, we are translating from an unconscious mode *across-into* a conscious one. When we attempt to communicate our dreams, we are translating from one dreamer to another, each with her/his own idiolect, comprising personal idioms and accents and cultural biases. It is engrossing to read unidentified dream records of one's analysands, to find that one can recognize each particular dream idiolect, highly personal individuating of cross-cultural symbols, a dreamer's own dialect. In this activity, we move ever *toward*, inclining-forward to the one with whom we would communicate. From me, to you. Our body postures often mirror our grammar. I was once surprised to hear from an analysand a detailed description of his sense of my attentiveness manifest in my physical posture and gesture. In this way, he translated me. We usually reflect on how analysts read their analysands.

Perhaps the most primitive and energizing prepositional paradigm is *from-to*, with its ineluctable trajectory. This syntactic dynamism is spatial, temporal, and logical, as efficacious in metaphoric as in literal utterance. In postmodern science, space and time as cosmic co-ordinates have proved inadequate. In our old cosmologies, death and life as time co-ordinates ran parallel with earth and heaven as space co-ordinates. Life lived on earth ended with death. But the Christian doctrine of life-after-death teased that simplicity. Earth life ended with death, but then heaven life began. The *from-to* movement could also be complicated by the fact that heaven might be experienced on earth. All these paradigms connect, for earth/heaven, just as here/there, also co-ordinate with up/down. In Western thought, there is a subliminal moral dimension, for *up* denotes the good, *down* the bad. Lakoff and Johnson conclude that "symbolic metonymies that are grounded in our physical experience provide an essential means of comprehending religious and cultural concepts."[58] *Up/down* modalities meet us everywhere in myth and religious imagining. Here all the directional energies of Latin *super* and *sub* come into play, with obvious implications and entailments for depth psychology. These same prepositions have been worked mercilessly as prefixes for our spiritual lives. As we will explore later in relation to actual unconscious material, the vertical axis seems most often to take precedence, at least in value terms, over the horizontal. For example, we might speak of the breadth of human experience, but we are not drawn to speak of the breadth of bliss or ecstasy, either in emotional or religious contexts. Bliss and ecstasy are measured in height. But we do not experience heights of depression! *Up/down* also constellates light and darkness, and collocates lexically with them. Olympus and Hades, heaven and hell.

We make-up, we cover-up, phrasal verbs that can be used with striking wit, especially in women's dreams. They can play especially around persona issues. When used as part of a phrasal verb, *up* often implies some kind of improvement. A man dreamed of a bridge for which he was somehow responsible that needed more radical attention than it had received, for it had simply been patched-up, rather cosmetically. He was intrigued by this, and the process of psychological patching-up led us to consider important defensive dynamics. He went there, to the patching up of the bridge, before amplifying the bridge motif.

The old Aristotelian model taught that earth tends downward, which has a moral undertow. In the quest for heaven, we work against gravity. St. Paul said this for us unforgettably: "For the good that I would, I do not, and the evil that I would not, that I do," Phillip Sidney's tension between the "erected wit" and the "infected will."[59] This is the matrix for the confessions of the West such as Augustine's primary text about the anguish and deliciousness of tension between upper and lower. We are for-ever struggling against moral gravities. One of the most graphic depictions of this prepositional experience is that of Faustus, desperate to repent: "O, I'll leap *up* to my God: who pulls me *down*?" I might well have enough ego strength to leap toward my spiritual goal, but am hindered by what might be articulated as instinctual, or diabolical, dynamics.[60] Mary Midgley traces our anxiety about the loss of heavenly co-ordinates that feels relevant to daily psychological practice, throwing bioethical light on the up/down paradigm.

> One of the lasting nightmares caused by Copernicus was the fear that up and down could no longer function properly. From the notion that we are perhaps in free fall, seasickness follows. But it ought not to. Up and down concern our relation to this planet, which is where we are....The notions of up and down, however, function as symbols. To worship is to look up. And for God to be in the sky, looking down on a universe of which we occupied the centre, was certainly a satisfying symbol. Before the Copernican Revolution, as afterward, it was not supposed to be relied on as literal truth, but seen, like all images of God that man could conceive, as provisional, as expressing men's ignorance as much as God's glory. So the Copernican Revolution ought not to have injured religion.[61]

Archetypally it would seem that the *up/down* paradigm has not been emptied of efficacy. The heavens still seduce soul upward into endlessness. In fact, *up* feels magnified since we have been *up there* seeing how much more there actually is than we could ever have imagined. We cannot domesticate archetypal heavens. *Up* has lost none of its symbolic potency, even though we now feel more familiar with unknowable space and even fill the aether with our technological litter, part of our pervasive desacralizing of the universe that so oppresses psyche. Contemporary dreams as well as ecological literature elaborate our distress. In his profoundly reflective collection *The Spirit Level*, Heaney plays with the experiences of the fluctuations of the spirit, especially in the metaphor of the swing, that makes rising and falling, up and down, possible. Soaring high above and beyond, the soul is tempted to rise above, but then inevitably descend, to the human domain of swollen ankles.[62]

There is significant unrest with the inevitability of cultural assumptions of the up/down hierarchy. We saw it in Hillman's early urge to invert sky-driven paradigms in depth psychology. Perhaps not unrelated are the ideas of late twentieth-century theological work such as *Above Us Only Sky,* with its attempt to demythologize what is deemed an already empty sky.[63] Here I am engrossed by three of these words: *Above, us, only*; especially *only*, a potent diminisher. Of course, in a tricksterish way, such projects remythologize earth and underworld, while invalidating *from-to* vectors of the *up/down* axes of ancient religious paradigms.

    Death need not be so much the end of life, but its goal. This model enacts a structure of passage that Jung elaborates in his paper on the "Stages of Life," where he uses with disarming freshness the ancient *topos* of the passage of the sun rising-up-from the east and sinking-down-into the West as analogy for psychological maturation. This particular *from-to* is organized by an instinctive orientation, our diurnal rhythm. Inherent in his passage is a sense of progress, often with an incremental sense of increase. It epitomizes the *from-to* paradigm's purest expression of a directional archetype. We are very much attuned to the psychological necessity of rites of passage and keenly aware of the paucity of such rites in our present culture. It is interesting that today, with significantly fewer marriages to mark the passage from single to partnered life, the birth of a child can activate the need to manifest a passage into family life through ritual. Baptism of new infants is now often celebrated with family gatherings and feasting with the largesse of the marriage rites that were omitted. Passing into this new state is one of the multitude of minor rites of passage that punctuate the overarching transit from life to death. Funerals continue to be felt as necessary, experienced as the final passage into *after*-death, if not experienced as passage into any kind of *after*-life, or life *after*. We encounter the more archaic articulation of such passage in King Lear's philosophical remark to the blinded Gloucester: "Men must endure / Their going hence, even as their coming thither: / Ripeness is all."[64]

    The journey, as going-hence and coming-hither, is the most obvious model of the *from-to* schema, and it varies according to mode of transport, purpose, and destination. It can be quest, pilgrimage, holiday, business trip, exploration, and so forth. Picaresque or peripatetic modes are prevalent in most literatures, manifesting life's passage by land, water, and even up through the empyrean. Literal traveling *from-to* is no longer exclusively horizontal. Hitherto, upward could only be an imaginative thrust, as in early science fiction, or yearned for and spiritualized in the Hebraic psalms. Such a spiritual trajectory is graphically represented in Quarles's seventeenth-century emblems.[65] His initial invocation uses the inevitable words: "While to high Heav'n our fervent Thought arise, / The Soul all Earthly treasure can despise." The invocatory poem urges the soul to "rouse" and "screw up the heighten'd pegs / Of thy sublime theorbo four notes higher" in order to join human music with that of the Seraphim. Higher notes in the musical scale register the soul's upward ascent to the divine. The upward/downward traffic is visualized in the emblem by the descending sunbeams, with the arm and eye reaching up into its light. (Fig. 7) The same trajectory of the heart's prayer to the ear of an all-seeing, all-hearing God who looks down on the yearning soul is represented by the arrow shot from the heart, recalling the ejaculatory prayer tradition recommended in Renaissance spiritual manuals. The soul, always feminine anima in the emblem tradition, is entangled in earthly suffering and temptations, and longs to rise above the vale of tears. "On Thee, O Lord, is fix'd my whole Desire; / To Thee my Groans ascend, my Pray'rs aspire." (Fig. 8). The language needed to present, to modify, and perhaps to transform this vertical axis of aspiration will be explored further in dreams of individuation. Language strains to catch the soul's pining. We have created a theological grammar to say what we can about God, while acknowledging the impossibility, for words cannot house that which is utterly beyond our understanding. These theological "ways," the cato-phatic and the apo-phatic, demonstrate how the mind works and how soul experiences.[66]

The limitations of language to speak our yondermost craving typically collapse into the seeming banality of *all that*. Such is Herbert's experience in his "something understood," quoted earlier. We know that something is there, and sometimes it has to be enough to say no more than (but so much as) "there is a there" and even "there is a there there." The theologian's *reductio* of the *there-ness* of God carries a sense of total assurance such as an infant might feel in the psychological embrace of the containing mother. This is sometimes what guides and sustains our halting therapies.

Perhaps the *from-to* paradigm is most rich and polyvalent in its temporal, rather than its spatial, application. For in this movement is history, personal and collective. Steiner reminds us that "memory is articulated as a function of the past tense of the verb," often asserted through auxiliaries. Although there is amazing flexibility in the tense system of most languages, nevertheless, there is inflexible rigor, too.

Figure 7. Quarles, *Emblems*, Invocation. Bk. 1.

We cannot speak of anything having happened next week; we concede that "conjugations of verb tenses have a literal and physical force, a pointer backward or forward."[67] Steiner makes the bold claim that in

Figure 8. Quarles, *Emblems,* Desire. Bk. 3.

our play with "tense-logic and time-scale beyond that of personal being, private man identifies, however abstractly, with the survival of his species."[68] More specific tribal memory is elaborated in the family psyche. One terrible sense of loss for the orphan is the rupture in the progression of generations, cleavage in the genealogical family tree, the *from-to* of its history. Jung urged the importance of roots and the necessary passage from origins to future becoming required by individuation. But unconscious psyche is not limited as is ego functioning in relation to time and space. Rowland claims that in *Aion* Jung introduces a new myth-making discourse, comprising "the present-in-touch-with-psychic-past-and-future." So *Aion* becomes "history as a map of the psyche in four dimensions of space-time...an attempt to offer history as a form of psychic energy."[69] Prepositions, adverbials, tense auxiliaries are needed to effect such moves through time and space, always at work as a kind of undertow to our grammar. We heard e e cummings sing his *didn't* and dance his *did*, and we can feel similar energies at work in analysis, where verbal auxiliaries block or excite psyche. The patient's "I've never been able," "I can't do," becomes re-framed as "I'm not yet able to," "I can't yet do that," and eventually, "I might yet...." *Yet* introduces possibility, promising to transform past dis-ability. So much expressed by so little, shifting from stasis to animation.

We are familiar with the Victorian terrors of the newly formulated evolutionary passage from ape to humanoid to *Homo sapiens*, but we have grown out of their turmoil. We are at home with paradigms of evolution, encountering such formulations in our developmental psychologies, and more dramatic metamorphoses in dream narrative. "I am racing through a wood, being chased by some creature...I think, a wolf. But suddenly, I am the wolf." I shall discuss such miscegenation in later chapters.

Sometimes such passages manifest as oppositional, as for example, *from* bondage *to* freedom or *from* indigence *to* wealth. The latter is engaged in lottery and grand draw cults, where *from-to* is very different from, though wrongly compared with, fairytale rags to riches conversions. In any one of the many developmental trajectories, there is movement between levels. The distinction of levels is not only exercised in the upper/lower schema to which I have already alluded. In one frequent dream terror, there is the experience of being stuck *between* floors in elevators, machines that raise-us-up and lower-us-down. Upper in this paradigm can be suspect, associated with ambition or inflation in negative ways. In such cases, getting-back-down is of major significance. It might also suggest that the analysis is momentarily stuck.

In the rhetorical field of psyche and psychic reflection, the paradigm of *here-there* is critical. Voicing the convictions of twenty-first-century eco-psychology, Roszak says,

> Simply by raising questions…we assert the existence of intelligence in the universe. The question may be a great one. "Why is everything the way it is?" But even greater than the questions is the statement we make by the act of inquiry itself. "We are here."[70]

In relation to this he, too, accedes to the power of *there* to affirm indelible reality. Responding to questions such as Why did you climb Everest? climbers have notoriously responded, "because it is there," *there* performing an un-trans-lateable engagement of psychic necessity with created existence. How do we make this absoluteness? We have no adequate ways of explaining such a *there*, with its load of proof, purpose, and necessity for the human psyche. Roszak suggests that "to see the world as a realm of interrelated ideas places us in a condition of dialogue; it connects In-here with Out-there as a continuum. It places us on speaking terms with the universe."[71] This is a contemporary here-there paradigm, very different from earlier Western Christian spiritual adverbials. As we have seen, in that paradigm, *here* and *there* were most often vertically opposed, vividly exposed in Marvell's seventeenth-century lyric, *On a Drop of Dew*.[72] Here the antagonistic relationship between here and there crystallizes in the couplet, "Dark beneath, but bright above, / Here disdaining, there in love." I will quote the whole poem, since it illuminates so poignantly a psycho-spiritual paradigm that we still encounter in praxis, often needing to be deconstructed or at least reimagined for Self's constellation to be accepted in consciousness.

> SEE, how the orient dew,
>   Shed from the bosom of the morn
>   Into the blowing roses,

>   (Yet careless of its mansion new,
>   For the clear region where 'twas born,)
>   Round in itself incloses;
>   And, in its little globe's extent,
>   Frames, as it can, its native element.
>   How it the purple flower does slight,
>   Scarce touching where it lies;
>   But gazing back upon the skies,
>   Shines with a mournful light,
>   Like its own tear,
>   Because so long divided from the sphere.
>   Restless it rolls, and unsecure,
>   Trembling, lest it grow impure;
>   Till the warm sun pity its pain,
>   And to the skies exhale it back again.
>   So the soul, that drop, that ray
>   Of the clear fountain of eternal day,
>   (Could it within the human flower be seen,)
>   Remembering still its former height,
>   Shuns the sweet leaves, and blossoms green,
>   And, recollecting its own light,
>   Does, in its pure and circling thoughts, express
>   The greater heaven in an heaven less.
>   In how coy a figure wound,
>   Every way it turns away;
>   So the world-excluding round,
>   Yet receiving in the day;
>   Dark beneath, but bright above,
>   Here disdaining, there in love.
>   How loose and easy hence to go;
>   How girt and ready to ascend;
>   Moving but on a point below,
>   It all about does upwards bend.
>   Such did the manna's sacred dew distil;
>   White and entire, though congealed and chill;
>   Congealed on earth; but does, dissolving, run
>   Into the glories of the almighty sun.

The Christian-Platonic orientation of this regretful aspiration is still fairly habitual in the modern psyche even when it sits fitfully and often enigmatically alongside postmodern spiritual intuition. The dismissal of the soiling *below* (shadow underside of the rose leaves) asserts the *super*-eminence of the supernal. The distress of the self-enclosed dewdrop, yearning for its upper home, is caught by the trembling, resisting *lest*, with its verbal subjunctive, grow. It trembles lest it grow impure. The soul still seems to be teased by this particular antithesis between here and there, and resists deconstruction. Jungian theory favors reconciliation and paradox, not substitution or reversal.

An episode in the Glasgow art gallery throws light on this spiritual predilection for the upward gaze. In 1961 the canvas of Dalí's *Christ of St. John of the Cross* was damaged by a viewer who was distressed because the viewpoint of the artist looked-*down-on* the figure of Christ, rather than looking-*up-to* him. (Fig. 9) Dalí's challenge to this human perspective was felt to be blasphemous. In addition, Christ was felt to be looked-at *from behind*, rather than more reverently, *from before*, from the front.

Throughout *The Red Book*, Jung wrestles with these issues, seeking inclusive reconciliation. Drawn to the shadow beneath the leaves, he reflects on the urge to seek "the highest truth in banality," insisting, to a female *someone* who becomes "she" to him in dialogue,

> But tell me, what do you think of the divinity, of the so-called ultimate truths? I found it very strange to seek them in banality....
> ...Only what is human and what you call banal and hackneyed contains the wisdom that you seek.[73]

Then "a destitute" comes *toward* him, who becomes the "he" who leads to the depths, and the realization that

> without the depth, I do not have the heights. I may be on the heights, but precisely because of that I do not become aware of the heights. I therefore need the bottommost for my renewal. If I am always on the heights, I wear them out and the best becomes atrocious to me.[74]

Values need to be lodged *somewhere*, and before we were made to affirm the incremental scheme of evolution our values were housed in the Great Chain of Being, which called us from the depths to the heights, from the animal to pure spirit. Jung's call to the depths

Figure 9. Salvador Dalí, *Christ of St. John of the Cross*. (Glasgow Art Gallery).

was not romantic, but the danger, not always resisted by fervent followers, was that the depths might become the old heights. We sense that soul must be anchored in ground, beautifully observed in the poet's listening in to the gossip of women, in whose talk "was woven / Such earth to cool the burning brain of Heaven."[75] Anchoring soul in the banal or the domestic is often crucial in therapeutic process, as we will see in the dream chapter.

We may have little use now for the archaic *hence-hither, thence-thither* lexical forms, except in poetic prose, but their movement and orientation are still as active as ever in psyche, and it is hard to express their meanings without considerable circumlocution. Jung suggested that "if the image is charged with numinosity, that is, with psychic energy, then it becomes dynamic and will produce consequences."[76] We might see these directional paradigms as silent images, charged with numinosity, especially in art and in creations from the unconscious. The current liveliness of these paradigms can perhaps be felt and understood in a seminal statement by Lakoff and Johnson:

> Since we are where we are and exist in the present, we conceive of ourselves as being HERE rather than THERE, and NOW rather than THEN. This determines what Cooper and Ross call the ME-FIRST orientation: UP, FRONT, ACTIVE, GOOD, HERE, and NOW are all oriented toward the canonical person; DOWN, BACKWARD, PASSIVE, BAD, THERE, and THEN are all oriented away from the canonical person. (Capitals in original).[77]

Our work in analysis is to explore and perhaps to transform this so-called twenty-first-century "canonical person." This is particularly urgent in the postmodern environment that attempted to deconstruct the humanist sense of unique personhood.

Man is a dialectical creature, dependent on relationship. Dialogue is essential to this relating, *within*, *between*, and *without*—depth psychology's *intra*, *inter*, and *extra*. In *Aion*, Jung insists on the necessity of relationship to inner complexes, discoverable through *intro*-spection but more typically through *pro*-jection. This is a newly charged *here-there* asserting relationship between partners. We know the arrow as symbol of movement between. Eros's arrow is always at work creating connections, and not only sexualized erotic ones. Jung urges that in relationship projections become operative, hence our need to engage with those who collude with or carry our complexes, shadow, animus/a, and other psychic complexes. We are inextricably involved in the ubiquitous Greek preposition, *dia* (δια), indispensable to our psychologies. Dia-lectic and dia-logue are the essential means to psychological development. *Dia-* works ceaselessly to create paths across, through, during. Its opposite, in Latin, *dis*, can defeat or thwart that movement, pushing asunder.[78]

Just as the arrow connects, so also bridges cross *between*. A bridge can be logical or intellectual, uniting ideas. Conjunctions can fulfill that role. Especially interesting are the adversative conjunctions, *but* most prominently. How often we hear analysands grieving over *but*s, with their blocking of forward-moving energy: "I so wanted to leave, but I couldn't." As we move from utterance to utterance, our grammar establishes relations between them; sentences bridged by *nevertheless* or *however* inevitably relating in adversative ways. As James says,

> If we read "no more," we expect presently a "than"; if we read "however," it is a "yet," a "still," or a "nevertheless" that we expect. And this foreboding of the coming verbal and grammatical scheme is so practically accurate that a reader incapable of understanding four ideas of the book…can nevertheless read it with the most delicately modulated expression of intelligence.[79]

Grammatical fore-boding is an interesting proposition. It is indeed useful to be alert to it in dialectical therapeutic engagement.

Co-ordination by means of the copulative *and* can unify and join un-problematically. It can be promiscuously absurd, as in the many things the Walrus catalogues for Alice, "shoes—and ships—and sealing-wax—cabbages—and kings— / and why the sea is boiling hot— / and whether pigs have wings."[80] When such seemingly indiscriminate couplings of things appear in dreams, this absurdity is not in the least problematical, for there we accede to its logic even when we cannot discern it. James's comments, with which we began this chapter, echo a Sufi teaching: "You think because you understand *one* you must understand *two*, because one and one makes two. But you must understand *and*." *And* can extend and it can contract, yoking together mundanely or mysteriously. Yeats spoke of the "rag and bone shop of the heart"—we might also speak of the rag-and-bone-shop of psyche's lexicon. Not one little word can be denied full attention. *And* is, in fact, a mighty and indispensable atom.

The grammatical bridge can be analogical, as in metaphor, and even systematically analogical as in Renaissance frameworks of Correspondences. Such material things as gifts can also function as bridges *between*, joining giver *and* receiver in special bond, as in many dreams. This might be one purpose of gifts in therapy, which should not be refused without conscious deliberation. And as we have briefly reflected, aspiration and desire habitually cross *between*. Many people come into analysis with no real connection to their desire, with no idea of what they really want in their lives, no idea of what they are *after*. Sometimes that is discovered through engagement with unconscious fantasy. One analysand articulated his dilemma: "There's a something else I want, that prevents me from seeing what is offered." Desire traverses gaps between a current *here-and-now* and new *there-and-then* possibilities. Homeric Aphrodite with her initiatory son or Lucretian Venus may here be constellated.

Hermes/Mercurius is also bridge builder, arch navigator through the multivalent prepositional energies of *trans-*, as trans-former and especially as trans-gressor. As Jung remarks, "Mercurius is the process which lies between." Mercurius as process, symbol of δύναμις, potency, function, force. *Trans* is Hermes' preposition, tireless in Jung's psyche. His mind was constantly bridging disciplines, seeing correspondences between myth, scientific theory, poetry, anthropology, theology, and the arts. Our grammar of *between* becomes symbolically loaded in our thinking and imagining. Images need not be pictorial but can manifest kinesthetically, because "archetypal forms are not just static patterns, but dynamic factors that manifest themselves in spontaneous impulses, just as instincts do."[81]

The following chapters will continue to play with these dynamic factors as they manifest in our human, psychological trans-actions and trans-lations. We are constantly crossing between our conscious and unconscious existences, often with a speed approaching simultaneity. For this is not a "stable relationship, but a ceaseless welling-up, a constant shifting of content; for, like the conscious, the unconscious is never at rest, never stagnant. It lives and works in a state of perpetual interaction with the conscious," even in sleep.[82]

CHAPTER THREE

Psyche's Grammar:
Discourse of Analytical Psychology
(ἐνέργεια, action, energy)

> There is not a conjunction or a preposition, and hardly an adverbial phrase, syntactive form, or inflection of voice, in human speech that does not express some shading or other of relation which we at some moment actually feel to exist between the larger objects of our thought.[1]
> —William James, *Psychology: A Briefer Course*

At a conscious level, we typically behave as though we have read, marked, learned, inwardly digested, and are practicing the guidance offered at the beginning of John Bunyan's seventeenth-century allegorical novel, where he imagines progression not so much in this world, as through it. His full title is *The Pilgrim's Progress from This World to That Which Is to Come: Delivered under the Similitude of a Dream.* He provides a startlingly visual entrance into the world of his pilgrim hero, Christian, who is Everyman. Such an opening itches for translation into film.

> As I walked through the wilderness of this world, I lighted on a certain place where was a den; and I laid me down in that place to sleep: and as I slept I dreamed a dream. I dreamed, and behold

> I saw a man clothed with rags, standing in a certain place with his face from his own house, a book in his hand and a great burden upon his back. I looked, and saw him open the book, and read therein; and as he read, he wept and trembled: and not being able longer to contain, he brake out with a lamentable cry; saying, "What shall I do?"
>
> In this plight therefore he went home, and restrained himself as long as he could that his wife and children should not perceive his distress; but he could not be silent long, because that his trouble increased: wherefore at length he brake his mind to his wife and children....O my dear wife...and you the children of my bowels, I your dear friend am in myself undone, by reason of a burden that lieth hard upon me: moreover I am for certain informed that this our city will be burned with fire from heaven, in which fearful overthrow, both myself, with thee, my wife and you my sweet babes, shall miserably come to ruin; except...some way of escape can be found, whereby we may be delivered.[2]

Christian's family, fearing that he was suffering some "frenzy distemper," wisely put him to bed. (We might gloss his behaviors with our own twenty-first-century clinical diagnosis, but we might also see a reliable image of necessary psychic dis-integration.) All attempts to settle him were futile, so he retired, to "talk solitarily in the fields," reading and praying, bursting out with his cry, "What shall I do?"[3] In this bewildered condition, help appears:

> I saw also that he looked this way and that way as if he would run; yet he stood still, because...he could not tell which way to go. I looked then and saw a man named Evangelist coming to him, and asked, "Wherefore dost thou cry?"

A conversation ensues, about judgment and death, after which Evangelist directs him to a prescribed path.

> Then said Evangelist, "If this be thy condition, why standest thou still?" He answered, "Because I know not whither to go." Then he gave him a parchment roll, and there was written within, Fly from the wrath to come.
>
> The man therefore read it, and looking upon Evangelist very carefully, said, "Whither must I fly?" Then said Evangelist,

> pointing with his finger over a very wide field, "Do you see yonder Wicket Gate?" the man said, "No." Then said the other, "Do you see yonder shining light?" He said, "I think I do." Then said Evangelist, "keep that light in your eye, and go up directly thereto, so shalt thou see the Gate at which, when thou knockest, it shall be told thee what thou shalt do."
>
> So I saw in my dream that the man began to run. Now he had not run far from his own door, but his wife and children perceiving it began to cry after him to return: but the man put his fingers in his ears, and ran on crying, "Life, life, eternal life." So he looked not behind him, but fled towards the middle of the plain.

I quote this at length not only because it is superbly cadenced, evocative prose, a stirring invitation into a story, and not only because something like it often comes to mind in the first session(s) of some analyses, but because it illustrates so energetically the forward propulsion of a narrative trajectory through the prepositional and adverbial flow of the language, piling up the kinds of words I am exploring. It also illuminates what we might call a grammar of the urge to individuation. The goal of individuation is wholeness, clearly a goal that can be achieved only partially in one lifetime. Many come into analysis looking for Evangelist, who will direct them *where they should* go. But all the analyst can do is support the analysand's compulsion from a *whence* within, rather than giving direction from without. Evangelist asks the pilgrim soul, "Do you see *yonder* shining light?" having determined that he cannot see details of the distant gate distinctly. Light attracts when forms are not yet visible. Many analysands would recognize truth here.

What is of particular interest to me is the energy of the *as if...but...for* in the almost onomatopoeic rhythm of the sentence, "He looked this way and that way as if he would run, but he stood still, for he did not know which way to go." His restless energy collides with an impeding *but*. He is immobilized by confusion about his meaning and purpose.[4] At this stage, his goal is constellated as no more than a distant *yonder* that must be obeyed, a compulsion that brings people into analysis, a *yonder* that feels both personal and supra-personal.

This *whence* and *whither* is a valid concern of analysis, but too much whence-and-whithering might indicate a neurotically restless condition that can seriously hinder active presence in the *here-and-now*. This we might diagnose as provisional living. All will be well once *whatever-it-is* is discovered or accomplished; meanwhile, I live with the immobilizing sense that *this is not it*. (A bald but profound statement.) Most typically, there is an overarching heuristic of whence-to-whither, in which we can assume that whither is *something, somewhere* as yet unknown, but dis-coverable. Though it seems that we set out from a known *here*, this can itself be bewildering when probed. We offer Jungian "exercitants"[5] a fantasy, a model of the journey (through our theory) that may well appear, at the end, as it did for Christian: "So I awoke, and behold, it was a dream." Christian's dream enacts the Way, elaborating directional energies that push and pull *hither-and-thither*. The helpful guide Evangelist, with his authoritative book, seems to know little about human nature. His instruction, "go up directly thereto" is Ego's illusory goal. For hither-and-thither are not only normative, but necessary. What needs to be kept alive is "that light in [the] eye," which will perhaps enable one to glimpse the *it* that awaits. It is deceptive to promise, *so shalt thou see*, though this is often demanded by analysands, both of themselves and of the analyst. When asked for directions, the analyst can only confess, "I do not know your way, and if I did, I ought not to tell you." Our maps are related, but different, and they can only be represented authentically at the end of each journey. As Alfred Plaut has warned, it is all too easy for the map to become the territory.[6] *Pilgrim's Progress* does come with its own prescriptive map, as do many quest logs from Rider Haggard's *King Solomon's Mines* to St. John of the Cross's *Ascent of Mount Carmel*. (Figs. 10 and 11) Maps that locate the treasure are not on offer in psychoanalytical work, in contrast to the habit of some other therapies of offering clear guidelines as to what goals should be and how they must be reached. This is most prevalent in how-to coaching and therapies employing medical models of cure with definable outcomes. In different therapies, there is significant divergence in establishing a *here* and *there* for therapeutic process. Cognitive Behavior Therapy does have a definable *there*. In Britain, Health Service psychotherapists were required to administer a CORE questionnaire at the beginning and

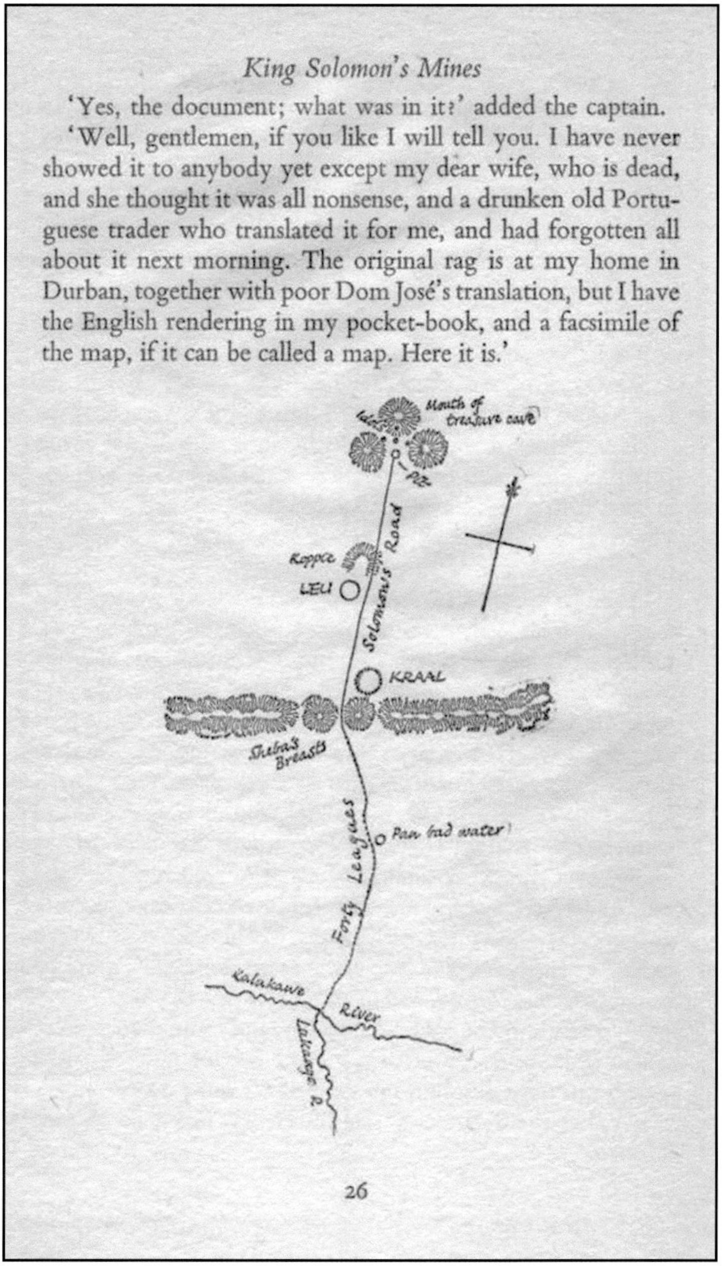

PSYCHE'S GRAMMAR

> ### King Solomon's Mines
>
> 'Yes, the document; what was in it?' added the captain.
>
> 'Well, gentlemen, if you like I will tell you. I have never showed it to anybody yet except my dear wife, who is dead, and she thought it was all nonsense, and a drunken old Portuguese trader who translated it for me, and had forgotten all about it next morning. The original rag is at my home in Durban, together with poor Dom José's translation, but I have the English rendering in my pocket-book, and a facsimile of the map, if it can be called a map. Here it is.'

Figure 10. *King Solomon's Mines.*

Figure 11. St. John of the Cross, *Ascent of Mount Carmel.*

end of therapy, tracking a determinable here and a there between which paradigms of improvement were clearly defined.[7] These have been replaced by new questionnaires, administered at every session, to measure "depression scales" and assess clinical "range of wellness." This determines diagnosis and the contract for work toward specified therapeutic outcomes. These are blatant enactments of the *from-to* transfer, from sickness to health, from madness to sanity, from pain to relief, in which it is circum-scribed what wellness looks like. Such clinical myths of progress bedevil the practice of psychotherapy when the goal is cure. Jungian therapy would rather promote transformation and enlargement, its myths having an insistent teleology but no prescribable *there*. We are often more in accord with the bare, liberating principle that the goal of life is death, to be approached with as much fullness of life and consciousness as possible, transforming neuroses into new meanings. Jung insisted that the "goal is important only as idea; the essential thing is the opus which leads to the goal; that is the opus of a lifetime."[8]

Nevertheless, we do often get a sense of what might be involved in the journey quite early in the analysis, dreams identifying and pointing to an individual *beyond*. A sensitive, intelligent man came to analysis at a time when he needed to connect with repressed feeling, proscribed in boyhood. The collusion of marriage had been that he was incapable of feeling. Dreams offered images that he was able to draw, something he had not done since childhood. He first brought a picture of himself looking into an inviting *yonder* that held the energy of a yearned-for *beyond*. We know this experience from our cultural store of images. Friedrich's paintings come to mind, especially those with romantic hero figures gazing out into a vast yonder. We might also think of Keats's verbal image of the explorer, Cortez, gazing out to new worlds, "silent upon a peak in Darien." Horizon often represents *beyond*, that elusive horizon, which according to Alfred Lord Tennyson's Ulysses, "moves forever as I move."[9] We see Jung's own sense of yonder becoming his beyond in the opening of *The Red Book*, when he encounters the Red One in the initial "Images of Erring." He describes his predicament poetically, not clinically, though we might translate one into the other.

> The door of the mysterium has closed behind me. I feel that my will is paralyzed and that the spirit of the depths possesses me. I know nothing about a way. I can therefore neither want this nor that, since nothing indicates to me whether I want this or that. I wait, without knowing what I am waiting for. But already in the following night....
>
> I find that I am standing on the highest tower of a castle. The air tells me so: I am far back in time. My gaze wanders widely over solitary countryside, a combination of field and forests. I am wearing a green garment. A horn hangs from my shoulder. I am the tower guard. I look out into the distance. I see a red point out there. It comes nearer....[10]

Such attending is crucial, though painful. It is entirely different from Godot's waiting endlessly for the one who never comes. Jung records productive waiting for the coming of the Red One, who arrives and speaks: "I greet you, man on the high tower. I saw you from afar, looking and waiting. Your waiting has called me." As often happens in fairytales, active waiting constellates Self figures.

Direction to a place that is simultaneously unknown and familiar becomes recognizable Self-country that ego consciousness begins to reconnoiter. That we are culturally captivated by this phenomenon is illuminated by the film *ET*, a popular film predicated on an achingly nostalgic relationship between *here* and *there*, the insistent pull back to a lost homeland. Hill comments,

> The long finger of the strange little spaceman pointing upwards to his lost home awakens thoughts of a final dwelling place beyond the horizon of human understanding, a home not of this world.[11]

These are psychic gestalts familiar in everyday praxis, for which we might introduce technical vocabulary in our professional discourse, but our native adverbials and prepositions charged with directional energies are soul's more natural vernacular.

Bunyan's Christian, Jung's pilgrim soul, and typical analysands set off. We cannot know what enlargement looks like, for we know not what Self requires of each individual. We must follow the lead of the unconscious, always one step behind the dream, even when all direction seems lost in the hither-and-thither, the this-and-that of the individual path. The traditional concept of progress is alien to analytical therapy. Most of us share Hillman's suspicion of myths of progress. Bunyan used the word "progress" in his contemporary sense of an official visitation, such as a monarch might make through his kingdom, or a bishop around his diocese. That sense we might allow, as we traverse our own inner kingdoms, where even the hills and streams before and around us in dream landscapes are us.

The Latin verb *gradior* meant to take steps, moving in gradations. It is from this verb that pro-gress and re-gress derive. In Jungian psychology, some directional sense of movement is essential, but it is not usually straightforward, or does not seem so to Ego's struggle for orientation. Though hither and thither may feel distracting, we are always subject to the tension between movement forward and movement backward, clinical pro-gression or re-gression. Re-gression is often a response to a call inward, "as an adaptation to the conditions of the inner world, spring[ing] from the vital need to satisfy the demands of individuation."[12] Therapy must support seemingly backward movement when it calls ego consciousness inward, sometimes even back-to primitive instinctual underpinnings of psyche. In the encounter with Nicodemus, Christ gives regression a symbolic meaning. We are born again, born psychologically as individuals. We can know this backward movement through the working mantra *reculer pour mieux sauter*. An analysand's dream stated specifically, "I must go back to the last turning to find the way." We must often back-track in order to find genuine ways forward, collecting rejected or unconscious bits of ourselves, retrieving past selves lost or selves as yet unknown. We cannot know what positive progress looks like. We do not even know whether or not it is desirable, even as we formulate it as movement onward or forward, always seeming *toward* something better or higher. Though with the psalmist we pray that we might be led on a level path, we know that there needs to be *abaissement* and re-gression in the service of enlargement or re-vitalization of spirit.

Despite his explicitly heaven-driven theology, Bunyan does understand erring, as do the mystics. He wrote his allegory from the literal *here* of a prison cell, entering that "Slough of Despond" just as John of the Cross must enter his soul's dark night. In our daily psychological experience, meandering along the horizontal plane, backward and forward, is constant, frustrating, and necessary. Such is the natural flow of rivers. Analysands are keen to make progress—"*How am I doing?*" is often their plea. Or, "I don't seem to be getting *anywhere.*" They demand of themselves that they should go-up-directly-thereto and yet they cannot manage that, nor may they, if the demands of individuation are authentically to be met. We assume a trajectory from (supposedly) known to unknown, the unknown becoming the new whither. We might localize this condition, symbolized as place, an as yet unidentifiable *somewhere*. But it is more than anything else an extension of consciousness, which is theoretically "capable of indefinite extension."[13] However (Jung's habitual and stubborn *however*), empirically, "*it* always finds its limit when it comes up against the unknown." How much of the unknown is any of us able to approach, and with how much can we cope? This unknown *it* constantly incites us.

Jung found the *before-after* energies of individuation in the profuse symbols of alchemy, which perform a conversion of value, lead into gold. But as myth and fairytale warn, gold might itself be problematical and is usually found *in stercore* (in the shit). What compels, in this symbolic model, is the uncannily exact likeness of the stations of transmutation to the stages of individuation as observed in human experience. The underlying story of transformation of some kind of lower to some kind of higher resonates in the soul. At a popular and trivial level, waiting room magazines manifest the desperate need to engage with this archetypal dimension, and the thorough misunderstanding of it. Advertisements and confessions confront us with images of transmutation: wrinkles to the smoothness of baby's bottom, from hippo to sylph. All at bargain prices. But—a big *but*—this commercialized state is in fact the treasure hard to find and hard to attain. It is a labor of consciousness. Behind the popular make-over fantasy for person, garden, or home lies an ineluctable archetypal drive, exploited so irresponsibly by advertising, which seduces us against our better judgment and the reality principle. At its root is the archetypal structure of transformative possibility built into the psychic system, performed so vividly in Hopkins's "The Leaden Echo and the Golden Echo." These are for Hopkins spiritual, theological resonances, moods, prophecies, whispers, hopes of emergent life, liveliness, and transformation in the face of fears of despairing finality. But whatever philosophic orbit we are caught up in, with or without consciousness and reflection, in the end none of us can help being a human being, a "self-infinitizing creature who is impelled to search for the beyond."[14] We have experienced this as our glory and as our misery. Herbert expresses this tension, assisted by his usual complex metrical patterning. It is the same torture that many analysands discover on their way. Feeling "Broken in pieces all asunder," the poet identifies himself as,

> Once a poore creature, now a wonder,
>   A wonder tortur'd in the space
>   Betwixt this world and that of grace.[15]

Much of our work transpires here, in this particular *betwixt*. But it is also the betwixt and the between of transitional space, offering the same psycho-spiritual possibilities. We might define transitional space as a way of being *here and there*, it is play space within which we can experiment with relationship, that space between self and other, even self and God. When Bell speaks of the compulsive striving of "self-infinitizing" beings as "the insistence of the imperiousness of the self" he is defining and valuing "self" very differently from Jung. But we might take the imperiousness he observes as the supreme soul-urge for realization, what we prize so keenly in Jung's reflections on the child archetype, with its "ineluctable urge to self-realization."

   In the Jungian lexicon, "Self" is the most profound and enigmatic term. It is for him the center to which all else is radial or circumferential. The ultimate etymology of the word *self* is uncertain (possibly related to reflexive *se/sich*) but its uses are in-tensive and ex-tensive, taking up many inches of column space in the multivolume *Oxford English Dictionary*, even before branching out further into all the proclivities of its prefixing activity, self-evident, self-serving, self-supporting, and so on…and on. It is a monosyllabic kaleidoscope, with the working-class energy of Coltman's *but* and the aristocratic influence and cultural breadth of his cherubim.[16] It has the humility to abut onto any word, fore and aft, pointing to or emphasizing a specific identity or functioning reflexively. Then "self" can spread its feathers like a peacock's tail, and Jung provokes it to do so. All the yearning of the human soul, the magnetic field of the Jungian Self, is (or behaves *like*) an autonomous complex. It seems to be or to provide the driving power at the root of the ego-complex, animating our longing. For we must ask, "What is it aiming *at/for*?" *What for* might be framed as the most vital on-site working particle of Jung's teleology. When writing of the various approaches to such imperious aims from within psyche, and about various techniques to keep the mind concentrated on these in meditation, Jung says of a yoga text and of the Ignatian exercises that "both methods, Eastern and Western, try to reach the goal by a direct path."[17] But such a direct route would be impossible for ego consciousness to fathom and would no doubt, quite sensibly, attempt to avoid darkness, bewilderment, and diversion. Fairytales and most human biography show us the necessity of circuitous minor roads. *La route se roule.*

In analytical work, interpretation must follow sinuous paths as ampli-fication and circum-ambulation. We cannot explain a dream or a symbol. To ex-plain (*ex-planare*) is to smooth out, to remove the bumps and the roughness. Similarly, ex-plicate (*ex-plicare*) is to get rid of the creases, to make plain. In this regard, I do not tire of quoting Phillips's wise warning not to make our analytical work into a "science of the sensible passions, as though the aim of psychoanalysis was to make people more intelligible to themselves rather than to realize how strange they are."[18] An explanatory compulsion has governed our habits of inter-pretation, which instead of closing the gap between, can create wider gaps through mis-understanding and mis-alliance with the dreamer's unconscious. We can do no better than the symbol itself, being more than content only to point *toward* (not *at*) possible meanings and emerging intimations. Our interpretive work must be subject to a receptive *perhaps*.

I began the chapter oddly but not unfittingly with a literary episode, affirming Freud's rather gracious remark about surrendering priority to the insight and instinct of the artist. The psychologist is always a few steps behind. Having surrendered to the primacy of story, we must also tell soul's story in our other language, our professional *langue*. From our native form-words, our whence and whither, our yonder and betwixt, to which we will constantly need to return (because we cannot escape them), I also play with our Jungian psychoanalytic glossaries, our hyper-glossaries, perhaps even our glossolalias. This is the *langue* of our discourse but not of talk at the soul face. Nor is it the speech of the unconscious. However, it does exercise its own alchemical power, as well as carrying a seductive aura of *gravitas*. Browsing the index of a volume of Jung demonstrates quickly that we could scarcely function without vital Greek or Latin affixes. At one glance we meet ab-reaction, an-amnesis, auto-nomy, circum-ambulation, com-pensation, com-plex, con-sciousness, con-iunctio, dia-lectic, onto-geny, tele-ology, endo-geny, endo-gamy, exo-gamy, in-flation, sub-liminality, re-pression, sym-biosis, syn-chronicity.[19] These formations help to make our discourse appear respectably scientific, more universally trans-lateable and possible. Valuable, necessary, and professional language, but not the soul's natal home, a perspective offered by Heaney in "Bone Dreams," where he speaks of pushing "back through dictions…the ivied latins / of churchmen / to the scop's twang."[20] (The intonation of the poet!). In the midst of such speech, he delights that

> In the coffered
> riches of grammar
> and declensions
> I found *bān-hūs*

Ban-hus, that house of bone that is our implacable reality. Heaney finds his home in native language as he demonstrates our common bi-lingualisms, moving between the soul's playground and the mind's more technical workshop. These languages need not be in conflict. My own experience of psychological discourse is rather like that of Heaney in this poem, and it is my experience of reading Jung himself. There is a *langue* that is appropriately technical, but we need to keep it for professional communication; it does not belong in the *temenos* of therapeutic encounter.

The meta-language of Jungian psychoanalysis must be learned, and learned afresh even when, especially when, the words are already in our working vocabulary in other contexts, or even in other psychological discourses. *Vide* Freud's "libido" or Kohut's "self." It is instructive to see how large is the number of Jungian index entries for words employing the *trans-* prefix: trans-ference, trans-cendence, trans-cendent function, trans-formation, trans-gression, trans-lation, trans-mutation, trans-personal, trans-figuration, trans-substantiation. We might add trans-itional, for though the concept of transitional phenomena was not used explicitly by Jung in those exact terms, he would have resonated with its current usage. For the moment, I will survey certain technical terms that articulate central concerns and theories of Jungian psychoanalysis, without which professional dialogue would be less possible. Most of these words were already in use but they are re-loaded or re-imagined to serve analytical psychology.

As prefix-preposition, *trans-* occupies almost as many pages of an English as a Latin dictionary. This is probably true of it as near-universal compound in all Western languages. Implicit in it is directional movement. It does not just shift things, keep them in motion, but it changes their place, it directs passage *over, across, beyond*, to an-other place. *Not here, but there*. We have looked already at many of the *from-to* constructions ubiquitous in daily talk; but *trans-* serves large therapeutic and psychic purposes very specifically. It underlies the whole course of the individuation compulsion, which pursues transformation toward wholeness rather than cure.

We might situate the stirrings of transformation rather grandly, as Jung often does, in the influence and action of numinous dream figures, such as Self, anima/us, wise old man, etc., but he admits that

> the process itself involved another class of archetypes which one could call the archetypes of transformation. They are not personalities, but are typical situations, places, ways and means, that symbolize the kind of transformation in question.[21]

I am particularly interested in his "ways and means" as indicators and carriers of energy in this process. It is exceedingly hard to find a synonym for "process" in this sense, for it is not entirely neutral; some sense of increment or progression sticks to it from its origin. Once the Latin *pro-* was added to the verb *cedere*, it indicated movement forward. It no longer implied just motion, being on the move. Psyche's journey may well need to go backward; in fact it usually does entail re-gression. It was true for Psyche herself in her dealings with Eros and we follow in her steps. Perhaps "course" of transformation is less value-driven than the few potential substitutes for the word. Course might deliver us from the myth of progress, which is usually associated with relief of symptoms. In analysis this can be mis-leading. The actual getting-there is often the transformation, enabling us to be on the road in a different way. Transformation lies less in the *there* than in the getting, which rarely feels like progress. The state reached after years of analysis can feel nothing like the improved, cured person fantasied at the outset. The terrible truth is that the transformed self often seems simply to be an accepted version of the personal self that had been rejected. I become more keenly who I am, my unique self.

It is our daily experience that meaning and meaning-ful-ness can in and of itself be a means to, and assurance of, transformation. Loss of meaning is the harshest suffering and it is commonly what drives people to therapy, especially therapies with potential spiritual bias. To ask, *What is this for?*—a *whither* question—introduces the teleological aspect that is the hallmark of Jung's work. We might consider this in relation to *where from* questions typical of a reductive approach. Jung did value the re-ductive method in the early stages of an analysis, when the foundation complexes needed to be made conscious; and he did not expunge such reductive work altogether, either in actively confronting complexes or in dream play. But he gave greater value to pro-spective approaches, compelled by the *yonder* of the complex or the dream symbol. This pro-spection did not necessarily infer a sense of incremental betterment associated with pro-gression. His most typical inter-rogative purpose lay in where symptoms lead us, rather than where they come from. The symptom was to be circumambulated like a symbol.

In relation to our deepest suffering, once meaning is found, even practical daily experience can feel transformed. At the end of analysis, one woman exclaimed, "*Nothing* was *ever* the same *again*." She could return to the dream that had thrown new light on her pain. Then she reflected, "I cannot say *how* or *why* this is so." This is working language at the soul face, not professional lexis. Such frequent utterances enact the rhetoric of the archetype of transformation, and in *praxis* work in its energy field. In our re-current and per-vasive Latin compounding, the force of *trans* exerts its own alchemical force.

Still working within the paradigm of trans-formation, I offer an unsystematic list of some of the movements we commonly encounter in analysis, positing a *before-and-after* structure. In each case, however, the categories are ambivalent and the nature of the process will always depend on the point from which the process began. A typical analysis might involve such shifts as from literal to metaphoric/symbolic; from (seeming) madness to a deeper sanity, or even the reverse; from isolation to community, or the opposite, from collective to individual; from past to present to future; from forgetting to remembering; from refusal to acceptance; from voice-less-ness to speech; from inflation or diminishment to authentic value; from false self to true. Underlying all such paradigms is some stirring from unconsciousness to consciousness. There are no guarantees and it is not always obvious how these shifts are accomplished, and all energy dynamics are subject to a mysterious *deo concedente* and the operation of grace. Here I posit grace as an energy, an *operatio*, not exclusively as a theological category. Sometimes, psyche plumbs its deepest grammar in the transformation of our paradigms of yearning, lodged in *if only*, impelled to paradigms of possibility expressed through *what if?* It is hard to find a technical language that could really accomplish so much, the transformation of *if only* into the wish-provoking possibility of *what if…?*

Symbols act as catalysts to change, functioning as generators and transformers of psychic energy, converting libido from a "lower" to a "higher" form.[22] Such conversion is accomplished through intensities of suggestion and feeling, carrying "conviction and at the same time express[ing] the content of that conviction. It is able to do this because of the numen, the specific energy stored up in the archetype." Sometimes the con-version is so great that it transposes into its opposite through a psychic strategy of *enantiodromia*, a word pressed into service by Jung to express a particular relationship of opposites in which one transmutes into the other. *Enantiodromia* "happens" when the intensity of a thought, a feeling, a position, is so great and so absolute, having moved so far into its own excess, that it turns into its own polar extreme. This functions as a psychic means of creating equilibrium, restoring balance. Jung was clearly influenced by Heraclitus's elementary observations about cold things becoming warm, wet things becoming dry, and myriads of similar properties and processes inherent in nature. Such a model has explanatory value and provides insight even into our large mysteries, approximating the principle of equilibrium in the natural world. In his paper "The Phenomenology of the Spirit in Fairy Tales," Jung comments pithily that

> the grand plan on which the unconscious life of the psyche is constructed is so inaccessible to our understanding that we can never know what evil may not be necessary in order to produce good by enantiodromia, and what good may very possibly lead to evil.[23]

This becomes a central energic model for psychic functioning. When any particular tendency dominates consciousness, an increasingly potent counter-position unconsciously develops that finally erupts into consciousness. When this is revealed through dream or active imagination, equilibrium can be restored or achieved. If it is ignored or resisted, a disastrous explosion can result, a severe neurosis that disables ego functioning. All the affixes that work through our professional language carry these archetypal orientations, *for* or *against*. The very word *enantiodromia* demonstrates this: *enantios* (against, Latin *adversus*) followed by *dromos*, running, racing as in a hippodrome where horses competed. The horse, in dreams and mythic material, typically might symbolize the source of exertion, an energy quotient.

Such turning of one thing *into* its opposite is more radical, more dangerous even, than re-conciling opposites, one goal of therapy. The energy of *counter* is strong. It might be that the sudden near simultaneity of psychic conditions, such as bipolar configurations, can be subject to this same mechanism. An analysand observed this shift in herself most keenly, registering a "leaping from one extreme to the other," opposite to opposite, manic to depressive or vice versa, with no incremental movement along a modal axis. It was dis-orientingly instant. This is most intense in what has been diagnosed as a pathological condition, but a movement along that modal axis is common to all human experience. Mood is a fascinating and neglected phenomenon, usually dismissed and/or diminished by a common judgment, "it's *just* a mood," deemed inferior to feeling, perhaps because it is more inchoate, less subject to identifiable cause. English "mood" was once a prouder word; mind, heart, even fierce courage are recorded attributions, but being circumscribed by time, moods were therefore deemed unstable. Mood is determined on a vertical scale, up or down. Clearly people have different ranges of mood and feeling, generally innate, but often supporting unconscious motivations. An older analysand narrated his very colorful and diverse life history. For years he had been living exhaustingly between highs and lows, desperately needing to be noticed, experienced as extra-ordinary, as he slid from peaks to pits, commanding admiration during "ups" and parallel sympathy during painful "downs." Using the word "swings" to describe these vacillations in mood is apt. In one session, he reported a dream of climbing over a stile and "ambling-*across*" a large plain. I remember his wry smile as he confessed, "I seem to have achieved flatness." *Along* and *across* felt oddly affirming, he could embrace what he had feared as ordinariness, which released him from an anxious vertical axis; he could begin to find stimulation and satisfaction in the horizontal modal axis that could serve genuine relationship. To relate is to be side by side, not in a constant relational missionary position. In fact his truth was remarkable.

Another analysand medicated for mood change came into a session saying that she was feeling *up*, explaining that this was because she was handling highs and lows better. A musician, she used the metaphor of modulating between minor and major keys. She reported keeping what she called a meta-log, which enabled her to see some things more easily now, since she was feeling more distance between *me-as-I-am-now and me-as-I-used-to-be*. We will keep encountering this *then-and-now*. With an early history of convent education, the same dreamer was always on the lookout for her own inflation, to rebuke and prick it. She reported that she dreamed of being given a stately home by a Lord, and in mock panic she confessed: "I woke up *depressed*, thinking I must be really *in-flated*!" This was a typical self-destructive put-down. For such psychic action, we often press affixes into service.

To aim for constancy of attitude and demeanor is to conform to St. Paul's ideal of accommodating reality, "I have learned in whatsoever state I am, therewith to be content." Herbert is psychologically more astute. Described as the poet of the English inner weather, he logged his moods from exaltation to despair in a disarmingly lyrical manner. Feeling his vulnerability to polar moods, he cries out,

> These are thy wonders, Lord of power,
> Killing and quickning, bringing down to hell
> And up to heaven in an houre;[24]

Such to-ing and fro-ing of mood from one end of the affective spectrum to the other is something we need not pathologize, unless it is seriously and unbearably disabling. As soon as we allude to two ends, we posit a tension between. Jung's theories about psychic functioning depend on this tension, the phenomenology of the source of tension, necessarily *between* (Jung's *zwischen*). *Between* inevitably provokes *trans*, *across*, and *inter*. Consider all the new uses of these pronouns in computer technology and contemporary life. At every level of domestic and political experience, life is now inevitably *inter*-national. Our *inter*-national and *inter*-regional societies are typical. We are always inviting relationship and cooperation, never having lived *inter* so pervasively. Most potently perhaps, we live through the Inter-net, webbing all connections, all inter-alia experience, making us permanently, virtually, connected. Psyche must adjust to this extreme way of inhabiting trans-phenomena.

Another preposition that has come into current usage more exactingly is Greek *meta* (μετα): after, beyond, with, even adjacent to. *Meta* can even stand alone now in English, as when we speak of "going meta." But we use it nowadays mainly to denote a concept that is an abstraction of another concept; in linguistics, meta-language is a kind of language for describing another language. For Freud, meta-psychology was coined to cover the general theory of psychoanalysis at its most abstract level. This is echoed by Dale Mathers in relation to supervision. He suggests that "supervision is a 'meta narrative'; outside the intimate space between therapist and patient, within which a patient's story is narrated." Later he points out that "supervisors make up fresh narratives, construct images from images of the therapist's view of the patient."[25] Psyche can embrace such meta-connections as simultaneous narratives; the creation of one does not displace or invalidate the other(s). All contribute to the attempt at whole-ness. How very impossible it is to dis-criminate Ego's ideal of truth, whole truth, and nothing but *the* truth! What a difference is achieved by the addition of that insignificant but lethal definite article, *the*, as in "the truth," exclusive preserve of the convinced.

In more traditional usage, certainly in Jung, *meta* carries the valency of *beyond*. He insisted that his concerns were not meta-physical.[26] In our psychology, we meet this active prefix most frequently in meta-phor, meta-noia, and meta-morphosis. Meta-noia, at its most basic, signifies change of mind, denoting profound spiritual experience as in healing religious conversion (*meta* + nous), a transformative turning-*around*. In English coinages, *meta* might seem quite esoteric, but in native Greek contexts, it was a comfortably domestic crossing over. Turning around or going across is the language used within praxis, where the prepositions carry soul's direction.

Metaphor is one of the most indispensable terms in our discourse. It is hard to imagine any Jungian project that does not use, does not need to use, the word. *Meta-pherein* (μετα-φερεῖν) is to transfer, carry over. Again, it is active, the carrying over, bearing across fields of reference and meaning. Most of our work happens in the realm of analogy, the realm of the *as though* and *is like*. Emphasis is always on the image that follows, asserted by these innocent lexical atoms. This kind of analogical functioning is necessary, given Jung's insistence on the fact that the archetypes are in themselves ir-representable. In our work, as in our theory, we are always trying to represent them nevertheless, through likening. We come closest to apprehending them through the emergence of symbols, energy generators that enliven and manifest in psychic life. But they are always, they must needs be, inadequate fully to communicate the essence of the archetype. This is the universal, age-old dilemma formulated for centuries by theorists and wrestled with by poets. It is a form of the inexpressibility *topos*, the feeling that "there are no words," a common distress in deep therapy.[27] In such situations, various rhetorical devices become essential, as accessible to theologian, philosopher, or psychologist as to poet. I cannot say what it is, so I will say what it is like. Eliot's poetry experiences this urgently because of the kind of inner experience he is trying to voice. In "East Coker," he attempts it in the violent language of London besieged by war.

> And so each venture
> Is a new beginning, a raid on the inarticulate,
> With shabby equipment always deteriorating
> In the general mess of imprecision of feeling…[28]

Representation is always approximate and as Eliot concludes, "For us, there is only the trying. The rest is not our business." Analysts would do well to heed this insight. For the symbol, potent though it may be, charged with libido and numinosity though it is, is still, paradoxically, only approximate. Our symbols, true symbols (as opposed to what he devalues in contrast as mere signs), however potent, are never more than "intuitive idea[s] that cannot yet be formulated, in any other or better way." The symbol attempts to express something for which no verbal concept yet exists. (*Something* and *yet* are crucial here, carrying significant Jungian freight.)[29] Even our most sacred and treasured symbols can only ever be expressed as "the best possible description or formulation of a relatively unknown fact."[30] Even the pregnant language coming from the pen of Goethe or Shakespeare must always "mean more than [it says]."[31] However, the symbol can accomplish the task of reconciling opposites, of pointing to the unsayable, more than any other medium. This brings into play other crucial compounds, exploiting the energies of the prepositional prefixes that we are exploring.

Symbol itself derives from the Greek *sym-balein* (συμ-βαλεῖν), to put or to throw together, making one *out-of* two. The opposite mechanism is to throw apart, a dia-bolical action (δια-βαλεῖν) making two *out-of* one. Anthony Stevens adds a useful third to this opposition with his *amphi-ballein* (ἀμφι-βαλεῖν), a more complex and wide-ranging action, gathering perhaps many more than two, throwing as it were a net to capture dispersed possibilities, on both or all sides, that is, *all around*. Symbol making can ransack the whole psychic repertoire of images, conscious and unconscious. However polar the ideas, however opposed the feelings, the symbol, the "amphibol," collects and contracts into one image, be it visual, aural, conceptual, or energic. It creates associations and relationships among phenomena where none were thought to exist.

Between assumes and asserts relationality. This is the essence of trans-ference, an inter-personal mechanism by which *there* becomes *here*. *Trans* energy is at work, crossing between, reaching across, carrying past imagos and presences into new and contemporary contexts. Pronouns come into play. In this place, this here, this relationship, there is an *I* and a *you*, a functioning *us*, communicating in and through the inter-active field *between us*. But there is also an inter-ference of a her/him, an-other, who disturbs and commingles with *us*. *Someone else* whom I am identifying as you. Transference is involved in all relationships, but especially in the analytical dyad where, transferred from *him/her out there*, there is a new dynamic in a *you here*. In analysis, this con-fusion is welcomed and explored. And not only is there a personal here and there transfer, but there is also a temporal dynamic, accomplished through the paradigm of *once*, a *then-and-there*, transferred to *here-and-now*. Once upon a time becomes all time in this immediate now. In the end, transference is about you and me, us, here and now, caught in the field of a new and potentially fruitful *whence and whither*. Post-Jungian writers such as Giegerich elaborate this further, arguing that

> The soul is mediation, a "between." But this between (e.g. of transference) is not to be imagined as a (one-way or two-way) arrow, a rope strung between analyst and patient, but rather as something which surrounds and encompasses, as well as transcends, both persons. Even if it is also in each of us and as such has an empirical aspect, it is nevertheless in actuality "a single all-embracing soul" (*CW* 10 §175, modif.), the "very soul of humanity" (*CW* 16 §65), mirroring Being as such, a world of cosmic dimensions (*CW* 10 §366).[32]

Yet another trans-dimension, significantly transcendent. Earlier, Giegerich talked about soul as the "third person in the room," and he imagines both analytical partners focusing their attention on this objective third presence, the Third, a therapeutically constellated *it*, most difficult of all pronominal forms to define, yet most valuable, like empty hands waiting to be filled.

I would that I had sufficient time, space, and ability to search these things through in other languages, especially Jung's native tongue. Unlike the fundamentally Germanic English language, German did not have its Norman occupation, its Norman transformation, so does not have the same "contamination" from Romance sources. But the native compounds offer similar explorations to those I pursue in English. It would be perhaps even more provocative, evocative, to play with Jung's *Über-tragung* and *gegen-über-tragung*. *Über* can be used as preposition or adverb, signifying transfer or transition, an across that in some contexts might also suggest *above*. These are all sources and exponents of psychic energy. As we ponder our psychological discourse, we can observe a constant foundation of directive energies at work, prepositional, adverbial, and conjunctive, supporting a whence-whither movement of psyche (*woher/wohin*), always establishing tension between the two points. The classical model of the arrow flight must always function so. Intro-jection and pro-jection, the latter provoking counter-projections. *Counter*, against, related to *contra*, in its multiple uses as pre-fix, always indicating oppositional direction (*gegen*). In the case of counter-transference, it can also imply flowing back whence it came. About counter-transference Jung uses words like force and compulsion, creating an "unconscious identity with the object."[33] But as Giegerich insists, there is even greater complexity than this simple two-way trajectory might imply.

All of my exploration to this point has explicitly or implicitly drawn on Jung's energic model of psychic functioning, serving an all-encompassing and multivalent dynamic of thence and thither, and the temporal tensions of individuation's then-now-then, creating a new then. One might even play with the initiating *dia*-gnosis and the intuitions of *pro*-gnosis as psychotherapy's whence and whither. I have been illustrating the synergic and contrapuntal syntactical flow of our speech and writing about our theory and praxis as Jungian therapists. What is clear is that at every level of our work and reflection, we are drawing on this, Jung's distinguishing core theory, shifting it from a causal-mechanistic view of the psyche to an energic-finalistic view. Jung's conviction that psychic function is governed by tension would seem to be strangely corroborated by the adversative conjunctions that express some oppositional energies even while conjoining. We have already encountered Dostoevsky's pregnant adversative *mais*. We will encounter psyche's *nevertheless* in later chapters, but here we might reflect on the massive *nevertheless* of the Christian West, Christ's words spoken in Gethsemane: "Father, let this cup pass from me. Nevertheless, your will not mine be done." Though I have colluded with the judgment that form-words are simple, I am also very aware that simplicity is a complex concept. And such formations as *never-the-less* are patently extensive, offering both contradiction and possibility. We use nevertheless when we want to contain opposing positions; it is frequently used in speculative thinking, in theology, and in philosophy. And other simple conjunctives can contain massive significance. One might look at the compound *instead of* in relation to atonement theology. If one belonged to that theological persuasion, one might use the technical term sub-stitution, but the soul's home, in that experience of the cross, would be *instead-of* me.

The semantic field of *nevertheless* is large and ambivalent, and its energy is operating habitually in the relating of Ego and Self, captured in Jung's own perception that "human nature has an invincible dread of becoming more conscious of it. What nevertheless drives us to it is the Self."[34] Such a profound construction is needed by psyche to catch her essentially paradoxical performance. Like *and yet* and *not only-but also*, the conjunctive allows the soul's both/and, releasing us from Ego's *either/or* and the extreme misconduct of the *nothing-but*. Jung harangues the latter soul-offending construction that has no stretch, and yet he often falls into it. I have taken particular (petty) delight in marking the times Jung falls into his own proscription of *nothing-but*. His use of it is usually rhetorical, expressing conviction emphatically with a sense of an adversary ready to pounce. But in the end, this illicit usage is nothing but a nothing but, alien to psyche's com-prehensive nature. There is a specially precious fall into this phrase in the *Red Book*, where in desperation of soul, in his attempt to ward off the challenges of his soul guides, he dismisses them as "nothing but symbols." Perhaps he was aware of Alice's similarly defensive logical maneuver in her Wonderland when the imperious Red Queen was finally annihilated by Alice's dismissal, "You're nothing but a pack of cards!" Jung uses the same strategy of ironic rejection in his imitation of the skeptical reception of dream theory in his day, the charge that they are "only"—i.e., nothing but—dreams!

Psyche is particularly active in adamant negatives such as *never*, as in positive assertions such as *ever*, intensifiers such as *really/very*, restrictive intensifiers such as *almost/nearly*. Jung is usually alert to grammatical signaling of psyche's activity. For example, his sympathy for religion's *simul* and *sicut*. In comments on the liturgy of the Mass, he speaks of the "famous *sicut*," which he says, "always introduces an analogy by means of which a change is to be produced."[35] The grammatical particle, *sicut*, itself participates in the transformation.

His psychology is always sited in the midst of a potent *otherwise*, always sensitive to both of the sides no coin can be without. Like Jung, Steiner is also and always friend to the *and yet*, *nevertheless*, and *otherwise*, speaking of alternity, saying otherwise. Steiner asks, "When did falsity begin, when did man grasp the power of speech to alternate on reality.…it may have been the most important in the history of the species—from the stimulus-and-response confines of truth to the freedom of fiction."[36] Jung's sense that every truth, every theory, is a fantasy is perhaps related.

All such phenomena arise out of currents and crosscurrents flowing together and apart in our speech as in psyche's unspoken libidinal circuits. Syntax effects the movement of an utterance and determines its relations. No matter where one turns in the *Collected Works*, on well near every page, there is some reference to these operations and mechanisms. The major source of tension is crucially that between consciousness and unconsciousness, which has often become conflictual or competitive, as between Ego and Self, that primary psychic axis of classical analytical theory. Jung associates this dynamic with any other energic system that depends on the tension of opposites, maximum stress inevitably felt in the middle between two opposing ends. He locates the unity of the psyche, where two opposites exist in connection, by likening it to "the living unity of the waterfall…in the dynamic connection between above and below."[37] Friction is also created by systems other than direct counteraction. Jung claims that psyche's evaluating system is also a source of influence and power, "namely the *system of psychological values*. Values are quantitative estimates of energy."[38] Some values are constant, but many differ from culture to culture as well as from individual to individual, and will perhaps be most strongly, if unconsciously, directed by psychic function and attitude. Values will vary according to typology, the word *attitude* actually positioning energy in terms of its own bias. Bias is an interesting energic phenomenon whose individuating force is always *toward*. The *from-to* task in typological work is to nurture the bias *toward* wholeness, *away-from* the one-sidedness that comes so much more easily to us as individual pre-judice. This prejudice supplies the lure of the *either/or* predisposition that slants us to one side or the other.

Typological bias is crucial to our functioning, to our turning, the *intro*-vert with-drawing energy from the outer object; the extra-vert's turning is positively *toward* the outer, and *away-from* inner contents. Jung comments that the "introverted thinking type…will follow his ideas, like the extravert, but in the reverse direction: inwards and not outwards. Intensity is his aim, not extensity."[39] Such bias is crucial to survival, for each feels endangered, the extravert by the inner world and the introvert by the outer. The creation of balance in place of one-sided orientation is accomplished by re-con-ciling the two opposite energies, in-tensity and ex-tensity.

This pondering the obvious has ranged widely, randomly, over the labor of lexical particles that we rely on but usually overlook. Many more remain but will be visited at play, especially in dreams. Clearly, pronominal forms constitute a *sine qua non* of both our formal discourse and our talk, our conversation and our narratives in face-to-face sessions with analysands. But I would like to prepare for that discussion here by reference to a foundational statement by James, a psychological thinker whose fore-sight is quite remarkable. In his inventive chapter on "The Stream of Consciousness," which proved so useful for twentieth-century reflections on art and literature, as well as psychology, James doubted the existence of a "mere thought 'which is nobody's thought,'" adding that "the only states of consciousness that we naturally deal with are found in personal consciousness, minds, selves, concrete particular 'I's and you's." He concluded therefore that "the universal conscious fact is not 'feelings and thoughts exist,' but 'I think' and 'I feel.'"[40] This is true in the unconscious dramas of our many and varied dream Egos as it is of our discriminating ego consciousness.

This chapter intends to illustrate the dynamic aspect of psyche, manifest in her rhetoric, in the individuation process itself, and in the ways we have found or designed to formulate and talk *about* it. In all of the multivalenced particles of language so far discussed, energy of thought is constantly e-mitted, trans-mitted, asserted, and renewed in our professional use, in our particular lexicon. We have the full panoply of our full-words charged with meanings new and old, those other parts of speech, substantial, bursting nouns and adjectives and verbs. But the language at the soul face makes different demands in the idiolect of the dream, its recording and its relating. The same syntactic flux is at work, accomplished more vividly. This is not only my experience, it is implicit in Giegerich's comment about consciousness having "irrevocably dropped from the level of semantics to the deeper level of syntactical form."[41] He is of course using this linguistic image metaphorically, distinguishing between semantic content (truths about the gods) and what he calls the syntax of consciousness. But his remark makes sense linguistically and rhetorically, too. Rowland seems moved by the same force. She remarks that "rhetorical emphasis on self as the most potent energy-image in the psyche is accompanied by a further warning against conceptual language as truth-bearer."[42]

How vital is our own consciousness of language as we use it and as we read it, as we hear it and as we respond to it. But hyper-consciousness can be dangerous, too. We can fall into the trap of Randolph Quirk's centipede if we have too much awareness in the process of articulation. (I must put my 34th foot in front of my 67th foot, and my 82nd foot in front of my 2nd foot, etc.…the poor creature would spend its life on its back.) I do not want to give priority to either of our languages, that of our professional discourse or that of our analytical conversation. At the heart of the Jungian enterprise is the inter-rogation of, and challenge to, absolute hierarchies of value. The old paradigm of heaven and earth is much threatened or rendered obsolete in its original form anyway. But that project, begun with the Enlightenment has not been, cannot be, completely successful, working against deep unconscious structures. Pope's dictum, "presume not God to scan," and the corollary that "the proper study of mankind is man," is a typical, perhaps patriarchal, either/or prescription.[43] Jung exhorts us to scan both, reflecting psyche's totality. Nevertheless, in our analytical work as in our supervisory dialogue where we seek to converse in a language that registers the idiom of experience (Richard Wainwright's apt phrase), we do need to "suspend Husserl's rule of the vertical, ordering in hierarchies, for the rule of the horizontal, where things are allowed equal weight. To witness is to be a natural phenomenologist. You surrender to complexity."[44] Such surrender is harder to achieve in conceptual exposition than in the wit and symbolic prodigality of unconscious drama. To that we now surrender. This kind of awareness of functioning on two lexical levels is captured by the poet who clearly felt our dilemma as he reflected on his own political formation: "I moved like a double agent between big concepts."[45]

CHAPTER FOUR

Whither of the Dream:
Foretaste of the Terminus

"foretaste of the terminus."[1]
—William James, *Psychology: A Briefer Course*

We live in the energy field of such a foretaste. This chapter explores the fore-taste of the pleromatic psyche through dreams.[2] We played with the yonder of Hopkins and Bunyan, a yonder responding to anxious ego questioning, *where*? Bunyan's allegorical *yonder* was literally spatial, with a destination, the gates of heaven, finally reached but not passed through. Dream yonders are more typically transformative images, intimations of full Self-hood, full becoming that is not yet perceptible. The word *yonder* may not be used, but it is implicit in much recorded dream experience.

We cannot admit others to join the dream drama as it happens; we can only share it via verbal or visual iconic representation. However, psyche plays with this reality. I remember my young daughter's impatience at my seeming ignorance of her dream experience as she related it, "You know mummy, you were there!" So at the outset I acknowledge that the dream reports I explore are generally conscious speech acts re-living unconscious drama, reported "via the screen of language." Intriguingly, Steiner adds, "if animals dream, as they manifestly do, such 'dreams' are generated and experienced outside any linguistic matrix." He argues further that

> The phenomenology of dreaming is imbedded in the evolution and structures of language. A theory of dreams is also a linguistic, or, at the very least, a poetics. No account of any human dream, whether provided by the dreamer himself, by a secondary source or by the dream-interpreter, is linguistically innocent or value-free. The account of the dream, which is the sum total of our evidence, will be subject to the exactly the same constraints and historical determinants in respect of style, narrative convention, idiom, syntax, connotation, as any other speech-act in the relevant language, historical epoch and milieu. Dreams were not less splintered at Babel than were the tongues of men.[3]

This offers us another way to conceive of the collective unconscious in which all our dreaming en-volves us. While accepting the primacy of the image, we work with verbal equivalence. It is also true that the dream can be reported through the language of the image, in painting, sculpture, or the sand tray, but that is a different language needing different translation.

I begin with innocent dreams typically brought to the session without much anticipated excitement. One dreamer brought much day residue to the beholding of his dream and at first it seemed like a bit of mere psychic hygiene, until we entered it, or rather, let it draw us into it. The energics of the dream took over.

> I'm at some sort of conference… I am meeting the people… we're greeting each other, as at the beginning… they are off to the first session. I haven't yet found my room… haven't got one arranged… I'm not aware of luggage. They go off. I notice in the near distance a hotel that I will try to book into. On the way, I'm caught up exploring another place. It's like going into a large pub… I'm looking around wondering whether they have accommodation. I see food… golden chips… they look very good. I go towards the exit but I can't get-out. I'm in the wrong place. I have to get out in order to go in the right way, find the main entrance to the hotel I'd come across on the way. I have an image of the name… Welsh or Gaelic… The dream ends with me going into the entrance of the other place, not back-to my colleagues.

We became oddly engaged with the phenomenon, spacial and psychological, of "in the near distance," where "another place" was situated. This began to feel subversively central to the dream's purpose. It is a location, not far off, but not close by, so very ordinary, and yet, somehow remarkable. In the dream there is continual going-off, going-in, going-toward, getting-out, going-into rather than going-back; experience of looking-around and wondering-whether. This directional bustle became more urgent than the substantive items of conference, colleagues, luggage, hotel, pub, and food, which would of course need subsequent amplification. But at first, the exits and entrances, the right way, the other or another way, coming-across while on-the-way, all these involved us as they did the dream's ego. Once one becomes sensitized to this kind of compulsion from the unconscious, finding the dream ego's place and trajectories in familiar and strange sites, dreams come alive in unexpected ways. We reflected that "in the near distance" is reachable, but it is a subjective location, visible but probably further away than it seems. It is not just outside the hotel or just down the street, but simultaneously near and far. It was where the dreamer needed to be. He was being led to the plate of golden chips (French fries), which the dreamer associated with a comment by *Shirley Valentine* in the film of that title. She claimed that if her husband had attended the Last Supper, he would have asked for chips! A strange and circuitous path to this seemingly mundane food, nevertheless associated with the sacred last supper of Christ. The dreamer was a priest, whose daily traffic was with the sacred. It was as though his relationship to the divine needed to be revitalized by association with a plate of chips, potential vehicle for the holy in their golden warmth, as numinous as communion bread. There is often such a circuitous path to the transformative symbol, which is never just *there*, standing alone like a museum piece, labeled and on exhibition for reflecting consciousness; it is not reached by a go-up-directly-thereto trajectory. This way-to is often accomplished by means of syntax and verbal relationships within the reporting sentences. The way seemed to have more significance, at this point, than the goal. The way to the unremarkable treasure felt labyrinthine, reminiscent of another dream about finding the way out-of a church onto a city high street that was also tortuous.

> *Nearly there* had similar force in an African woman's ascent dream.

> I am going to places where other people walk up easily. I join them. As I am about to get to the top, I realize that the wood is weak. Even though they say, "come," I know it's not strong enough to support my weight. I am nearly there… and I see a gap. Others get over easily but I cannot. I can't cross over the gap.

About to get to, even though, and crossing-*over* claimed attention. The gap felt like a postcolonial empty space. So near and yet so far. A tantalizing psychic place needing gradual negotiation. The gap was perhaps the goal of the dream, a fact that needed to be brought to consciousness. At this point, it is still hindered by a syntactic *even though*.

In dreams the wit of the unconscious is often at play. We might consider dream metaphor as the work of wit, which the Renaissance mind saw as human sharing of the divine creativity as in the *concetti* of artist and poet. The art of the conceit was to compel acceptance of likeness, while conceding unlikeness, thereby begetting the strangely familiar. This was the response of one dreamer to a vivid dream.

> I am in London, near Tavistock Square, surrounded by tall Georgian houses. I go into one of them and start to climb up steep winding stairs. They go up and up and I go on climbing. At last, I come to an attic room and I go in. On a table in the middle is a huge round fish bowl with fish swimming around in it, multicolored fish, most beautiful. They swim round and round. I realize that they are swimming around in white wine. It is luminous and sparkling. I am silent. I can almost hear the movement of the fish swimming round and round.

The directional movement was remembered kinesthetically, the effort of climbing *up and up, on and on*, and then fish going *round and round*. Initially this registered more keenly than the colorful fish in wine in Bloomsbury, only much later associated with Virginia Woolf's "room of one's own." The syntactic energy was centri-fugal, winding the dreamer *into* the mystery stored in her own soul's attic. She remembered childhood homes with attics for storage of the dust-covered detritus of the past. But here were living fish and wine. First the kinetic syntax had to conduct her to the numinous fish, in a round bowl of wine, which might have distracted us from the energic charge of verbal direction that she felt in her body. Fish and wine later offered many vital associations.

The innocent ordinariness of such language causes it to be overlooked. It offers humble service to the higher and amazing things psyche makes conscious. Prosaic language "helps keep the lid on things."[4] But it also invites peering under that same lid. The innocent dream texture can be misleading in a dream in which affixes are at work.

> I dream that I return a supermarket trolley, in the middle of the night. When I get it there, I'm accused of damaging it and told to pay for its repair. I say that I'll pay, but I will never go back.

Subsequent discussion foregrounded the affix *super* in the accusatory super-intendent, an innovative authority figure who evoked Kafkaesque guilt feelings in the dreamer. The witty ditty "Tesco ergo sum" came to the dreamer's mind, reminding him of shopping in super-size stores, where he sees people caught in a "sort of shared regret that they have to be there."[5] This *there* where it is necessary for people to be had tremendous power. It touched the compassion of a man who lives a vivid inner life that enables him to find satisfaction and purpose in the mundane, as illuminated by such a dream. So "regret that they have to be there" becomes potential soul territory. Such domestic dreams show how, in common language, psyche accomplishes her task, here also to make conscious such apparently harmless but tyrannical inner super-figures who police the super-stores, "dressed in a little brief authority."

Much attention has been given to the core symbols in a well-known dream of Jung that merits careful exploration for its function-words. Observe all the prepositions, adverbs, conjunctions at work—and I mean, at work—in Jung's vivid experience of a descent into unconscious depths.

> I was in this meadow. Suddenly I discovered a dark, rectangular stone-lined hole in the ground. I had never seen it before. I ran forward curiously and peered down into it. Then I saw a stone stairway leading down. Hesitantly and fearfully, I descended. At the bottom was a doorway with a round arch, closed off by a green curtain. It was a big, heavy curtain of worked stuff like

> brocade and it looked very sumptuous. Curious to see what might be hidden behind, I pushed it aside. I saw before me in the dim light a rectangular chamber about thirty feet long. The ceiling was arched and of hewn stone. The floor was laid with flagstones and in the centre a red carpet ran from the entrance to a low platform. On this platform stood a wonderfully rich golden throne. I am not certain but perhaps a red cushion lay on the seat. It was a magnificent throne, a real king's throne in a fairy tale. Something was standing on it which I thought at first was a tree trunk twelve to fifteen feet high and about one and a half to two feet thick. It was a huge thing, reaching almost to the ceiling. But it was of a curious composition: it was made of skin and naked flesh, and on top there was something like a rounded head with no face and no hair. On the very top of the head was a single eye, gazing motionlessly upward.
>
> It was fairly light in the room, although there were no windows and no apparent source of light. Above the head, however, was an aura of brightness. The thing did not move, yet I had the feeling that it might at any moment crawl off the throne like a worm and creep toward me. I was paralyzed with terror. At that moment, I heard from outside and above me my mother's voice. She called out, "Yes, just look at him. That is the man eater!"[6]

Jung is reported to have commented, "This dream haunted me for years....I could never make out whether my mother meant, '*That* is the man-eater,' or 'That is the *man-eater*'" (italics Jung's). It is clearly significant that the open-ended deictic *that* precedes the identified symbolic object, preserving its identity *until* it could be known. There is much information in these innocent particles, generating energy, relating symbolic things, *even somethings*, kinetically. The upward gaze of the phallic something resonated in another man's dream:

> It's as if I'm watching a scene from a drama being played out in front of me. Some sort of detective (Sherlock Holmes?) is walking across a room... He's holding a snake, as if he is about to eat it, as though he's picked it up as food. He is about to bite into it, as if it was an imitation snake. But it's real, it bites him. For some reason I know it's a dangerous, venomous snake, a puff-adder. After biting, it sort of fades-away. I don't actually see it leave, but I know it's a puff-adder. The front enlarges, near the head.[7]

The dreamer reflected on the psychology of inflation and of being drawn to the dangerous. But more importantly, in amplification of the snake's position, *upright*, the dreamer related its charge to John Beebe's discussion of "uprightness" in his work on integrity:

> For Jung, the masculine was a position taken towards the unconscious, a standpoint (and to this image we can associate the bodily image of "uprightness" that we have seen is an archetypal, and I think masculine, representation of integrity).[8]

The same man dreamed: "*just very* vivid image of a snake, *like* a python, long, coming *along* a branch *towards me*." This snake is not upright like the last, but approached him horizontally, coming *towards* him *along* a branch. His analysis had begun with a disturbing image of a coiling mass of writhing, undifferentiated anacondas. Now the energic texture of the fantasy had become as vital as the central dream creature, the snake, with all its symbolic substance. Even as Jung's mysterious *something* is introduced, perhaps it already carried numen into his dream. Something is enigmatically loaded, even before being filled out and more fully identified. In both dreams, the uprightness is crucial, but so was the movement along and toward, its purpose achieved. Jung speaks of the *something* enthroned ithyphallically (ἰθύς), the Greek suggesting purposeful movement upward.[9]

A woman dreamed starkly and enigmatically: "Must stay right there, standing upright." No more. She had a sense that she was being instructed by a reliably authoritative masculine voice. She was also very aware that *there* surprised her; she would have expected right *here*. Upright both had a sense of being ready to move but also of uprightness in a biblical sense. Clearly, she had to move from her present station, though where to was still to be revealed. *Here* and *there* were powerfully charged with new bearings.

Observing the facts of a dream is only part of our task. The syntactic context of a recording sentence is also important. The upward trajectory of the snake felt as significant as the snake symbol in and of itself. It is easier to translate substantive snake than directional bearing. The approach I am intuiting is complementary to Jung's response to dream report: "I therefore proceed in the same way as I would in deciphering a difficult text."[10] Dream as strange text leads us to translation as much as inter-pretation. In this act of carrying one experience across into the experience of another medium, we might be mindful of the forty-nine levels of meaning that the Talmud finds in a revealed text, to keep us mindful of how much our translations miss![11] We are forever translating one experience into the language of another, echoing the pertinent question, "How does this world of translation work, what men have shouted or whispered to each other across the bewildering freedom of the rubble of Babel?"[12] One might say that each dream needs its own language and idiolect, just as Shakespeare endows each character with his/her own particular speech. Whereas in our usual pre-occupation with the dream, interpretive emphasis falls on objects, actions, qualities, here we are considering relationships between them. The symbol, as transformer of energy, can inhere in syntax and interior syntactic motion. Such is the energy generated in the prepositional movements of this dream:

> A king or queen needed some kind of healing. I was telling them the story of the white seal. We were all looking-out of a window of a wooden hut by a lake. Birds were flying above. I told her that if she followed the flight of the three geese she would get to where the white seal was. Owls were landing on an island in the lake, one of them looking-at me as he landed. I watched in awe as the owl, a white seal, and another creature moved-towards us. I reached-out to touch the seal. It moved-back a little and I respected that.

Reaching-out and subsequent moving-back reflected a necessary attitude to unconscious experience that was drawing near, for which the waking ego was being prepared. These indicators of psychic development were as vital as the gathering of creatures: geese, owl, and seal.

So far we have been drawn to what we might call positional energies. In the next dream, the adverbial image of *sideways* is crucial. It is a transformational dream energized by affixes met already in reflections on analytical discourse. The dream was amplified through reference to Christ's trans-figuration. It often seems that the charging of grammatical form-words is especially important in big dreams.

> I am walking through a wood. There is a clearing ahead. I see a person in the middle of the clearing, changed or transformed in some way, as if subsumed into a radiance. I reflect on what I

have seen and try to understand it. I'm on the edge of it. I realize that it is Carl Jung… as though he is involved in something religious, standing sideways to me, as if he's looking at something. Then subsumed into radiance… brightness… sunshine.

Jung, as inner figure, is transformed by radiance, in the middle of a clearing, *just ahead* of the dreamer who comes-across him having walked *through* a wood. The event is couched in tentative language, *in some way, as if, as though*. This layering of vision is vital to the experience. It allows it to be so, and not to be so, simultaneously. Such visionary reticence is also captured in the position *sideways*. Jung is not encountered full frontal. And it is not Jung who is the source of translucence; rather, he is reflecting *something*, a religious something, that he is looking-at. He is *sub*-sumed-*into* its radiant energy field. The dreamer was mindful of the assertion that "God is a con-suming fire." He was struck by his dream substitution of *sub* for *con*. As this dreamer was becoming more deeply engaged with Jungian thought, he was increasingly aware of the potency of the archetypes, the force of the constellating Self and the dangers of inflation.

One might explore other recorded big dreams from this perspective, like the seminal meta-morphosis dream (from caterpillar pupa to butterfly) that Stein explores, that is dominated by a temporal grammar:

> I am walking along a road, feeling depressed. Suddenly I stumble on a gravestone and look down to see my own name on it. At first I am shocked, but then strangely relieved. I find myself trying to get the corpse out of the coffin but realize that I am the corpse. It is becoming more and more difficult to hold myself together because there is nothing left to keep the body together anymore.
>
> I go through the bottom of the coffin and enter a long dark tunnel. I continue until I come to a small, very low door. I knock. An extremely old man appears and says: "So you have finally come." (I notice he is carrying a staff with two snakes entwined around it, facing one another.) Quietly but purposefully he brings out yards and yards of Egyptian linen and wraps me from head to foot in it, so I look like a mummy. Then he hangs me upside down from one of many hooks on the low ceiling and says, "You must be patient, it's going to take a long time."

> Inside the cocoon it's dark and I can't see anything that is happening. At first my bones hold together, but later I feel them coming apart. Then everything turns liquid. I know that the old man has put one snake in at the top and one at the bottom, and they are moving from top to bottom, and back and forth from side to side, making figure eights.
>
> Meanwhile, I see the old man sitting at a window, looking out on the seasons as they pass. I see winter come and go; then spring, summer, fall and winter again. Many seasons go by. In the room there is nothing but me in this cocoon with the snakes, the old man, and the window open to the seasons.
>
> Finally the old man unwraps the cocoon. There is a wet butterfly. I ask, "Is it very big or is it small?"
>
> "Both," he answers. "Now we must go to the sun room to dry you out."
>
> We go to a large room with a big circle cut out of the top. I lie on the circle of light under this to dry out, while the old man watches over the process. He tells me that I am not to think of the past or the future but "just be there and be still."
>
> Finally he leads me to the door and says, "When you leave you can go in all four directions, but you are to live in the middle."
>
> Now the butterfly flies up into the air. Then it descends to the earth and comes down on a dirt road. Gradually it takes on the head and body of a woman, and the butterfly is absorbed, and I can feel it inside my chest.[13]

Spatial, behavioral, modal, and temporal directives guide the *from-to* narrative, accomplished through phrasal verbs, adverbs, and qualifiers. I can imagine time spent pondering the spare words, *just be there*, and *there is nothing but me*, as indescribable psychophysical experience of death-like incubation. There is a necessary time frame for transformation: the prick of *suddenly*, initiates the first stage, *at first*, *until* completed in the first *finally*; *then*, *then*, lead to another *at first* in a second stage of dis-solution, with a disturbing *but later* and *then* seeing it through. The next stage begins with a waiting *meanwhile*, *then*, and *again*, ending with the *finally* of the last part of the process, moving from past to a present *now*. With a liberating *finally*, *when*, there is a releasing upward *now* and a descending *then*, a coming-*down-into* the dreamer's embodied life. So many other aspects of this necessary narrative deserve reflection, especially the repeated *but* that speaks soul's vernacular, marking difficulties that might resist transformation. The dream ends saying *yes* to resurrection as in Walcott's poetic proclamation (see page 19, above).

Near the beginning of an analysis that immediately delved into hitherto uncharted territory, a man's initial dream invited him to engage with his inner life symbolically. The force of the dream's positional energy did not fully emerge until the man painted the dream, an activity wholly new to him. He had never taken dreams seriously before.

> I kissed a woman. She had long black hair. I was helping her over a gate or fence. I have no recollection of her face. Just the hair. I kissed the nape of her neck.

The ensuing drawing demonstrated that the woman was experienced *from behind*, a crucial position, not yet allowing her face to be visible. (Fig. 12) Eventually, she would turn round and they could engage face to face. But he had to stay with the fact that at this point, contact was from *behind*, hair and neck. The act of drawing enthralled him, clarifying particular details about "the woman and I" standing on *this*

Figure 12. Dream gate and meadow.

side of a fence. He looked-over, then climbed-over. But his drawing not only showed a gate, but a gate with a latch that he could easily have opened. Then in another drawing, the field became wide moorland, extending his vision to a horizon. (Fig. 13) There was suddenly a rich palette of color. "I wanted to use every color in the box," he said. The movement was toward the beyond. Across the field

Figure 13. Dream horizon.

in the first painting (Fig. 12) there is a village, a source of life and community, which also drew his gaze. This was a world he knew, but without an intimacy for which he yearned, though with no sense of what it really was for which he longed. But they were now over the fence, legitimately through the gate and heading into ample, liberating space, felt to be beyond anything hitherto imagined. The new path was zigzag, shadow on one side but moving into what he described as "some sort of sunrise." It was his *yonder* and there was freedom and exaltation in this engaging with creative space, lost to his life since boyhood.

This positioning in front of or behind was especially charged for a young woman who dreamed of a spider. She had no fear of spiders, but *suddenly* the creature turned-round and she saw that it was a scorpion, not a domestic spider. The dream made her realize her own well-established attitude, a fixed expectation that anything that looks good, once encountered, is bound to turn destructive. "You can't trust what looks good from the front... the sting in the tail is always threatening, once it turns-around," she said, realizing keenly the implication of this for the way she approached life. Another woman dreamed of being "sucked-*down-into*" mud *up-to* her head, and wondering *when-or-whether* she would be pulled out by "a man I know to be *behind me.*" His position *behind* had great significance, a newly emerging ally, not prescribing or leading the way, but following, perhaps protectively.

The movement of the gate and field dream is horizontal, moving *away from and into* new territory. Another analysand experienced many dreams that charged the vertical plane. He was an intelligent man, extremely well read and immersed in psychological and philosophical literature. He had left university after the first year and became a gardener. He was specially engaged with early twentieth-century writers associated with Oxford and Bloomsbury. In one dream, he was gardening for Vita Sackville West, *Vita* (life) having special intent.

> I am tidying-up a sunken garden for an aristocratic lady. She is sitting over-looking the garden as I work. I have a hoe and stretch-out with it as I lie-on the ground above the sunken garden to hook out a piece of recalcitrant weed, just below where she is sitting.
>
> Then a grey-haired man who seems to be very skilful and wise watches me playing on a snooker table. I am struggling. He rolls three eggs across the table and indicates smilingly that this will transform the way I play.

The interplay of levels is fascinating. Lawns are on different levels, beds are raised, he looks down from above, she sits above him. He associated a well-kept lawn with a billiard table, a common mantra for gardeners. Other dreams situated him on the top deck of buses, looking-down on rather idealized intellectual figures from his reading life. The mechanism echoed Jung's exploration of the compensatory function of dreams, which corrected one-sided conscious attitudes. The psychological task of this man was to find his true level, his true self. His sense of this had been damaged in early experience of parents and teachers, which had prevented him from fulfilling considerable intellectual potential. This he must acknowledge and live. The perfect, smooth flatness of the dream table felt oddly numinous, now the surface for rolling live eggs, not dead balls.

Many dreams negotiate between upper and lower planes, via elevators, stairs, and escalators. More dramatically, planes, helicopters, even spaceships, move between a lower *here* and a higher *there*. Sometimes it is crucial to descend rather than ascend, whichever directional pull or thrust is required. We do have to guard against automatic and cliché responses, as for example, that the snake's upward bias "represents" spiritualization of phallic energy. The pull between upper and lower might indeed register movement between spirit and instinct. Vertical movement in dreams is always important, signaling a change of psychic level and perspective. The compensatory function is equally active in this way in people who are living too spiritually or cerebrally, losing contact with earth; or too stuck in soil and needing to look up. A profoundly religious woman who lived ascetically finally dreamed that as she was "going down two small steps, I notice some large ripe blackberries at my feet. I stoop down and pick one and eat it." Going down to ripe fruit felt especially nurturing, and this was the first time the food in her dreams had actually been consumed. The dream felt deeply grounding.

A highly speculative man's dream indicates a directional correction by the unconscious. The dreamer found himself enclosed in an elevator that rises steeply, then stops, then goes sideways. It shifts from vertical to horizontal, as though on a train. The dreamer felt that he couldn't (perhaps shouldn't) rise above an outer situation. He felt constant tension between sexual libido and spiritual aspiration. The dream presents no solution, though it illuminated the dilemma. At that stage, what dominated his consciousness was his desire for punishment and overcoming, rather than integration, of what he judged to be his lower self.

Another man was compelled through his dreams to engage more specifically with a native religious self. He had rejected Christianity and lived his spiritual life increasingly through Buddhist practice. But as Jung warned, one cannot sever oneself from roots without loss, and so some kind of accommodation of his early Christian beginnings had to be made before he could forsake them, if that was to be his way. He dreamed:

> I go to a church. It seems a little like the church where I was baptized. I am going in as a lady and a couple of children come-out. She is locking the door, but she gives me the key to allow me access. She is very trusting of me and I feel pleased. I go-in and it is quite dark. I feel some fear and put some of the lights on. There are other lights but I decide not to put them on as it may be too bright if I do. There is a small congregation there and a male priest, but it is as if they are in another dimension and don't see me. X is there in the church, sitting down. I am behind her. She has recently been diagnosed with some illness… I hug her from behind and feel very worried about what I'll do without her.

Apart from the directional energies of the dream movement into the church interior, the adjusting of light is most precise. It is only *quite* dark, and he puts on only *some* of the lights, measuring the amount of light needed, not *too* bright. He feels as though he is in *another* dimension from priest and congregation, though the dream posits that it is they who are in that *other* realm. In this old and sacred space, he comes to a deeper appreciation of the dimension of human love, hugging his wife *from behind*. This position can sometimes carry shadow aspect, but it might also indicate that the spiritual aspect of the feminine cannot yet be approached directly. Such adverbials and qualifiers are illuminating. Gentle and discriminating light was needed, not solar brightness or clarity.

Our development often requires a new relationship between the life of spirit and instinct, living in tension *between* the two poles. The polar pull was represented in one dream through the experience of pole dancing, endowed with a whole new spiritual dimension and taken out of the more sordid environment in which the dreamer usually conceived of it, the sex club.

> I was in a workshop. Large building and large grounds. I was with another woman. She was a little neurotic/anxious. She was running a class but we had forgotten something and we needed to go-back to the town to get it before the class began. There was also a man there. I remembered I had left my brown handbag in a different room, so I ran down the corridor to get it. In that room there was a woman running the next class. Something like dance and yoga. As she placed a pole in the center

of the room she told me how she began this work. I was really looking-forward to the class. Then the first woman arrived and she told me that the class in this room was really good. I said, "I know, I'm really looking-forward to it." She said I couldn't go to it because we needed to go to get something first. My alarm woke me but I had the words "Sacred Polarity Dance" in my head. It was the name of the workshop.

There is fascinating detail in the comings and goings of the way to the Sacred Polarity Dance, hindered by the demands of *something* (not yet specified) and *but*. The connection of body and spirit was a vital element in this woman's work, graphically represented in this movement toward redeeming the pole and the flesh. Many other things in the dream obviously needed amplification, but the dream's grammar also needs reflection.

Jung imagines the relationship between spirit and instinct with helpful clarity in his model of the spectrum *from* the *infra*-red *toward* the *ultra*-violet. One can observe the unconscious playing the axis, many dreams enacting the push and pull between spirit, culture, and nature, negotiating between instinctual and spiritual poles. This tension *between* was captured humorously in a question that climaxed a long dream action: "Do crocodiles eat lettuce?" The lettuce in outer reality grew in flowerpots on the dreamer's urban patio.

I went-out with a tribe of people, primitive, Inca-type people to take eggs from giant crocodiles. We took some, a lot of them, and were canoeing-back with them. Everyone was laughing. We had outwitted the crocodiles. There was an animal in front of us, pulling the canoe. I noticed a wound on its back. I mentioned it, saying that it could leave a trail of blood for the crocs to follow. But someone said there was no problem. We got back to a large Inca-type settlement, a platform and then a huge wall rising-up from the water, with iron steps anchored to the wall. As we landed, someone shouted, "They're coming." I'm on top, looking-down-into an enclosed area below, like a meeting place or a temple. At the bottom, a huge crocodile has been carved-into the stone, like a god, like an effigy for worship. I notice this from the top. Because someone had shouted, people were running, frightened, climbing-up the ladder. A man passed up a medallion, made of bone, carved-

> out. When I (but I am also another woman) looked-at it, she cried-out and dropped it, shouting, "It's an omen that the crocs will get us!" Next I am back at the bottom of the wall. Lookouts are checking for crocs. Someone near me pulls-up a lettuce out of the ground and someone said they shouldn't do that as the crocs could smell the disturbed earth and come-back. I had both of my dogs with me and I was concerned because they wanted to relieve themselves… but I am worried about the crocs if I let the dogs go free.

The dog was experienced as median creature, nature tamed, somewhere between the lettuce and the crocs. The dreamer had lived an urban life but was feeling urges such as learning to fish. Something primitive and ancient summoned her from her own depths. With some apprehension, she followed where it led, enabled by energy generated through transformative symbols. Her dream offered integration of culture and a fresh experience of nature, which Jung described as "psychic processes [that] seem to be balances of energy flowing between spirit and instinct."[14] He observes that in the psyche, as in the above dream,

> multiplicity and inner division are opposed by an integrative unity whose power is as great as that of the instincts. Together they form a pair of opposites necessary for self-regulation often spoken of as nature and spirit.[15]

This integrative unity moves between levels, river and castle ramparts, embracing the twenty-first-century city dweller in rhythmic unity with ancient Inca canoers, gliding to safety. But the earth has been disturbed and the crocs are feared to be waiting. The dream was not yet over.

The *from-to* energy of metamorphosis is often encountered in dream shaping, where whence and whither are posited in provocative ways. The fact that the last dreamer, merely in parenthesis, has become another woman, goes almost unnoticed. But the changing of one dream figure into another, a special parameter of *from-to*, the force field of *meta*, is always significant. Speaking of the dynamism between physical and spiritual passion, Jung suggests that it can take "the merest touch to convert the one into the other."[16] Such shape shifting is often accomplished suddenly. Typical dream experiences of turning-*into* include conversions from age to youth (and vice versa), a man becoming a pregnant woman, a child becoming a kitten. Our contemporary response to these transmutations is surely affected by the current film and fiction culture of "morphing," a con-version even every child of television-watching age now takes for granted. The ancients were much closer than we have been, until our recent fiction, to the commerce between animal and human forms. Balance between our two natures is essential to psychological well-being. An African woman dreamed,

> There is a big snake… People are around it but can't kill it. I said, "Give me a stick, I'll hit it." I did hit it, but it became something else, something became a human being. Half of it. The other half was still a snake. It was trying to bite me. It was only interested in biting my hands. I struggled to hide them. It just kept coming-after me.

The only half-trans-formed aspect is important, reinforcing the value of both/and, transcending the restrictive ego preference for either/or. Consider the half-human, half-animal creatures of myth. These liminal creations have vital functions in negotiating our connection to the animal within. They are manifestly held between two natures. They can embody untamed nature, but they can also be wise teachers, such as Chiron. They are hybrids: man and horse (centaur), man and bull (minotaur), human and fish (mermaid). In the dream just quoted, the snake remains partly human, perhaps affirming this woman's need to remain embedded in her own African context and identity, even though she needed to integrate certain Western ways.

Swans often participate in dream transformations, reinforced for many by Hans Christian Andersen's "ugly duckling" fantasy, where changing-into is in fact a maturation or evolution of what *is-already* present, rather than a radical change in essence. A movement therapist's dream brought to consciousness a relationship between body and spirit evolving through dance. Within the dream, she feels dull when leading a session where she was moving like a cat. She awakes in the dream and goes to a

> communal courtyard with seating area. It is walled. In the courtyard, there were some amazing giant swans, electric blue color, all glowing. I thought I'd never seen anything so beautiful. I wanted to ride on one. I got-on its back and it took-off into

the air. Then it turned-into my dog. I worried in case I was too
heavy… he won't be able to carry me. But he could.

She used the word hybrid in amplifying the dream, reminded of a Harry Potter creature. The dream hybrid brought her into contact with her own en-spirited body, which she could get-on-to and take-off. The flight motion itself was as transforming as the puzzling swan-dog that could bear her weight. Midgely comments on our hybrid nature.

> We ought not to feel that dignity threatened by our continuity with the animal world. And I have compared the threat people feel here with the threat Christian thinking detected in the Copernican Revolution and in the theory of evolution.[17]

The traditional Christian attitude to the flesh as beast made us fear degeneration into our lower nature. But in dreams our unconscious wholeness of vision tries to seal our dignity and promote at-one-ness with the animal self we carry within.

A very different kind of *from-to* energy operates through contemporary re-cycling imagery, using what is already there to re-organize whence and whither. An old whence is remade by adaptation, by re-cycling, not by destruction and reconstitution or by wholly original creation *ex nihilo*. An emerging contemporary dream site is the re-cycling station, which can throw light on the process of integration. This is sometimes how we formulate the treatment of projections and shadow phenomena, re-cycling invaluable psychic energy needed elsewhere in the psychic economy. Psyche wastes nothing.

I return to dreams already explored to engage with the mystery of *some*. One might speak of "The Somehow of the Dream," which can expand into play with all the *some* compounds, a closed-category lexis that renders powerful service to the mechanisms of the dream: the modalities of somehow, pronoun identities of somebody or someone, locations of somewhere, substantives of something.[18] In all these formations, *any-* can be substituted, creating *anywhere, anybody, anyhow, anything*, with their extensive and expansive possibilities. There is in these form-words a very special energy, a tincture of paradoxically recognizable unknown-ness.

Jung's dream, quoted earlier, became a founding dream for his personal psychology and for analytical psychology itself. The curiosity behind his discovering things not seen before makes him peer-down-into the unknown, penetrating the hitherto closed-off. He pushes-aside the curtain *it* was hidden-behind to disclose the climactic *something*, thereby formulating his own definition of the symbol as presentation of the not yet known. This *something* is never actually identified, nor could it be, except insofar as it was eventually classified by mother as potential "man-eater." Such a functional identity is somehow subordinate to its naming as *that*, following his mother's affirmative recognition of *yes, that* is to be looked-at. *Something* gets near to the crucial, indefinable known thing that is yet to be revealed, not yet accessible to consciousness, though already active in the psyche. It was Jung's special gift and particular experience to formulate such psychic phenomena for us. To that he dedicated his work. It is not only in dreams that we have this need for a word to hold a familiar and yet unknown reality. In speaking of the anima/us, Stein also feels this necessity:

> The anima/us, strictly speaking, is a scientific hypothesis about "something" that exists but cannot be observed directly, like an unknown star whose position and size are known only from measurements of gravitational pulls in its vicinity.[19]

It is typical in such explorations that the portmanteau *something* is followed by an image that gives sensible sense of what is being reached after. So Stein's *something* becomes *like* a star. This enables us not to see or know what it is, but what it does, what it makes us feel or imagine.

In contemporary experiences of a dream's critical *something*, curiosity and tension are aroused in both dreamer and analyst. This undefined but palpable *something* must by no means be explained; the worst service we could pay the dream is to define it prematurely, a mistake it is easy to make, especially in light of our indomitable curiosity. There was such an urgent *something* in a recent dreamer's unconscious fantasy, lodged in a familiar but terrifying *there*:

> I go into my study. There are three things in there. My maternal grandfather is sitting there. As soon as I go in I am aware of fear. Aware of two other things with him. I am too frightened to look.

WHITHER OF THE DREAM

> One seat is occupied by a dead dog. Terror. I back out, unable to go in. Sense of menace. Something on the chair.

This sense of undefined menace reminded him of other dreams. His report was halting and bare, though he was extremely articulate. Later, he dreamed again:

> This time it is in a dining room, emptyish. I am going in the doorway, sensing something bad emanating from the empty grate. Tiny beads of light, pea-sized and orange, spheres of light on bare floorboards, part of something in the fireplace.

He spoke of the pure menace of the *something* in the empty grate. He said it was a bare room, but *somehow* he knew it was a dining room. The nonspecific *something* remained more terrifying than any identifiably nameable form. This something was inchoate terror, something left over from childhood, never integrated and demanding attention at a time of outer crisis. Very slowly the work of disclosing the essence of this terror might be accomplished, but like Jung's *something*, it could not be exposed to consciousness before the fullness of its own time, when there is enough ego strength and insight and compassion to meet it. In this case, the compassion (for himself) was most crucial.

The as yet unidentified dream-something can provoke positive awe as well as menace, as in the dream already quoted in which the dreamer sees Jung looking at "something religious" in a forest clearing. More personally, a man, a scientist in midlife, dreamed:

> Einstein beckons to me. There's something he wants me to do for him. I am thrilled, but then I realize that I have already arranged to do something else, for myself. I must do that instead.

There are two distinct *somethings* here. Something for Einstein and something for the dreamer's own self. The nature of the dreamer's creative project is not yet disclosed, but as it came closer to consciousness, it took more specific shape. What has to be trusted and obeyed in dream time is the fact that something is waiting to be brought to consciousness in some creative way, something related in value to Einstein's something that must become *something else*. Another dreamer recalled

> a sense of moving-through huge buildings, on the ground floor. I come to the end. I reach a door. I open it and stand looking-out-on a vast landscape. I have a sense of reaching the end of something and experiencing something more, a wholly new vista.

She could not say what she had reached the end of, though some sense of it resonated in conscious awareness. She had what she later described as an "itching sense of something new." "Somewhere" is not used here, but the sense of a new *somewhere* is potent, and it is more than merely some place she could not name, but somewhere recognizable and yet mysterious. A new there, discernible from here, but only known on arrival.

Death itself can be a psychic locus, a dream's *there*, Hamlet's "undiscovered country" from which no one can return. But other somewheres might also be accessible to a sick soul. A dreamer reported:

> I am in a nursing home, on a balcony. People are flying out of the window to fly somewhere for healing. Someone comes-back and was standing-at the door. I had my hands out. They had theirs out. There was a rainbow color around the hands.

This is rich soul country, affirmed by the rainbow that brought associations to the end of destructive flooding. The dreamer was not sure that everyone returned from this healing place, but a crucial someone does come. Here *somewhere* collocates with a soul's *someone*, and the ambience of *somehow* that hovers over the drama. The layering of indistinctness is provocative. Someone is often allied to something and somewhere:

> I am standing in a queue waiting to receive communion. The priest holds-up the host to each person, who then receives it. My turn comes. I am at the end of the queue. But there is no host left for me. The priest searches in the chalice, consternation on his face. But there is nothing. I am devastated. I've missed it. He then starts to search beneath his vestments, in his jacket and inner pockets. Nothing. I turn-away and weep.
>
> Then I'm being given something by someone. It could be a priest, perhaps the same one. He has most carefully put something together that had been smashed.

Before a numinously new *something* could be experienced, hands have to be emptied and there has to be an experience of *nothing*. An amazing space is opened up for the restoration and repair of *something* of even greater value, once known, but smashed. The concerned priest, who could not find a host to supply soul's need, then becomes an emergent figure, an unknown *someone* who can provide this new *something* that is felt to have even more efficacy than the missed host. *Someone* is not yet close enough to consciousness to be personified, and *somewhere* not yet close enough to the threshold to be distinguished. But it is on the radar.

We have considered the significance, sometimes the terrifying energy, of the *something* of the dream, but equally significant and equally terrifying can be its opposite, *nothing*. This can echo through inner emptiness as pronoun, subject, or object of numberless verbal actions. Imagine such scenarios as these that I now imagine, composites of actual dream experiences. The analysand brings a vivid and unnerving recurring dream in which s/he searches desperately through various strange or familiar buildings or cities. But they are all empty and in some indefinable way feel both fearful and inviting. The frantic searching for something ends in the same way. The lysis is refusal of lysis. Waking in a sweat, *yet once more*, they find nothing. This ardent *nothing* is as palpable and numinous as any *something* and is sometimes qualified further as "absolutely nothing." There is always nothing, never anything. The copulative verb "to be" carries weight. This *nothing* has real substance; it really exists in the psyche. There *is* nothing. It is qualitatively different from *not anything*. Sometimes very slowly, sometimes swiftly, the problem of *nothing* can materialize in awareness that the actual problem is that they do not know what they are looking for. This *what* suddenly hits them; that's the first thing to search for. And so often, as Jung knew early in his long life, that particular *what* is me. I look for myself. The nihilistic sense of this nothing opposes the sometimes pleromatic sense of something.

Two books on autism, by a woman who suffered from that condition and who has now become a therapist, load these words poignantly. The first, *Nobody Nowhere*, is answered by *Somebody Somewhere*.[20] Her task was to find, to get to somebody somewhere from that desolate condition of being *nobody nowhere*. This is also often the process of people not diagnosed as autistic, but who have an abandoned, autistic part-self equally in need of integration and relationship.

Collocated with a *here-there*, *from-to* structure in the next dream, a new and helping someone appears from unconscious depths, leading the dreamer from imprisonment to freedom.

> I am in a town. It's dark. A bunch of men dressed in army uniform are capturing people and putting them in prison in the town. Along with someone else, I am captured. We're looking for a way-out. This person then said, "There are no walls… no fence. What are we doing staying here?" I am concerned in case they come-after us. This same person said, "No they won't, because they are not aware of who is here… they're not keeping track… they're just rounding people up." So we just went… we just walked-away.

As this helping *someone* becomes more liminal even within the dream action, s/he becomes *this same* person, a highly specific use of the deictic article. This person is not that one. In terms of the dream's narrative structure, there is a liberating climax in the final *no* that charges the final *so*, a conclusion of such obviousness that it throws into absurd relief the ignorance of the complex that has kept the dreamer captive. "*No*, they won't…" "*So we just* went." *Just* is by no means redundant. What was it like, just to go. *Just* breaks through the complex with amazing ease. It reminds me of a dream from long ago of an analysand caught in very bourgeois Swiss rigor, who also suddenly realized that the door of her prison had never actually been locked. She sat in it for years, never trying the door of her jail until after a year of analysis she too realized, through a similar dream experience, that she too could *just* walk out to freedom. These adverbials carry multilayered implications beyond explicable context.

The dream someone, the as-yet un-named, anonymous, newly appearing someone, can carry a sense of the supraordinate personality, conceivable as Self.[21] That it can express a culmination of value, climax rather than bathos, is affirmed by the Greek *ho ōn* ("Ο ὤν), the self-proclaiming "I am," ultimate, non-named Being that Moses encounters, that has reverberated through Judeo-Christian culture. Moses is commanded to speak of God as unqualified and pure Being, hence the ultimately emphatic self-identifying, un-translatable and in-comprehensible, "I am that I am," or "I am who I am, I am the one who is, I am whatever I will be," all these un-naming names deriving from the Septuagint's "the existing one."[22]

Compounds formed with *some-* or equivalent forms like *some sort/kind of*, bring tentative analogical links to dream narratives, perhaps making the waking ego more comfortable with unnerving challenges, or preparing for something familiar to unconscious psyche but disturbingly strange to the waking ego. Such might be the impact of a dream beginning, "*I am at some kind of* Nazi rally…" The terror felt by attendance at such a horrific event is ameliorated somewhat by the modification, which allows the dreamer to go forward into the experience and then allows the waker to assimilate the dream memory. This is the effect in similar dream situations: *I am in a sort of* psychiatric unit; *I am somewhere rather like* an extermination camp. These formulae serve the over-arching purpose of psyche's *somehow*, which evokes a special attitude, a sort of how-can-these-things-be?—a question that needs no answer and defies any. It is a rhetorical attitude that accepts the question as a container for the waiting to see how these things will be, a strange aspect of dream grammar. *Somehow* can normalize oddities in dream circumstance, and often has camouflaging naiveté. It introduces the very well known and the not yet formulated, but already existing and active in the psyche. Sometimes we do not even notice it, since it has its own tact, mediating between the revealed and the hidden. But there are very important "big" dreams where *somehow* secures transformation.

> I was with three different people, traveling. One was X, though he looked the opposite of how he is in outer life. Another man just joined us. And a woman is there. It was the end of the world. Something strange was happening in the sky, in the movement of the planets… it was very unsettling. At one point, I am on the beach, in a beach hut. I came out and could see a strange object in the sky. I run to X to come to look… it's at the end of the world. When he came it had disappeared. The constellations are still moving…
>
> Then somehow it was the next day; things were still strange but the end of the world had not happened. There was still a strange light, and a rainbow over things.

The dreamer had seen a television program on the solar system, describing it as "awesome... expanding and humbling." The strange object in the dream sky felt "not part of nature ... it was made," reminding me of Jung's response to flying saucers. The dream location was a shoreline, hinterland between land and sea, *between* conscious and unconscious perspectives. Something crucial was con-stellating in the dream's actual astronomical language. The dreamer was unsettled; the known world felt threatened. New inner figures were congregating beneath new constellations. Something quite alien needs integration into consciousness. Celestial perturbation felt rather like the sky at the nativity. Just as that era ended, something unknown pushed the narrative to a different reality. But *somehow*, despite the ominous omen of ending, a new day begins, with a rainbow as a hopeful source of light arching over things. Such hope was not yet accessible to consciousness.

Here *somehow* feels needed as a qualifier against too much formulation, guarding the mysteriousness of what must, nevertheless and notwithstanding, come to pass. Perhaps it signifies some preparation for inner process, warning off the defining ego to make space for something yet to be actualized. *Somehow* takes up a position in opposition to consciousness, re-imagining opposition, inviting the dreamer to adopt a different attitude to reality. A similar possibility lies beneath another dreamer's "wonderful flowers" and records that "somehow they feel like violets but they look like clover." Simultaneity holds together the contradiction; these plants are *somehow* violet *and* clover, both of which were later amplified in startling ways.

When *somehow* appears in the midst of a dream sequence, it can signal a turn in the action, as a new attitude is claimed—a transformation that is not, and cannot be, the work of consciousness. In it the transcendent function might be activated.

> Two threatening youths are somehow dealt with by a mouse. I don't know whether the mouse changes-into or is just associated-with some marvelous crystal, later related to a deep green emerald.

The enigma is not solved. We cannot tell how these things came to be, but the mouse/emerald preserve the dreamer from danger. *Somehow* is reconciliatory, making paradox productive; or it prevents the dream proposition from having to make too much sense. *Somehow* can become the matrix for metaphor, the assertion of impossible truths, and we concede to an abdication of conscious logic that might threaten the dream transmutations of conscious expectation. We often step into the dream experience through an initial or early somehow.

> I am creating color. Somehow, as I color circles, they fill in with new original colors. I feel my hand or arm circling. But the dream is in black and white and I am aware of that, and know that my colors' hue would be seen as black and white, though they are authentically quite new colors.

The alchemy of *somehow* transubstantiates the strange into a familiar zone of the mundane, a why-should-these-things-not-be? attitude. So the dreamer can create circles with colors never seen before, *but* the dream is in black and white. *Though* functions in the same way, assuring the dreamer that being simultaneously black and white *and* in *whole* new shades of authentic color is an original reality. This is a conspicuous substantiation of both/and, refusing an either/or that prohibits totality.

Unconscious dream experience can feel threatened by conscious logic, despite somehow's web, so it often finds an accomplice in adversative conjunctives such as *yet, nevertheless, although*, especially *but*. Consider the snake dream of the upright snake carried "by some sort of" detective (see above, page 96). In the dream record, *as if* it was gives way to an unarguable *but it is* a real puff adder. Another dreamer wrestles with alternative realities held together through *but*. The dream begins with an encounter with a "giant," a massive and fearful man. But I realize "he's really quite tiny," followed by the insistence from within the dream, a tenacious "*but* he's still a giant." So the dreamer could be freed from a powerful complex, massive and pathetic, that had long dominated inner and outer life.

Adversatives that tolerate, establish, or encourage paradoxical simultaneities function rather like the clutch mechanism in a motor engine. Such grammatical particles can work like a synchro-meshing lysis, not unlike the activity of the transcendent function. There is dynamic and dialectical energy in them, moving through contradiction and opposition, enabling both to be engaged. These are positive aspects of oppositional conjunctives and prepositions. There is unassailable adversative energy that must not be gainsaid.

The energy of *contra* and *anti* can oppose all linkage between, enforcing and re-enacting fragmentation and isolation, especially between body and mind, because

> the self care system of early trauma cannot allow the elements of whole experience to be present at once and...this results in an attack against links between somatic and mental components of experience.[23]

This happens, Donald Kalsched illustrates, when psyche, the linking agent, can only de-link, its goal being survival, not integration in the service of individuation. Such people do not have the capacity to hold together both/and possibilities. They cannot sustain paradox and so are extremely difficult to work with analytically. Kalsched loads the preposition *against* in this way, speaking of a daimonic force, aggressive to healing, resisting change, that we often encounter in analysands with early trauma. This force *against* works strenuously to refuse rather than relate.

Tertullian uttered these notorious words about his faith, *certum est quia impossibile est*. For him, the very impossibilities of his creed provided assurance of a truth that can house contradiction. This is not the kind of truth espoused by the enlightenment mind, which valued a truth not true enough to accommodate psychic or poetic reality, which is necessarily paradoxical. Of such profound human need for more comprehensive truth Steiner comments:

> Human speech can never do without falsehood. It may have arisen out of the necessities of fiction, of the manifold need "to say what is not" (Swift's lapidary phrase). Our subjunctives, our conditionals, our optatives, the "if" clauses in our grammars, make possible an indispensable, radically human counter-factuality. They make it possible for us to alter, reshape, fantasticate, cancel out the material constraints of our biological-empirical world....The fictive genius of our grammars.[24]

Somehow, with its synergies, embeds us in that fictive genius of our grammars. I am arguing for more conscious awareness of such dream grammar, active awareness that supplements our engagement with substantive dream symbols.

We are used to discriminating between the dream-I and the waking ego, and the various rhythms of relationship that get activated between them, harmonious, contra-puntal, conflictual, oppositional, cooperative, or collusive. This *between* is often the stuff of our explorations. There is interesting play between the two in this extract from a longer dream:

> A black horse is in a field. I see a sore bit on its neck, exposed skin. I knew it needed help. I brought it into the stable, and then saw that it was sore all down the chest. I go to the edge of the wood. I know that in the wood is a man who could cure the horse… I asked him to come with me. The horse was restless. The man had knowledge of plants. I wondered whether I was feeding the horse enough… but I knew I was, as it was in the field… with good pasture.

The dream "I" is extremely active here: "I see, I knew, I brought, I go, I know, I wonder." So the deliberations proceed, building to a climax about the quality of care for the dream's sick horse. The limits of consciousness are reached at the edge of the wood, where the deliberating "I" encounters a mysterious forest wild man. (This forest man contrasted starkly with dirty mechanics who haunted her early dream world, chasing her through oily garage underworlds.) The force of *whether* was strong. She doubted her capacity to nurture her inner world, cope with the energy of horses now wanting to gallop in her dreams. This wondering-whether formed a kind of transitional space between a false and true sense of herself. It culminates, syntactically, in the strongly affirmed *"but* I knew I was." The positiveness of this *but* was healing. Her inner world could support the healthy life of this potent energy symbol; the horse would empower her. We had often discussed the fact that we measure engine force in terms of horsepower. This woman was compelled from within to know herself as a powerful person before she could foster an as-yet tentative professional identity. Dia-logue between conscious and unconscious ego was enacted through pronominal play. The second part of her dream contrasted with an earlier action, where she visits a city. "We go-in-through one of the arched gates, down into a dip. There is a dark car park with spiral ramps. We start driving *round and round and round* these ramps at speed." They pass through the old part of the city, to circumambulate the car park to gather momentum. Then the car carrier is exchanged for the horse. But going even further back into this dream, she was involved in a very different activity.

> I was digging up roots beside a wood… roots like turnips that farmers fed to cattle. Loads of them. Underneath the roots, there were holes in the ground, out of which hens came, with chicks, dozens of them. I thought, "What can I do with all these? There are so many."

All the adverbials and ad-positionals here offer vital context for the numinous experience of receiving the multitude of hens. Turnips turn-into chickens, prolific life lies in wait for her to unearth. She is overwhelmed by such abundance and needs to trust herself more before she can integrate them into the meaning and purpose of her conscious life. All the pronominal action here suggests a strong ego engaged in soul's work.

These are strongly delineated ego subjects. I have drawn attention to the enigmatic *someone* so often active in dreams, representing the not yet knowable self (one of the many selves of Redfearn's valuable study).[25] Very often, this seems to suggest a self that is emerging from the depths of the unconscious, not yet close enough to the threshold to be personified. I sometimes suggest that analysands might compile *dramatis personae* of dream figures. It is fascinating to see how past life is ransacked for carriers of part personalities that need to be integrated into the conscious personality, bright Self-figures as well as dark shadowy ones. Past schoolmates, past workmates as far back as training days, people never met for decades, people met fleetingly on trains, all are pressed into service by the unsleeping unconscious, saving, storying, collecting data 24/7 for psyche's future animation. Some dreamers seem particularly prone to such assemblies of past lives. One analysand comes to mind, whose dreams were richly populated from past encounters in a very diverse life experience. But accompanying the familiar people, distantly known characters would appear, representing a who's who in fields of aspiration. One single dream hosted Roderick Main, Cardinal Wolsey, Henry VIII, Charles Williams, and C. S. Lewis, all together. In dream fantasy, we are entirely promiscuous, relating, even uniting, with anyone who proffers possibilities of new attitudes or challenges. These identities, sometimes appearing as only *he, she, they,* or even *it* before they can become *we* or *I*, might never be more fully realized, or might have to materialize in a different form to be apprehended. Positively or negatively, such splinter psyches, who are us, bring their ore to the surface.[26] And gendered identity is always flexible, for as Jung points out,

> Each of us is an hermaphroditic being, capable of uniting the opposites, but who is never complete in the individual unless related to another individual. The unrelated human being lacks wholeness, for he can achieve wholeness only through the soul, and the soul cannot exist without its other side, which is always found in a "you." Wholeness is a combination of I and You.[27]

In action and in dialogue, we engage with these pronominal bodies through the dream's *I*, not a simple figure by any means. The task of my *I*, my many *I*'s (in all pronominal forms and named essences), is to become unified, to contain the multiplicity of all required for wholeness in an ever-expanding coherence, but emphatically not in an amorphous, fused mono figure. The complexity of this lifelong task prompted Hillman to speak of the

> little devil of an I....the confessional voice, imagining itself to be the unifier of experience....a language game....the grammar of the first person singular creating ontology. But also...a confessional ontology of the personalistic heart dominating our grammar, persuading us by our very sentence structures that when our pronoun is singular then so must be our verbs; our actions too must be single.[28]

We actually experience a congregation of I—I am a novel; I might be the personae of the whole Shakespearian canon in fact. And what is said of the novel might well be said of psyche's dramatic play. Rowland suggests that "the dream is a (Bakhtinian) novel device in linking the cultural history of the past with the revolutions in current consciousness."[29] And further, that

> as the one literary form that delights in heteros glossia, the novel has a political dimension in counteracting the stratification of society in social classes. The novel's virtue is that it mixes things up without homogenizing them.[30]

This capacity to be multiple, united but with no loss of discreteness, begins to organize wholeness and equips us for the kind of inner dialogue with and in our dreams that Jung considered to be "a touchstone for outer objectivity."[31]

There is an essential set of opposites within the Self archetype, for "there can be no reality without polarity," a founding idea in Jung's psychology, a fundamental axiom being that anything psychic has at least two sides and should never be considered from a single viewpoint.[32] This claim prompted Joseph Rychlak to answer, "I can only wish he had called this a *principle of dialectic*."[33] Even in childhood Jung came up against serious "inadequacies of ordinary conceptual language" to formulate his experience of dualities in the unconscious.[34] At such an early point, he was struggling with pronominal realities. On the road to school, for a single moment, Jung says,

> I had the overwhelming impression of having just emerged from a dense cloud. I knew, all at once; now I am myself! It was as if a wall of mist were at my back, and behind that wall there was not yet an "I." But at this moment, I came upon myself. Previously I had existed, too, but everything had merely happened to me. Now I happened to myself. Now I knew. Previously I had been willed to do this and that; now I willed. This experience seemed to me tremendously important and new: there was "authority" in me.[35]

From now on "I," this freshly emerged *myself*, must accommodate two essential, permanent core identities, for the moment called Personalities 1 and 2. The foundation is already laid for his subsequent departure from Freud's seductive, ego-enhancing dogma that "the Freudian word for the biographer is the ego."[36]

Any reflections on our use of pronouns, psychologically (or theologically), cannot altogether ignore Buber's paradigmatic and discourse-shifting study, *I and Thou*. He endorses the questioning: What does it mean to have, or to lack, an I? What does it mean to relate *as an I* to an other as *thou*, or to reduce the other to an *it*? Buber's instinct toward communion is a profound human compulsion, but our collectivity is always to be balanced with our solitude and individuality. No one can individuate alone. Negotiating a coherent, non-monadic, whole self is assisted by the relationship between the conscious ego, the dream ego, and the various dream selves. The dream ego continually engages with others, human or any other formal figures. In response to the dream narrative, one often asks, Who is the dream's *we*? This is sometimes explicable, but often it is not, for those others can remain vague, just unrecognized people who participate in a dream *we*:

> We live in a huge old farmhouse that feels French. We are having the whole cluster of buildings sprayed from the outside, a sense of fumigating to get rid of vermin. But I see no such creatures. Strong sense of sealing and protecting.

This *we* is never identified more specifically, a gathering of part-selves active both protectively and as it felt, later, judgmentally. But often the newly embodied *we* takes a known shape. For example, an initial dream *we* subject was eventually recognized: "The people on the ship are mainly my work colleagues." The proliferation of pronouns in dreams is both intriguing and disconcerting, especially when figures appear as though from the deepest reaches of unconscious psyche. Such a *s/he* is often described as foreign, perhaps wearing a burka or unfamiliar clothing. "He seems to be an Arab, come straight from the desert" was how one such figure was described. *He* simply appeared, was simply there, as yet fulfilling no specific task or obvious purpose. Such cultural strangeness can stir the imagination, capture the waking ego's curiosity, and prepare consciousness to meet and integrate surprising selves in the service of a larger myself.

There is not room for an adequate discussion of the inter-play of pronominal identities in the almost kinesthetic field of empathic relations in therapy, where extreme consciousness allows the inter-mixing and inter-action of *you and I/me*, analyst and analysand in the *coniunctio* considered vital to our work. But apart from Jung's own wrestling to formulate this mysterious connection by reference to alchemy, there are numberless texts that explore the inter-mixture of conscious and unconscious selves. One clear articulation of this is offered in Stein's chapter "Transformative Relationships," where he quotes Jung's pithy claim,

> Wholeness is a combination of I and You, and these show themselves to be parts of a transcendent unity whose nature can only be grasped symbolically.[37]

The goal of this inter-action, that we might think of as "kinship libido," Stein asserts, is hopefully a means to generate a new sense (on both sides of the therapeutic equation) of individuality and the reorganization of psychic energy around a constellation of the self.[38]

Such inter-communion, inter-subjectivity, becomes even more complex in training, in the experience of supervision, explored in various collections of contemporary essays.[39] The ever-increasing networks extended through supervisory work, where a third is invited into the dyadic relational field, results in a proliferation of persons and pronouns. This becomes giddying when supervisors are required to have their practice of supervision itself supervised. Here more than anywhere else in our discourse the affix *inter* comes into play synergically, *inter* exerting energy upon, and being acted upon by, the pervasive *trans* of our specialized professional language of transference and answering counter-transference.

In the field of pronoun reference, the allusiveness of the lexical atom *it* demands attention. *It* is dismissed, if noticed at all, as a weed in the lexical garden, even more humdrum and overlooked than *something*. But it can point to psyche's treasure. Kalsched seems to be wise to this in his chapter on "The Fitcher's Bird."[40] He picks up on an insight into the process of "personalization or 'indwelling,'" which Winnicott leaves unspecified. What does come to indwell the body of the infant? Kalsched ventures to name this unnamed *it* as the individual's "inviolable personal spirit." What he highlights is that so often in our work we know we are dealing with something absolutely crucial, its effects observable as wind through trees, but so surfeit with content that too many words, ideas, concepts are needed to represent it. In that situation, until there is an epiphany of graspable reference, we fall back on the promiscuous generosity of *it*. This neuter and neutered pronoun will stand for everything and anything. How often do we hear in our consulting rooms the anguished question, *Is this it then?* Lying awake in the night an imaginative and articulate man wrestled with the big questions, reporting with distress simply, "*What are we here for? Is this it?*" This overflowing *it* can be replaced by *all* in the same interrogation, *Is this all?* A typical comment by another woman at the outset of her analytical explorations asserted, "I *can't do it yet*"; and later, "I don't know *yet what it is.*" Consciously, she did not know, but incubating in the unconscious, waiting to manifest a sufficient symbol, a painting was gathering that somehow could project something of that inexhaustible *it*. And what relief, that moment of seeing, of being seen, of being understood, when the analyst responds to something, points toward it, and the recognition is felt in the analysand's exclamation, "*Yes, that's it, that's just it, exactly it.*" The delight of this is matched by the devastating sense of abandonment at the not being seen, not having one's *it* understood, as in Prufrock's frustrated cry, "That is not what I meant at all, / That is not it, at all."[41] This might be regarded as the language learned at mother's knee, the mutually felt communication pathway that needs no more than *it* to be perceived, or to be missed. It is a language of transitional space.

The experience of union with another, first needed *in utero* and in *post-partum* life, perhaps reflects a participatory union with creator source that the Christian mystic acts out, or acts in. This is the traditional understanding of the Unitive Way, beyond contemplation, drawn even further by the *yonder* of the soul, that urges co-alescence with the divine.[42] The subsequent loss of individual discreteness, and loss of ego, goes beyond what we would typically recognize as the surrender of the ego to the Self in classical analytical theory. One might also see it psychologically as an experience of merging, which in human relationships is often pathological. Herbert indulges in fugal pronominal wordplay in a poem entitled "The Clasping of Hands." Through this physical clasping he patterns a series of interwoven pronouns from the essentially separate to the ultimately fused. In his *I/Thou* prayer, the poet claims to become even more *me* by being lost in *thee*:

> LORD, Thou art mine, and I am Thine,
> If mine I am; and Thine much more
> Then I or ought or can be mine.[43]

Through lexical play, he becomes so intertwined that he loses conscious identity, in union with the originating other.

> O, be mine still; still make me Thine;
> Or rather make no Thine and Mine.

Theology, too, exploits psyche's mystery of personal pronouns and possessives, making the most domestically tamed language serve the highest purposes of the soul and the deepest purposes of healing.

Just as inextricable in its pronominal density is Shakespeare's formulation at the end of *The Tempest*: "and all of us ourselves / When no man was his own."[44] This affirms the play's final reconciliation, words spoken by the supposedly virtuous Gonzalo, proclaiming a teleological sense of having found what was lost. All the phrases in this speech depend on the verb "find." Not one of us was authentic, we were all lost to ourselves, until we were shipwrecked together on this island. Like the young Jung, who "came upon [him]self," all these characters now acknowledge their self-discovery, an inner and an interactive journey *from thence to here*, en route to a future *thither*. Most of Shakespeare's dramatic action posits the *hither* of human experience, the human situation, *here, in medias res* where individuation begins. And many of them end with a sense of a new *thither*, a *yonder* opening up that can only be approached from *here*, where we have reached, *so far*. Each of these particles is loaded, highly charged with psychological possibility. All action is foretaste to an as yet unrealized terminus.

There is a curious Irish story about Ireland's physical and spiritual geography. The country is supposedly divided into four provinces, and yet the native word for them actually means fifth. Imagination has it that the provinces are North, South, East, West, and Here, the numinously inexplicable and indescribable *Here* of their soul geography.[45] A Here that only the spirit can imagine.

Wherever we turn, wherever language is used, the lexicon of function words is hard at work. We cannot speak without them. We must pay more conscious attention to them. Of course we do respond to them, but we are not often aware of the extent to which they carry psychic implication. For this reason, I draw attention to them anew as locators and interpreters of time, place, manner, and so much else.

First, time. Psyche is outside of time, but must be incarnate in our lives through it. Dreams and waking fantasy employ a necessary temporal diction, in which soul strives to assimilate its apprehensions of eternity, infinity, enormity, often through intersecting filters. *Ever* and *never* are constantly on our lips inside our praxis and in every mundane situation. *Always* gets drawn into that orbit, too. Our complexes often inhabit that *always*, as in a recent insistence of a particular action in a dream: "My mother always does that." As the negative mother complex dissolved, so did the dream's over-determined *always*. *Sometimes* becomes more flexible. We have already considered the *from-to* energies in relation to transformation, but we might also note how they inhabit time. *Now* and *then* are crucial. *Then* can point *backward* to a *thence* and *forward* to a *thither*. An analysand who had a history of near-psychotic breaks reported with some satisfaction that today she was "more here than there, more in the now," the need for escape to inner fantasy outside of inhabited time was no longer so indomitable. This *here* that we take for granted is precious to the healthy psyche. We are therefore shocked by recent brain research that elaborates the eternal now of the Alzheimer's patient, an excluding *now* affording no access to past or future.

Dreams often take the dreamer back in time and space to old haunts where history was made, especially early family homes, or sites of adolescent awakening. When work situations or past relationships have not been sufficiently assimilated, dreams compulsively repeat: "I go-*back to* school, to the sixth form library"; "I go-*back* to the X hospital…." This going-back is common dream stock, each return offering another opportunity to heal what was damaged or restore what was lost. *Again* can signal both neurosis and possibility.

One might come away from Kalsched's book on the inner world of trauma with a phrase that haunts, a phrase that lights up warningly in work with analysands with early damage. He quotes the Jewish Defence League's rallying cry, "Never again!" as the watchword for such patients.

> "Never again," says our tyrannical caretaker, "will the traumatized spirit of this child suffer this badly. Never again will it be this helpless in the face of cruel reality….before this happens I will disperse into fragments or encapsulate it…or…or…to keep it from hoping for life in this world."[46]

This negatived future is asserted with an absoluteness that the injured psyche constantly musters. In this way, "archaic defences become anti-life forces which Freud understandably thought of as part of the death instinct." The power of such a neurotic and defensive *never*, and of this *again*, is frequently enacted in dream fantasy where Persecutor/Protector dictates. In the force field of this *never*, and the fear of any *again*, hope is refused and destroyed, as "something more powerful than the ego continually undermines progress." This *something* is identified as an in-educable Protector/Persecutor, whose grammar is limited to the past historic tense; the future can only be re-enactment of the past. They cannot support subjunctive reality, a modal verb typically used after verbs that stir wishing or hoping. *Somehow* is not accessible to them, nor *perhaps*. Only *never* will serve.

There is insufficient space to respond to all the valences of *yet*, *still*, *at once*, and other mundane words with temporal undercurrents. As we open ourselves up to their charge, we heed them even more in our work. I suggested elsewhere that *suddenly* (*subito*) is the moment God/gods choose.[47] This adverb in dream record marks a distinct climactic moment, announcing some crisis in the action, as in most narrative progression. I reproduce here two sections of typical dream structures.

> I was feeling increasingly anxious, suddenly sensing a huge disaster looming. As I ran for the door I called, "Something terrible is going to happen," and the same clunk of the kiln happened. X and Y said, "It's only the kiln."

> There is a large building, a castle or a prison. I drive past it. Then I get out of the car. As the narrator, I don't know where I am. Suddenly, I am part of what I have driven past. I get out of the car. There is a group of men, Polish men near the castle/prison. There is another large building beside it, swarming with men. There is an inner courtyard. A child is advising the men that it would be better if they built a ramp rather than tunnel underground to get into the prison. It would be easier to invade, to release whoever is imprisoned there. In the courtyard, which has rooms off it, I go-into one room and say it would be better if you have more roof lights in these rooms. All through the dream I'm sliding-between being the driver, the child advising, and the narrator.

The sudden interruption of a time sequence that is simply going on registers a moment of crisis. This charged moment might be waited for, and so be experienced as relief; or it might be quite unexpected and feel shocking. *Suddenly* usually prepares for some kind of *perepeteia* that makes an unforeseen lysis possible.

By now I hope that you are paying keener attention to various other active grammatical particles in such dream narrative. How innocently adverbials choreograph or supervise the symbolic field. For example, a woman often dreamed of the horses she so adored in her girlhood that became a potent energy symbol for her as an adult. She brought a strange but critical dream shortly after the death of a close friend whom she admired. Its very grammar alerts us to the importance of this rich material from the unconscious.

> There is a beautiful sunset—plum color. I'm in a modern house with a big back garden. I'm in the garden and see X dressed in the purple suit he was buried in. We are talking. I am aware that he is dead, but he's come-back to talk. I say, "Shall we dance?" It's a dance where I dance in the air… He dances with me in the air. Someone else is there, also dead. I see but I don't know who it is… We say something, a remark about leaping. Then he disappears.

This helped the dreamer ponder afresh the mysteries of life and death, the passage from one to the other, the ultimate rite of passage. We know the archetypal structure of such rites from many anthropological studies that explore the movement from one stage of being to the next. This is perhaps the keenest of all archetypal trajectories. In this dream the ineluctable flow of life toward death is momentarily reversed as the revenant comes-back to engage with the living. The dream enacts both the dance of life and the dance of death, an exhilarating mutual dancing-with. Something vital arose from the amplification of the dream dance. It evoked a very powerful somatic experience of recent "leaping" in dance movement sessions, where she experienced it specifically as "transitional movement *between here and there*" (the dreamer's words). This introduced the puzzle of what lay in between, which seemed to be where the energy was needed. It invited her, in her mourning, into the necessity of the here-and-now, where life must go on, with spirit and body somehow thrown into kinesthetically heightened relationship, perhaps signified by the mysterious new *someone* entering psychic space. The energy was keenly generated in the intervening suspension before landing. Leaping provoked somatic memories of the horses of her childhood and her fascination with their power. She described with fresh emotion those calm chestnut horses and the white stallions of her recent dreaming. The memory was in every sense dynamic, an important word/concept related to the archetypal energies inherent in, and actualized through, prepositional and adverbial syntax. The word *dynamo*, root of the word dynamite, is often used theologically for the work of the Holy Spirit, *dynamis* (δύναμις). It is related to *energeia* (ἐνέργεια), divine power at work in creation. For this dreamer, the energy of spirit lay *in between the here and there*, the suspension, mid-leap.

In all of the above dream material, there are adverbial tensions at work. There are also certain moderating energies working through restrictive adverbials to which I will at least point. We met it in Prufrock's pained, "That is not what I meant at all, / That is not it, at all." I foreground the particles *at all*, and the more emphatic *not at all*. There is intense frustration in this phrase, a desperate crisis in a cluster of monosyllables. Such adverbials of degree that work significantly in dream record are *only, so, very, rather, really, nearly, even, quite, enough*, and especially, *too*. Consider the well-camouflaged *too* in the dream of being in church and needing light, *but not too much*. It was crucial to have *just enough*. I once met with a woman who in the very first hour exposed too much, for her need was limitless. Her soul story needed more discreet dis-closure. I turned-down the tri-light to minimum for the next session and was amazed that it made a difference. So the church dream gave some indication of how the work of un-covering psyche might proceed, the caution that must be adopted in dis-covering psyche. In analysis, dreams will make us heed such necessary modifications, with their counsel of too fast, too loud, too much, all supplies that exceed *enough*.

Along with such qualifying adverbials, we find various modalities in verb structures. Stein responds to the fascinating preponderance of conjunctives and qualifiers in contemporary attitudes and their embodying speech, remarking on

> the attitude and feeling tone of the modern person: secular, atheistic, perhaps slightly humanistic. A modern person's values seem hedged about with reservations, conditions, "maybe's," "not sure's." The modern person's stance is relativistic.[48]

Dreams are bolder than such conscious speech and do not fear asserting improbable realities. Nevertheless we miss a great deal if we do not attend to such things as verbal auxiliaries, the imperious *must* and *should* that need to be challenged. We converse with the dream in terms of its purpose, the standpoint of finality, pondering what its effect is

WHITHER OF THE DREAM

meant to be, as directive or illumination from the unconscious. Jung points the analyst/dreamer to the question of *why* and *wherefore* in receiving and hearing the dream with his urgent interrogatives, "*Wazu* dient dieser Traum? *Was* soll er bewirken?"[49]

I have not yet explored the dynamics of inside/outside that are central to analytical psychology and to dream composition. A claim made definitively in the *Red Book* is that "if no outer adventure happens to you, then no inner adventure happens to you either."[50] This is exactly what the earlier dreamer discovered after he had climbed over the fence, entered the meadow, and headed for the village where he could engage in a life of feeling. Some months later, he had a sudden urge to draw a spontaneous image.

> I just see a barred window. I'm on one side. Through the bars, I see the horizon. There's a person's face at the bars, as though parting the bars. I am puzzled about who is inside and who is outside.

This was followed by an exciting drawing of the outside/inside threshold, a drawing that once again clarified important details. He saw that he was now on the outside. The bars were prised apart and he was released from imprisonment. (Fig. 14) Such inside/outside dream phenomena often collocate with us/them distinctions, where the dreamer can behave as both prisoner and

Figure 14. Dream prison bars.

guard. This is the mechanism of the complex that enforces or subverts the possibility of liberation.

In anticipation of the chapter on fairytales, I consider a dream brought to a session the same day as the dream about the usurped super-market trolley, a trite thing in modern life. In that first dream, the trolley signified the affluence of super-market expectations, an image of plenty and a lack of reverence for supply. The second super-market trolley dream provoked very different and disturbing personal and collective images. In this linguistic record, I draw attention to the narrative flow:

> The dream was simply an image of a super-market trolley, filled with all of a person's possessions, being pushed off along the road into the world... forever. Exile, wandering, no resting place. No sense of destination.

In amplification, we shared images from World War II films where displaced people pushed all their belongings along tree-lined roads in prams or carts, leaving behind all that was familiar, moving toward they knew not what. The dreamer's words, which felt as though they were still inside the dream, spoke of there being *nowhere* to go. She was still feeling a politically induced existential dread from a film she had seen some days before. At the beginning of the hour she had commented that since our last meeting "so many things had happened" in her life, and she emphasized how important it was to relay those events "in their correct sequence." She outlined them in a temporal "then... then... then" structure, at the end of which she experienced "a big revelation. *I am still here.*" The step-by-step report of her experience and the dream itself brought home to her, very painfully, that in some ways, as life was changing radically and mysteriously, she had *nowhere to go* that she could recognize. There was not yet a representable *yonder*. For that she must wait. Her dream had left her a refugee on the road, in transit, in transitional space.

Steiner speaks of text as "homeland." Whether the dream is reported in spoken or in written language, it provides an imaginal place to depart from and to return to in the context of the analytical session. I end this chapter with two very different dreams that illuminate this particular native language of the soul. The first shows the two discourses co-inciding, both *parole* and *langue* of my applied distinction. A man dreamed of two women. The crucial energy within the dream was the going *back and forth between them*. The dreamer, who was familiar with William Sheldon's typological map of body personalities, could identify both dream figures and perceived them even within the dream as ecto-morph and meso-morph, associated with whiteness and redness. A third woman appears, suddenly *just there*, dressed in over-the-top hot pink. But though the language of the reported dream was rich with flowers and colors, and even technical language of ecto/mesomorph, the felt energy was in the traffic *back and forth between* the two women. As yet, the third had not much intensity (apart from the hot-pink dress) and she seemed to arise out of the tension between the other two.

The other dream's dynamic energy arises from this record:

> I was going from somewhere to somewhere else, with my baby in my car. The headlamp was broken so I couldn't continue in the car. I got-out and carried my baby down the street. The baby kept changing from bigger to smaller… we went for haircuts. After that we went to a stranger's house to rest. I put the baby down. It needed to be changed… I had no nappies but someone found some for me. The woman who owned the house came in… she had only one eye… we went out. We were on a big train traveling through South Africa. It was wonderful, the vast landscape. And animals. Turtles. Camels. Like a television image… animals in huge spaces, the veldt.

There are so many symbolic nominals here, all of them needing amplification. But it was syntactic direction and the functional lexis that reinforced the dreamer's sense that she needed to be on the move with the nascent part of herself, though the map at first could identify no more than *somewhere* and *somewhere else*. After much coming and going and baby changing, the elsewhere gained definition, opening up into a vast veldt landscape, which she traversed with the one-eyed companion.

CHAPTER FIVE

Whither of the Fairytale:
Between Once Upon a Time and Ever After

> I have a sense of moving-through huge buildings, on the ground floor, I come to the end. I reach a door. I open it and stand looking-out-on a vast landscape. I have a sense of reaching the end of something and experiencing something more, a wholly new vista.

The action of this dream is condensed into a single episode: moving-through, opening, and looking-out-onto. This single action might be significantly expanded into a story. Perhaps this is how fairytales began, dreams filled out and amplified by hearers who became tellers who told other hearers who also became tellers. Such succession of tellers and tellings leaves us both incrementally rich and perhaps distant from the original accounts of soul's journeying. Each of our own individual tellings and hearings and readings make us experience the narratives anew. Through such processes, our folk tradition comes to us, told and retold until the advent of print, when it was arrested in fixed text. From these evolved any sense we might have (and need to relinquish) of an authorized version. There is no such thing. Like someone newly literate, confounded by marks on a page, we need to turn those trapped words loose, back into speech. In what follows, I have needed to use such texts, reshaped, perhaps hijacked, from oral form to print, with all the losses and the gains that this development entailed. The larger picture of this process is documented in W. J. Ong's seminal work on "the technologizing of the word."[1] I will use and adapt several standard versions of published fairytales translated from various European sources, including my own.[2] My purpose once again is to pay attention to the lexicon of closed-class particles that are rarely noticed, despite the work they do. I see them like the mint that grew so profusely in the poet's garden, unattended. "Like the disregarded ones we turned against / Because we'd failed them by our disregard."[3] We might imagine these little words like our little dreams, a kind of undergrowth on the forest floor, not the tall trees of our big dreams, but equally important to the ecology of psyche's forest.

In the above dream we find a particular, hitherto unknown *whither* that brought an unspecified *whence* to fulfillment in the form of *something* that made unknown vistas visible. The precise whither is not yet known, or not yet able to be known. We cannot will dreams to a satisfactory lysis. In fact, the dream often refuses even the possibility of lysis, and this need not indicate an imminent psychosis! It may be that the dreamer has not yet reached that fullness of time that belongs to *kairos*. In one analysis, the dreamer's own sudden death was the lysis, when the fullness of his time came. He died very soon after his last session, to which he brought a dream of exultant cleansing in a humdrum but numinous shower.

The fairytale, however, does not usually rest until some resolving lysis is reached, no matter how magical or incomprehensible that might seem, or how convoluted the path to its accomplishment. In relation to dream structure, Jung played with the Aristotelian model for a work of art, asserting the fundamental need for a ground plan of a beginning, a middle, and an end. Aristotle laid out a foundation for any drama that is to move audiences to an experience of catharsis and so fulfill the purpose of drama.

> By entire I mean that which has a beginning, a middle, and an end. A beginning is that which does not necessarily suppose anything before it, but which requires something to follow it. An end, on the contrary, is that which supposes something to

> precede it, either necessarily or probably, but which nothing is required to follow. A middle is that which supposes both something to precede and requires something to follow. The poet therefore who would construct his fable properly, is not at liberty to begin or end where he pleases, but must conform to these definitions.[4]

A fundamentally archetypal directive! Fairytales, typically, do conform to this structure, but they do so kaleidoscopically and idiosyncratically. We do them an injury if we try to make them fit too precisely into our sense of literary or psychological structure. This is sometimes the weakness of the rich and compelling analyses of Marie-Louise von Franz. But the fairytale as a quest for a transforming *whither*, the accomplishment of the tale's *thither* from a problematical *whence*, is axiomatic. The whence of the situation is usually implicit, if not explicit, in the tale's opening setting. From this we usually see what is missing and what kind of transformation is needed. We must not make that too mechanically the realization of a final quaternal constellation. We might consider Aristotle's strictures about *peri-peteia*.

> In general, we may say that an action is sufficiently extended when it is long enough to admit of a change of fortune, from happy to unhappy, or the reverse, brought about by a succession, necessary or probable, of well-connected incidents.

Fairytales care little for the probable, nor for Aristotle's well-connected plot. But they comply with his insistence that a legitimate plot needs a reversal of fortune, only we might reformulate this as passage to transformation. A radical change between beginning and end might employ several reversals in order to accomplish the necessary individuating shifts in consciousness, manifest through action, rather than reflection.

Aristotle's *Poetics* established Western ideals for the creation of drama. He preferred drama, its action more controllable by constraints of time and credibility, while the epic was long and unwieldy. The novel and the short story were as yet uncreated forms, though he knew the tales of the gods, which he condemned, stylistically, even though they included reversals of fortune. The vulgar fairytale would have been wholly alien to him. He gave priority to tragedy, which adhered to unities of time, place, and action, while the epic roamed through multitudes of minor actions, thereby losing intensity of focus. The action of the fairytale is compact, though flagrantly defying the unities, continually leaping into the indefinite frame of "sometime later." One hundred years can pass in just one breath. And there is no unity of place when seven-league boots can, and do, cross impossible and impassable distances magically in two steps.

We can observe the same narrative strategies structuring the fairytale as the dream, acknowledging a common unconscious origin. Fairytales tell stories that move us through time and space, physical and emotional, driven by purpose that unfolds as we travel. We move between the most fundamental *and then*, via *eventually* and *suddenly* through a magnetic *until*, to the anticipated *at last*, and sometimes *ever after* and *beyond*. We move from a problematized *here* to a resolving *there*, through *further on* and *ever after*. This is profoundly the language of the soul, familiarly archetypal in its directional energies. One particular aspect of the telling that has become a language in which the soul is at home is the reliance on formulae. Early heroic poetry, as in the Anglo-Saxon canon, demonstrates the use of formulaic language in an oral tradition. Formulae fulfill all sorts of practical and imaginative purposes for listeners.[5] It is beyond the scope of this study to consider this subject in any detail. I simply want to register this kind of language, usually dominated by the particles, the closed-category items that we have been revaluing, and which are certainly in the working vocabulary of folk listeners.[6] *Once upon a* time, *long ago, ever after*, temporal formulae, often collocating with formulaic settings and formulaic situations. These are recognizable not only because we have been readers of, or listeners to, fairytales, but because we have *always already* been there in archetypal imagination.

First, a stimulating response to the language of tale-telling by Ursula Le Guin.[7] She establishes relationship, both tense and complementary, between what she describes as "mother tongue and father tongue," modes of speech used by both men and women. However, the cultural predicament of most women in the past caused them to rest more often, or more comfortably, in their mother tongue. We might associate this with the poet's feeling for "granaries of words like breasts."[8] Le Guin associates father tongue with the discourse of power, which does not need to be oppressive. It is a language more suited to disinterested analysis and action, a more distanced speech, more authentic when written and typically going one way and not inviting an answer. "It isn't anybody's native tongue," she concludes, but a learned language. She speaks about her own learning of three languages, all of them English.[9] It has been argued that

> a holistic, simultaneous, synthetic and concrete view of the world are the essential characteristics of a feminine outlook; linear, sequential, reductionist and abstract thinking defines the masculine....Whenever a culture elevates the written word, patriarchy dominates.[10]

We have considered some of the implications of the language of thought that values and seeks objectivity in the chapter on professional discourse, though even there, perhaps because its subject is psyche, our mother language constantly "breaks through." It is interesting to think of it as a tongue, or even a dialect, rather than more distantly, as a language. In this soul tongue are the idioms we feel at home in. Though we might question some of Le Guin's assumptions, as, for example, about the father tongue not demanding answers, it is fertile soil for reflection. Rowan Williams affirms her ideas but suggests that "what matters is not victory but keeping the conversation going." The mother tongue

> is about maintenance, the unobtrusive and hard-to-formalise ways in which people attend to the background regularities of a shared world, and so it values bare continuation, participation in the exchange, in a way that can be baffling or infuriating for someone conditioned to the idea of verbal exchange as an exchange of information or of signals about who is in charge. Death, for example, is surrounded by clichés....Some things require saying and originality is not what's looked for.[11]

Despite much richly colored symbolic substance, the fairytale is largely told under the auspices of mother tongue. That they were commonly told in spinning rooms by women would support this claim. Our familiarity with the speech and form of the fairytale constitutes much of its delight, but so do the oddities of the unexpected, the magical transformations and unimaginable outcomes. We enjoy both satisfaction of expectation, and surprise, two of the main ways by which fiction engages us.

In the twentieth century, before the post-postmodern deconstructions of fictive assumptions took hold, a novelist once spoke naively and illuminatingly about the construction of narrative. E. M. Forster distinguished between what he called "life by time" and "life by value," defining story as "a narrative of events arranged in their time sequence." But a plot is "also a narrative of events, the emphasis falling on causality."[12] He posits the most basic narrative structures: "The king died and then the queen died" tells the story. The smallest adjustment can change this. "The king died and then the queen died of grief" is a plot in which "the time-sequence is preserved, but the sense of causality overshadows it." Complexity can then be introduced by means of suspense: "The queen died, and no one knew why, until it was discovered that it was through grief at the death of the king." Telling life by time is most primitive. It is the way children first structure their experience, *vide* the child's breathless sharing of the school day's "and then... and then... and then...." So events unfold through time, grammatically via time's ubiquitous adverbials and tenses. This is perhaps paddling-pool perception in comparison with sophisticated contemporary narratology, but it is valuable. In fairytales, action is always condensed, the emphasis on what happens rather than detailed exploration of character. Le Guin wittily dispels our need to surrender to "heroic dominance."

> It is hard to tell a really gripping tale of how I wrested a wild-oat seed from its husk, and then another, and then another, and then another, and then another, and then I scratched my gnat bites, and Ool said something funny, and we went to the creek and got a drink and watched newts for a while, and then I found another patch of oats....No, it does not compare, it cannot compete with how I thrust my spear deep into the titanic hairy flank while Oob, impaled on one huge sweeping tusk, writhed screaming....This last story not only has Action, it has a Hero....All parts of the oat story have all been pressed into service in the tale of the Hero. But it isn't their story. It's his.[13]

And yet bald life by time alone does not enthrall us. She imagines instead a narrative that tells of

> that wonderful, big, long, hard thing, a bone, I believe, that the Ape Man first bashed somebody with in the movie and then,

> grunting with ecstasy at having achieved the first proper murder, flung up into the sky and whirling there it became a spaceship....I'm not telling that story. We've heard it, we've all heard all about all the sticks and spears and swords, the things to bash and poke and hit with, the long, hard things, but we have not heard about the thing to put things in, the container for the things contained. That is a new story.[14]

She establishes a new and more feminine narrative that might engage us anew.

Forster sees temporal sequence (and then and then) as "one of the lowest forms of the human faculties." More respectfully, C. S. Lewis spoke of the "easy excitement of what happens next," which kept people listening to the first human stories, and still has power to enchant even sophisticated postmoderns. Moving through time creates a reassuring sense of familiar order, which is partly why synchronicity disturbs us. Time moves on through *next*, and other temporal adverbs introduce more complexity, as with the anticipated *until*. *Until* brings tension, straining toward something posited in the future. *All of a sudden* generates even more excitement. This teleology of the fairytale drives toward resolution, but not through apotheosis. Le Guin makes a most provocative suggestion about story as a "stratagem of mortality."

> It is a means, a way of living. It does not seek immortality; it does not seek to triumph over or escape time (as lyric poetry does). It asserts, affirms, participates in directional time, time experienced, time as meaningful. If the human mind had a temporal spectrum, the nirvana of the physicist or the mystic would be way over in the ultraviolet, and at the opposite end, in the infrared, would be *Wuthering Heights*.[15]

Fairytales from around the world have the capacity to wander strangely along the axis of infra-red to ultra-violet, between now to always. This is both reassuring and disconcerting.

Bank advertisements accost us on city streets, vaunting the dream car that we are groomed to desire with the pledge, "Until your dreams are fulfilled, we will not rest" (United Bank of Switzerland ad). This is the stuff of current collective fantasy. What betrayal of the stretch of *until*, in relation to the treasure fullness of time offers; what a facile *until*, cheaply proffering the gold hard to attain. This is not what fairytales enact; their magical helpers are not of this ilk. Fairytales demand passage-through on a costly transformative path. The psychopompic fox only helps the one already embarked on the task.

In this psychic territory, Evangelist's seductive advice, "Go up directly thereto," is constantly thwarted. That is a heroic modality of which Le Guin warns us.

> So the Hero has decreed through his mouthpieces the Lawgivers, first, that the proper shape of the narrative is that of the arrow or spear, starting here and going straight there and THOK! hitting its mark (which drops dead); second, that the central concern of narrative, including the novel, is conflict; and third, that the story isn't any good if he isn't in it.[16]

The pilgrim's actual path demonstrates that Bunyan himself does know better, that he is tuned in to the vagaries of human motive and fallibility. Wandering is the prevailing mode, insistently getting things wrong but finally enabled to win the treasure.[17]

Dreams and fairytales urge that we must err. Although we note initial one-sidedness, whatever deficit is constellated at the beginning of a fairytale that compels a necessary figure to a necessary goal, we know that it will not be a direct path and may require actual circumambulation in order to bring the world into balance, or break the bewitchment of the complexes. This is enacted in "Jorinda and Joringel." The betrothed couple wanders-into the forest, falling deeply, and rather unusually, into melancholy. In the center of the forest lives the ever-vigilant witch, who captures Jorinda, turns-her-to stone, and cages her with all the other maidens. Joringel wanders far, grieving and searching for a solution to his loss. He works as a shepherd, and

> often walked round and round the castle, but not too near to it. At last he dreamt one night that he found a blood-red flower, in the middle of which was a beautiful large pearl and that he picked the flower and went with it to the castle and everything he touched with the flower was freed from enchantment.

Round and round, not too near, aware but not yet touching; *aber nicht zu nahe*. This circling is not the complex driving him round in circles. He circles inward and dreams about a flower. He then finds the flower of his dream, returns to the castle and can now get closer, just touching the door to gain instant access. Seeing the witch, "he sprang-towards her, touched the cage with his flower and also the old woman." The prepositional verbs release energy, allowing him now to act directly. The witch's enchantment is broken. Young maidens will no longer suffer paralysis, and the witch "could now no longer bewitch *anyone.*" Jorinda "was standing there…as beautiful as ever." *Now no longer* is fairytale time, soul time. Joringel did not go round in circles unproductively, though he had no sense of specific direction. He is impelled from within to ponder and con-centrate on the imprisoned center. This somehow constellates his dream, with its solution, not possibly imaginable beforehand. The language that proceeds from the action of the transcendent function could not be simpler, could not be more the speech of the mother tongue. Spatial and temporal aspects of the narrative are vital, communicated via that familiar formulaic lexis, which is both abstract and precise: Joringel walks "round and round but not too near"; the witch could "now no longer" bewitch; with Jorinda, just *there*, as beautiful *as ever.* Of necessity, "they lived happily *together* for a long time."

Happily *ever after* is the most commonly formulated ending that suggests that psychic well-being through the balancing of opposites has been achieved. The time frames of fairytale fascinate and shape our expectation. The equally common opening, *once/once upon a* time is deeply embedded in our sense of just so, how things must always be. As Roszak intuits, once upon a time is "actually before time itself existed—the world *In-here* and the world *Out-there* existed in the unity of a creative instant."[18] This temporal framing works subtly and with supreme differentiation in the tales. Marilynne Robinson goes even further, asserting,

> What is eternal must always be complete, if my understanding is correct. So it is possible to imagine that time was created in order that there might be narrative—event, sequence and causation, ignorance and error, retribution, atonement.[19]

We cannot escape time or sequence in fairytales, but we surrender to it willingly, carried along as in dream experience. This is disturbingly reassuring.

The Germanic tale of "Mother Holle" illustrates this surrender.[20] What is so interesting about this tale's journey of true and false individuation (one response to the tale) is that the second daughter, primed by the first girl's experience of her individual and unknown path, does in fact go-up directly *thereto*. This very directness to the known-beforehand, denied to the first, robs the second girl of the treasure. The first girl, who was required to descend into the well, was designated "the other" by the stepmother. The girl is hated, *even though* she is generous. The mother's own daughter is loved, *even though* she is selfish. *Even though* entrenches the stubbornness of the complex. After losing her spindle down the well accidentally, the first girl is forced by the stepmother to pursue it down into the subterranean realm of the lower mother. Landing underground, the girl finds green pastures and trees laden with fruit, bending down and asking relief; she finds and removes loaves that beg to be taken out of their oven. She risks herself to these tasks. Then, wandering *further on* (a necessary trajectory), she finds the frightful old woman in her welcoming cottage, which she enters despite the *but* of the risk. The girl's life is dominated by the Earth Mother's *must*. There are things she must do because the snow must fall. Both assert the imperative compulsion of nature. Then, in her own fullness of time, she yearns for home and asks to return-*back above* ground. She is led *through* the gate that leads *upward*, showered with gold as she passes. There is a crucial adverbial modality of time. The gold pours down only *just as* she passes *under* it. *Just as* is exactly the ripe time. The map of her journey can only now be inscribed. She can now take her underground, unconscious experience back into conscious living.

    The second daughter grabs her sister's map and follows it directly-to this final doorway. She pricks her finger, goes directly up to the well, directly up to the apple tree without relieving it of its fruit, directly up to the expected oven where bread is left to burn, directly up to the frightful old woman's cottage. She questions *why* of each *must*. She throws herself into the well, throws herself after the adventure she mimics. *At first* she shook the eiderdown *until* feathers flew, *but only this once*. There is no fullness of time when she felt the individuating need to return above ground. Instead, Mother Holle requires her to leave, pre-maturely. This *when* is ambiguous. The girl runs straight ahead to the doorway, places herself under the arch and waits impatiently for the shower of gold. Tar falls instead and she goes-back untransformed and black to the unchanged home. No spindle retrieved, no treasure attained. In a tale of true and false paths to individuating readiness, one expects a graduated temporal frame for the action in which *until* has special valence. Readiness is essential in the process of growing soul.

In "Briar Rose/Sleeping Beauty," the theme of readiness is even more urgent. Reaching the fullness of time takes a hundred years of fairytale time. In most tellings of this tale, the first paragraph is grammatically complex, then the progression is more direct. The formulaic temporal setting presents us with a King and Queen who are defined by their waiting. Every day they express their wish for the missing child through the aching *if only*, often intensified by an exclamatory "Ah!" The impossibility of fertility is enforced by *though* and *never*. This is usually the most intractable sentence of the whole tale, followed by the adversative *but* that introduces the next constellation.

> A long time ago, there were a King and Queen who cried every day, "Ah! If only we had a child!" though they never had one. But it happened that once when the Queen was bathing, a frog crept out of the water on to the land and said to her, "Your wish shall be fulfilled. Before a year has gone by, you shall have a daughter."

But introduces the opening up of a new temporal possibility, asserted through the verb *happened* and the closed phrase *once when*. The queen bathes and a frog creeps-out-onto land. The past tense of hopelessness transposes into a new futurity as the frog proclaims a confident *shall*. The schedule is not in a year's time you shall, but *before* a year has gone-by you shall. This is a mysterious passage of time, defying the ego's logic of *if I, then I*, which is often the expectation of analysands at the beginning of their work. Pain of barrenness must be felt, in tension with hope, until incubating life can manifest in consciousness. From here on the tale unfolds inevitably through time, connections almost entirely via the copulative *and*. There is little grammatical hindrance through *but*. Resistance is encountered through the thorn hedge that protects fullness of time and guards against pre-maturity. Temporal connections are direct, moving mainly through *and then* or *and when*, up to the *at last* of *as soon as* he kissed her. This effects a transformative *dénouement*. Narrative unfolds through spatially incremental ways, too, *through* the hedge and penetrating *still further into* the room at the center. Such narrative unfolding enchants listeners even more than readers, exploiting that easy excitement of what happens next.

To the center always impels, imperiously. Often the feminine is enclosed or imprisoned *there*, awaiting redemption, perhaps to be released back into process. Waiting to wake-up. Interestingly, we do not wake-down; consciousness is always symbolized by upwardness. The imperative to wait for fullness of time informs authentic psychic development. Wilfred Owen risks disturbing the incubation of this fullness in his sonnet, "Sleeping Beauty."

> Sojourning through a southern realm in youth,
> I came upon a house by happy chance
> Where bode a marvellous Beauty. There, romance
> Flew faerily until I lit on truth—
> For lo! the fair Child slumbered. Though, forsooth,
> She lay not blanketed in drowsy trance,
> But leapt alert of limb and keen of glance,
> From sun to shower; from gaiety to ruth;
> Yet breathed her loveliness asleep in her:
> For, when I kissed, her eyelids knew no stir.
> So back I drew tiptoe from that Princess,
> Because it was too soon, and not my part,
> To start voluptuous pulses in her heart,
> And kiss her to the world of Consciousness.[21]

This approach to the beauty that slept is punctuated by a reflective resistance, in the grammar of *though, forsooth, but, yet, so, because*. There is no simple sequence of *and when, and then*. The questing male figure's kiss to consciousness would be pre-mature. Too soon. The penetrative ego saw, acknowledged, and honored the unreadiness, recognizing that a necessary *until* had not been reached. This is a psychological tact needed in analytical praxis, knowing when, able to recognize *too soon*.

In the story of Briar Rose as it is most commonly told, this unreadiness, the not-yet, is reflected in the conscious attempts at rescue planned by several princes, in heroic mode trying valiantly to break through the hedge of thorns that protects the dormant girl's incubation. In many versions, the prince who does make it to the fortified center just happens to hear about Briar Rose just *as* he rides-out on his own journey. He just happens to reach the hedge just as a hundred years ends. It must be said that no self-respecting traditional hero would tolerate these *just-as* indignities of fairytale success. It would be most unheroic to have Joringel's victory, with only a flower just to touch the castle's door to open it, no need for battering rams. Briar Rose's prince is helped by a cooperative thorn hedge that bends like flowers. A Red Sea passage-through. But he had to approach the hedge vulnerably, humbly, in the right place at the right time with the right attitude. Le Guin has harsh words for conventional heroes. What she says about her own capacity to fight hoodlums off if needed is pertinent for the fairytale hero:

> I don't, nor does anybody else, consider myself heroic for doing so. It's just one of those damned things you have to do in order to be able to go on gathering wild oats and telling stories.[22]

Just so with this prince. He allows the story to go on, but it is not a "starting *here* and going straight *there* and THOK!" narrative. In those ways, however, the lawgiving Father-King is demonstrably heroic, with almost comical bravado taking on all the spindles of the kingdom, destroying them in a conflagration of protective love for his child. Such heroic defense is subverted in fairytales, often through a slippery *nevertheless*. Nevertheless, despite his magisterial authority, just one spindle survives. And so the princess is pricked; and so the unheroic prince does get to the heart at the center, as trickster-hero; and so the feminine is kissed to consciousness.

Many tales follow similar trajectories to the center, often to the center of a forest. Some denizens live *near* the edge, like Little Red Cap who lives where village meets forest. Foresters and woodcutters live in the depths, as do witches. The quest takes ordinary folk "deep" into these woods. (Fig. 15) We do not go higher into forests; it is always a descent. The symbolic atmosphere of this forest experience is captured by Roy Daniells, a Canadian poet.

> "So they went deeper into the forest," said Jacob Grimm,
> And the child sat listening with all his ears,
> While the angry queen passed. And in after years

Figure 15. Anthony Browne, *Into the Woods*.

> The voice and the fall of words came back to him
> (Though the fish and the faithful servant were grown dim,
> The aproned witch, the door that disappears,
> The lovely maid weeping delicious tears
> And the youngest brother, with one bright-feathered limb)—
> "Deeper into the forest."
>   There are oaks and beeches
> And green high hollies. The multitudinous tree
> Stands on the hill and clothes the valley, reaches
> Over long lands, down to a roaring sea.
> And the child moves onward, into the heart of the wood,
> Unhindered, unresisted, unwithstood.[23]

The sonnet evokes archetypal experience of the great forest, especially potent for those who were introduced to it, and entered it, in childhood. Most such wilderness has been lost, so it is hard to have a true fairytale sense of these directionless, lonely tracts. Into such usually pathless depths, exposed and simultaneously protected, we must make our descent fully to experience fairytale terrors and transformations. One such tale, often provoked in analytical experience, is "Hansel and Gretel." Here the journey to the center is demanded and accomplished despite strategies of avoidance. Moving *onward* is going *inward*. This trail is evaded in many psychotherapies that set goals for the work, quite certain of what paths should be taken.

Because of resistances, the flow of narrative conjunctives is halting in most versions of this tale. Father resists abandoning his children to the forest and Hansel resists by dropping pebbles to mark a path back home. (Fig. 16) Regressions are needful on these urgent ego-Self pathways. Initially, the way-back-home must be lost. Forest birds swoop down to eat the crumbs, obliterating the backward path, and then they alight on the witch's roof at the heart of the forest, guiding the lost children to their unconscious destination. The direction is ever inward, ever downward. The force of the re-gression is asserted through the temporal adverb *again*, and even *again and again*, that keeps interrupting the forward development of *and then, and when*. Again is the adverb of the complex, finally arrested in the witch's seductively sweet prison. Then the action moves forward to its climax. *Then, when*, and *now* speed up as the witch is tricked into her own oven. Then they could go into the cottage and gain the treasure. Re-turning home is very different from the initial looking-*back* that hindered the opening, when Hansel dropped pebbles on the path back to the empty pantry. This pantry could only be re-filled by imagining the destruction of the witch at the center of the complex.

The prepositions and prepositional phrases insistently drive *further into, even further into* abandonment. The rejecting mother had taken them "farther into the wood, so that they will not find their way out again….she led the children deeper into the forest, where they had never been before." They repeatedly fell asleep in the impenetrable wood, and when they woke, always, "They began to walk again, but they always came deeper into the forest." The travail of these helpless figures fuels Le Guin's perceptive questioning.

> Well, so that is our country. Why did we look up for blessing—instead of around and down? What hope we have lies there.

Figure 16. Anthony Browne, *Hansel and Gretel*. (Looking Back).

> Not in the sky full of orbiting spy-eyes and weaponry, but in the earth we have looked down upon. Not from above, but from below. Not in the light that blinds, but in the dark that nourishes, where human beings grow souls.[24]

That tantalizing *well* and *so* evoke what we know, resist, and invite, simultaneously.

The tension between the going-back, with its false perhaps-this-time-all-will-be-well solace, and the pull forward to the traumatic encounter with the witch is heightened through the numerous adverbial conjunctions. The story's movement through simple co-ordinating *and* is constantly disturbed by *but* or *nevertheless*, which is always a vital means of sustaining tension. "Nevertheless Hansel comforted his sister and said, 'Do not cry, Gretel, but go to sleep quietly for the good God will help us.'" In tales arising out of a Christian culture, we expect this formulation of the psychological need for the ego to surrender to the Self. Do not cry, but rest quietly. To feel this calm trust is as helpful in fairytale crisis as in the consulting room, where the analyst, more healthily the inner analyst, takes on Hansel's role.

In our speech there is a deictic potential that is considered universal. We will refer to it briefly here and consider it further in relation to other tales. In "Hansel and Gretel" there is a significant play of reference between *here*, *there*, and *where*, poles between which the plot moves. These demonstrative adverbs are stable semantically insofar as they maintain consistent dictionary meaning.[25] But they need context in time, place, and person to be fulfilled. Tune in to this aspect in the following quotations from the tale, as typically told. The unmothering mother plots: "We will take the children out into the forest to *where* it is the thickest; *there* we will…leave them *alone*." As they leave, the boy turns back to drop pebbles, and his father asks, "Hansel, what are you looking at there and staying behind for?" *There* is the familiar emptiness, familiar destitution. Anthony Browne's depiction of this emotional squalor is all too recognizable. Despite Hansel's active resistance, the children must be taken to, abandoned in, an unknown *elsewhere*. It is commonly accepted that the negative mother has at least one value: she compels her child to take to the road. There is nothing to stay home for. But it is traumatic to integrate the consequences of psychological abandonment. Meager crumbs of food are often sacrificed to find a way back, with false hope, to the old destitution. We witness Hansel's backward looking so often, when analysands feel helpless to sever the ties back to past emptiness, unable to let go of old complexes that have habituated them to insufficiency.

There is another potential inner and outer place that the children have to experience. The witch asks with feigned innocence, "Oh, you dear children, who has brought you here?"—a terrible *here*, home of false mother-provider who lies in wait for children in her enticing gingerbread house. What must become conscious is the core truth deep in the forest-unconscious, that the face of depriving Mother is that of the witch. This image must be redeemed.

Entering-in and finding the way-out are different paths. Hansel and Gretel must lose the way they came in; birds *must* eat the crumbs, for they *must* discover the witch's house. But they must also discover aloneness, like most fairytale figures, needing that time for new possibilities to incubate. How often the forest is the context for being *alone*, even *all alone*, Jung's requirement for being all alone in the world, the necessary orphan condition.[26] (Fig. 17)

Once the witch's power is outwitted, the return *will* be via another route, involving crossing-over a river that did not appear on the way-in. Their path lies between two cottages. One is empty of food, the other an edible cottage, made of all the sweet food they have been denied. It is a path between destitution and false abundance. It is common for the deprived and hungry heart to crave and pursue false nourishment, as witnessed in starved analysands who have repeated histories of exploitative and empty relationships. Once the devouring mother is devoured in her own heat, they can bring back the means to stock the old empty pantry. They cross-over to a hitherto unimaginable way of being.

Hansel and Gretel were actively lost; they were helplessly passive to deliberate parental losing. However, many fairytale figures, adult and child, are lost accidentally. The forest is an obvious place to be lost. In "The Six Swans," a hunting King loses his way in thick woods. He too must stay lost to encounter his Witch, who bargains his escape for marriage to her daughter. He takes this daughter *up behind him* on his horse as bride, though he cannot bear even to look-at her. The warring energy of these phrases introduces the tension for the whole tale. Commitment to the very thing we cannot bear to face is a good image for the complexes that we continue to carry behind us. The King's fear for the children of his previous marriage makes him conceal them even further into forest darkness. The path to them can only be found through the guidance of a magical Ariadne-clue. The Witch procures this and finds the six boys in the castle, whom she turns-into swans.

WHITHER OF THE FAIRYTALE 153

Figure 17. Anthony Browne, *Hansel and Gretel*. (Alone in the Forest).

Sentences race forward, *ands* and *buts* breaking through defenses, moving then halting, until the King's own daughter makes the kind of statement that echoes through analytical praxis. "*Here* I can no longer stay. I will go and seek my brothers." "I can no longer live like this" is an announcement that initiates individuation. The center of consciousness must shift.

To discover her brothers, the faithful sister must find another path *back into* the forest. She needs to connect with her own masculine energy, determining,

> "I can no longer stay here. I will go and seek my brothers." At night she ran-away, and went straight into the forest. She walked through the night and next day also, without stopping, until she was too tired to go any farther. Then she saw a forest hut, and went-into it, and found a room with six little beds, but she did not want to get into one of them, but crept underneath, and lay down on the hard ground, spent the night there.

She goes *straight into* the forest, walking all night and day *until* she finds the brothers' cottage. The brothers find her and insist, "*Here* you cannot remain." The *there* she risks is their imprisoning *here*. Again she must go "into the midst" of dense trees. She climbs-up-into the branches and there begins to weave the redemptive shirts for the swans, sitting safely *there* among the leaves. She is found, forced to come-down, and taken-up on the King's horse, in the silence required by her task. Married in her silence, married to her silence. Such incubating silence must be protected. The King's witch-mother questions, "From *whence* comes this creature who cannot speak?" and contrives that she be found guilty of devouring her children, a projection of her own destructive hunger. Throughout the tale's time, the young queen never stops sewing the shirts. We wait for a redemptive *suddenly* to rupture the remorseless sequence of events. This is withheld until the painful climax. Only on the last day of the six years during which she must not speak, *only just as* the fire "was *just* going to be lit," only *then* could the swans fly in. She is able *at last* to throw the shirts over them, and *as soon as* they were touched-by them, *at once* they turned-back-into human form. Except the left wing of the youngest brother. About him, with his all-but-complete transformation, another story is told daily in our praxis. We know what that un-trans-formed bit feels like, and honor Jung's insistence that we cannot and should not try to heal *everything*. At this last hour, *at last*, the silence is broken. "*Now* I may speak." Into this new thither the hidden children are brought and new prospects open up, a transformed *now* that looks toward a future.

In these stories, a liberating heroic feminine is activated. I use heroic here not in the sense that Le Guin condemned it, but in the sense that Jung suggests, seeing the hero/heroine figure as "self-representation of the longing of the unconscious," that propels it into "restlessness and wandering."[27] In such a project, inevitably, a kinetic grammar of movement will be exploited.

I suggested that in "Hansel and Gretel" a regressive pull *back* to the empty pantry fuelled the repetitive *agains* of the narrative. This is not always the force of *again*. The handless maiden's *never again* has more a sense of restorative movement than neurotic repetition. This mutilated but resolute daughter forestalls imprisonment in an old regressed *here*, subject to patriarchal *dictat*, positioned at the back of the house of her resource-less miller father. In a loaded, lexically bare threat, the devil had insisted that father must dis-empower his daughter: "If you do not do it you are mine and I will take you yourself" (Grimm is equally bare: "*Wo du es nicht thust, so bist du mein und ich hab dich selber*").[28] The girl at first met her father's pleas with the elemental monosyllables, "do with me what you will, I am your child" (reminiscent of Christ's "nevertheless your will not mine be done"?). Thereupon she sacrifices her hands and resolves to move on from her passive way of being. Such a *thereupon* has the *ipse dixit* certainty of a strong father-complex that clearly needs interrogation. The father offers her all the treasure he has gained from his diabolical deal, but she rejects him firmly, though forgiving him outrageously—clearly not for the first time. With a staunch *but* she comes to herself: "*but…here I cannot stay, I will go forth.*"

With the same resolve, the sister of "The Seven Ravens" "set out…and went forth into the wide world to search for her brothers to free them." She went "further and further, to the very end of the world." This uncompromising sense of the *here* that must be left behind and the transformed *there* that calls actualize the urge to move. There is archetypal momentum in this urge; psychic energy is constellating in an urge to consciousness.[29] A neurotic *here* is rejected. *Forth*, another valuable archaic adverb that has the same atmosphere as yonder, thither: going-forth, setting-forth, henceforth, and so forth, serving psyche's individuating purposes especially in fairytale narrative.

Figure 18. Anthony Browne, *Hansel and Gretel*. (Return to Father).

All fairytale figures must set-out. The handless maiden's tale plays on the experience of what constitutes *enough* to secure psychological health after searing betrayal. *Thereupon* signals her setting-out, hoping only for "as much as I require." *As much as* belongs in the same semantic and psychological field as *enough*. This is mother tongue and soul language. At nightfall the starving girl finds a paradisal garden guarded by a moat. "*Ah, if I were but* inside *that I might* eat of the fruit, *or else must I* die of hunger." No heroic assault on the garden's defenses can lead to satisfaction; rather, it offers an essential *inside* to reach-after. The conditional and subjunctive auxiliaries invoke prayer, not theft. Before action can resume in the indicative mood of fact, fantasy and longing have to be tasted. Le Guin regrets the reductive tyranny of living and writing in the indicative, while,

> beneath that specious and arrogant assumption of certainty all the ancient, cloudy, moody powers and options of the subjunctive remain in force. The indicative points its bony finger at primary experiences, at the Things; but it is the subjunctive that joins them, with the bonds of analogy, possibility, probability, contingency, contiguity, memory, desire, fear, and hope: the narrative connection.[30]

Fairytales are always voiced in this spirit, either in oral or literary form, for this is their soul tongue, a dimension perhaps most often voiced through verbal auxiliaries. "If only I could… if only I were to…" can mark the beginning of the dissolution of complexes in therapy as in these tales. Initially, it may release appetite, Winnicott's good greed.

Alongside the now handless young queen is the sympathetic Queen Mother, who affirms her determination and her acceptance of the unknown as preferable to the known. She also recognizes where the feminine must free itself from patriarchal manipulation, from subordination to the abuses of masculine power. She too urges: "But *here* you may stay no longer. Go *forth into* the wide world with your child and *never* come *back here again*." The language is uncompromising, its energy typically generated through prepositions and adverbials. The handless mother carries her child on her back into the wilderness, where she finds a house of grace, at last a healing "*here* all dwell free.*"* She is conducted inside, no moat now separating her from the fulfillment of need. She is introduced into a belonging she has not known, from whence her redemption will be accomplished. This can only happen after her husband-King has completed his own journey through forest paths. The tale weaves between the longing, the hoping and praying mood and tense, and the brave indicative action of the vulnerable maturing girl. When the King finds her, his response is protective, not heroic: "*If you are* forsaken by all the world, *yet will I not* forsake you." Much of the action proceeds through dialogue that depends on interrogatives—how, why, who—that try to sort out and counteract the work of shadow power play that disguises motive and confuses identity. The tale had begun in the shadow of *behind* (*hinter*), an unconscious state hidden to consciousness. Precious things are often positioned here, like a king's apple tree bearing golden fruit, behind his palace (Grimm's "Golden Bird"). The daughter is situated in this *behind* when the father's rash promise is made, sacrificing to the devil whatever lies *behind* his mill. Traditionally, fathers are not lawbreakers but promise-keepers, unremitting guardians of the given word. This can collude with the devil's manipulation of communication, as in the letter exchanges in this story.

The King who owns the palace and the apple tree in "The Golden Bird" belongs, initially, to the tribe of counting Kings. But he is able to loosen the counting neurosis to experience the treasure. Enumerating and tallying cannot ensure the mysterious quantity of *enough*, for enough is not quantitative. The handless girl's pear eating elaborates the quality of provision, the felt knowledge of sufficiency. There is much lexical play around the healing supply of *enough* (*genug*, *satt*), and the forms associated in Romantic languages with Latin *satis*. *Satis-facere*, to make enough. Satiety. Being fed by some kind of grace, feeling satisfied is the potent *enough*, rather than everything, that fairytales and analysis seek.[31]

Fairytale figures are often asked from whence they come, as they discover a new "here." "The Singing Soaring Lark" moves between various contradictory and related soul places, and as in all tales, the specific narrative context defines and realizes each *here* and each *there*. This tale's first *here* is home, the *status quo* from which one must depart. The tale's final *here* is the home of the lion-prince and the daughter-queen, where their own child awaits them. There are various here's and there's in the wandering of father, prince, and daughter. The first, provisional *there* is the lion's tree trap, home to the singing soaring lark. On the father's return home to his known *here*, he begs his child "not to go *there*, come what might." But the girl's soul is already compelled to sing and soar, and resisting father's energy, she too insists,

"I will go *thither*." Singing and soaring is a splendid image of psychic flourishing. After her sojourn with her lion-prince-husband, she desires to return to her father's home, so she "went *thither*, accompanied by the lion." Her roaming is far from finished. Her next *there* is edge and center of the sea: "Then she went thither, and found everything as the night wind had said." And still she must journey further, to the castle where the lion-prince is captive to a new bride, "the castle where both of them were living *together there*." Quietened by her grief, she has respite from movement forward. She went out "into a meadow, sat down there, and wept." Such postures incubate new possibilities, for "while she was sitting there, she thought of the egg." Each *there* reached becomes a new *here* from which further directions arise. We might call these stations of the soul, discovered and visited in each tale according to the particular constellation of each errand. But the final goal is always the soul's home, lost pieces of self, endangered parts of self, gathered together, individuating wholeness finding some haven for a future.

Mary Midgley, a moral philosopher, reflects on persistent patterns of motivation that she identifies as a homing instinct in most life forms. These she calls open instincts. Of this pattern she says that

> such general locomotive tendencies as the one to *come home*—which is common to many animals, including some very simple ones—an indefinite and unpredictable variety of ways travelling, routes to be followed…yet the creature must have a general ruling motive….the more complex, the more intelligent creatures become, the more they are programmed in this general way, rather than in full detail.[32]

Most fairytales log and enact innate homing tendencies in the human soul. We feel this portrayed urgently in the tales we have already considered; Hansel and Gretel cross the water back to father. Anthony Browne imagines father standing at an open door, now entrance into, rather than forced exit from, the original house with empty pantry. But now green shoots break through dark soil. Former dead home life is enlivened, its destitution replenished with treasure they have won. The homecoming of the young woman who desired the singing and soaring lark also passes-over water, on the back of a griffin. "Immediately a tall nut-tree grew up, whereon the bird rested, and then carried them home, where they found their child." In the grip of these tales, such creatures compel attention to their symbolic significance. That is where we usually go; but I am deliberately responding to less obvious facets of archetypal influence, through unexceptional, usually disregarded words that contribute so much to the psychic economy.

The syntactical flow of "The Singing Soaring Lark" is unusually complex. We do have moments when the strongly indicative sentences push forward resolutely, nothing allowed to hinder progressive movement: "So she took it out and put it on, and went up into the castle, and everyone, even the bride herself, looked at her with astonishment." But verbal auxiliaries are mostly complex from the beginning of a story that illuminates the individuation of a highly neurotic personality.

> There was once upon a time a man who was about to set out on a long journey, and on parting he asked his three daughters what he should bring back with him for them. Whereupon the eldest wished for pearls, the second wished for diamonds, but the third said, dear father, I should like a singing, soaring lark. The father said, yes, if I can get it, you shall have it, kissed all three, and set out.

The plot unfolds out of this nexus of complexes. The father "about to set out," asking what he "should bring back." The too-beloved daughter is marked out straightaway. While the first two daughters simply wish-for and later simply receive, the third "should like" and is responded to with the complementary, "if I can get it you shall have it." Tenses and moods are particularly dense, refusing indicative simplicities; there is a proliferation of subjunctives, conditionals, imperatives, modal auxiliaries: *must* and *should, might, could,* and *if* and *but.* Of course, these grammatical particles supply the nuts and bolts of any utterance. But we can also ignore the crucial part they play in carrying essential significance and nuance in fiction and in therapeutic anamnesis.

> Only spare my life. The lion said, nothing can save you, unless you will promise to give me for my own what first meets you on your return home, and if you will do that, I will grant you your life, and you shall have the bird for your daughter, into the bargain. But the man hesitated and said, that might be my youngest daughter.

Impatient of the father's caution, the practical servant insists, *why should your daughter be the very one to meet you*, *it might as easily be* a cat. Ego consciousness struggles to cope with new possibilities pragmatically. In this first encounter with the numinous lion, the father, the servant, and the lion itself have a potent *however*. But as obstacles to growth and reconciliation are transcended, the syntax loosens its modal intensity and the future possibilities become present realities. The complexity of mood is replaced by intensities of time. The whole tale has suspended the individuating figure between the lion's dark night and the intrusive light of day, alternating his animal/human identity. This diurnal movement is transcended as bewitchment is broken. The action speeds up, moving impatiently through *and then, and when*. This enforces the close texture of consequence, each incident dependent on the one before, the promise, threat, and anticipation of possibility. This density is typical of all fairytales, but especially interesting in this one. Such archaic diction as *whereupon/thereupon* is now lost to common speech, no longer found outside traditional tellings of myth or fairytale, but it houses a vital sense of psychological consequence.

As we have noticed in all the other stories, the prepositional forms urge action forward or backward; more journeys *into the midst* of forests, and *back again into* them, continually *further and further into* the wide world. And when this kind of prepositional energy infuses verbs, psychic tension is at its fiercest. The energy is also disturbingly and reassuring meta-morphic. There is much transforming into, becoming again, changing into, constant shape-shifting dynamics until authentic being can be stabilized, a stability perhaps endorsed by the child who appears at the end, waiting to greet wandering parents, heralding the ineluctable urge to self-realization.

One final tale vividly affirms the impossibility of ever going directly up to the treasure. In the Spanish "Water of Life," three brothers desire to grow rich and set off to win treasure. They accumulate wealth, build palaces and churches, but no matter what they create, there is "still something else needed." An old man diagnoses the problem: they need to find three things: "water of life, a smell that gives eternal beauty from the branch of a tree, and a talking bird." To procure these, they are told, "Go to the mountain that is *far off yonder*, and *you will* find what you seek." One paragraph in particular articulates the predicaments of the path most teasingly. Each quester in turn asks a giant the way. He replies:

> Many have passed-by seeking those treasures, but none have ever come-back; and you will never come back either, unless you mark my words. Follow this path, and when you reach the mountain, you will find it covered-with stones. Do not stop to look at them, but keep on your way. As you go you will hear scoffs and laughs behind you; it will be the stones that mock. Do not heed them; above all, do not turn round. If you do you will become as one of them. Walk straight on till you get to the top, and then take all you wish for.

Inevitably the brothers are unable to accomplish this; they do look-back and are able to turn neither right nor left, as instructed. *Only* the sister can withstand the temptations. *Only then* can she turn around and descend the mountain.

The title of this book speaks of coming home into the language of the experiencing soul and heart, as well as the reflective mind. Fairytales do this to and for us, receive us and send us out, refreshed and reassured that the path is worthwhile that leads to reconciliation and balance in each particular soul's kingdom. This language, as home, is fascinating and ambivalent. It is both the language of our hearth, the language of our everyday heart, but also, it is ritual language. Not what Yeats called "wideawake" language. When one has encountered such tales as a child, especially as mesmerized listener, one has a very secure imaginative home for them, from which to go out into the world of sense and fantasy, sensitively evoked in Daniell's poem. The sense of the specialness of this language is heightened if it was first heard *spoken*, though it is still efficacious as read-word. It is the domain of kings and queens, certainly, and of magical possibilities and life and death situations, never resolved by brute heroism, but by tricksterish manipulations, by a strange logic of eros, by engagement with the absurd. There is often a sense of the archaic in the language, words reserved for special occasions, but not for intellectual exchange, not meta-language of professional discourse. *Hither and thither, whereupon, thence* and *whence, yonder* and all points *beyond*. This early aural attraction by fairytale language with its sense of soul-occasion is captured in Sartre's account of his own initiation into the mystery of story. He heard its special language in its "Sunday best," ceremonial and bewitching.

> *De ce visage de statue sortit une voix de plâtre. Je perdis la tête: qui racontait? quoi? et à qui? Ma mere s'était absentée: pas un sourire, pas un signe de connivence, j'étais en exile. Et puis je ne reconnaissais pas son langage. Où prenait-elle cette assurance? Au bout d'un instant j'avais compris: c'était le livre qui parlait.*[33]

His book spoke magically. Of the narrating mother he confesses, "il me semblait que j'étais l'enfant de toutes les mères, qu'elle était la mère de tous les enfants." In this ritual, the teller becomes all mothers and the listener becomes all children. Sartre suggests that it is the language and the style of narration that activates archetypal experience, as well as symbolic figures like woodcutters (*le bûcheron, la bûcheronne et leurs filles*) or creatures like forest does (*des biches au bois*). Sartre remembers the deadly intrusion of patriarchal discourse when father's scholarly friend interrogated the boy about his understanding of the tales.

> *Il me sembla qu'on interrogeait un enfant: à la place du bûcheron, qu'eût-il fait? Laquelle des deux soeurs préférait-il? Pourquoi? Approverait-il le châtiment de Babette?*[34]

This wrenching from soul's experience into an alien analytical discourse silenced him, but could not rob him of delight, recalled as a transfiguring liberation.

I have visited only a few tales, using various translations, named and anonymous, illuminating common narrative language. All retellings use language in the ways I have suggested. I hope that readers will be encouraged to feel and respond to the urgency and efficacy of these lively particles of our grammars—not instead of, but in addition to, the more obvious allure of the symbolic objects and creatures that meet us: crowns, flowers, water, fire, ovens, spindles, edible houses and castles, forests, oceans, seashores, kings and princes, maidens and crones, griffins and lions and lark, beggars and merchants; and all the archetypal situations and experiences, wars, marriages, births, and deaths.

We might ask, where is soul in such a linguistic exploration? I would answer that we hear psyche in conjunctive modalities, for there we often hear the complexes speaking, as in *and yet*. We see Self working its alchemy through *nevertheless*, the transcendent function exerting its energy through *however*, and archetypal directions criss-crossing psyche's terrain. Fairytales speak through action and direct speech. Native tellings would never use words like "misunderstanding" or "failed communication." But where there is such failure, it is embodied through action, as when malevolent servants or the devil himself exchange letters or rewrite them, as in "The Handless Maiden." Messages are misrepresented, false documents substituted. In such ways, the tales imagine the way complexes interfere with mutual exchange, derailing it with traumatic consequences. The true message does not get through, and here the often insidious implications of the harmless conjunctive particle *instead* is engaged, with its limitless field of alternative possibilities. Soul also speaks through the shifting from indicative verbal realities into unlimited potentiality of conditionals and subjunctive auxiliaries, through *could*, *would*, and *might*, which especially initiate the capacity to wish and hope. In this ordinary everyday language there is a sense of mystery, sometimes coming even from archaic usage, as in the hither, whence, thither, and whither that set me off on my exploration. That world is made my world, the world I recognize; but it is also strangely other. I enter the familiar, unknown other-world. This was Sartre's experience. And he is right. The listener becomes every child, and the teller becomes every mother.

The Red Book wrestles with the phenomenon of bewitchment, but bewitchment not by the extraordinary, but by the banal, the trite, the platitudinous, the commonplace. One might include the formulaic in the unexpected term banality, Jung's *Banalität*. One might also describe the little particle words that I labor to dignify, as banal. Jung recounts that in his encounter, the first mysterious *She* admits:

> She: …I was bewitched by the banal.

> I: Woe is me, because you now become very fairy tale like.
> She: Be reasonable dear friend, and do not stumble now over the fabulous, since the fairy tale is the great mother of the novel, and has even more universal validity than the most avidly read novel of your time. And you know that what has been on everyone's lips for millennia, though repeated endlessly, still comes nearest the ultimate human truth. So do not let the fabulous come between us.[35]

CHAPTER SIX

Whither in Myth:
We Are All Part of It

…the question we ask of a myth…is not whether or not it is true or false, but whether it is living or dead.[1]
—Richard Holloway, *Doubts and Loves*

"Time is neither here nor there": "we are all part of it"[2]
—Salley Vickers, *Where Three Roads Meet*

In this chapter, I respond to content of myth but I am more preoccupied with its telling. No matter what one hears (for example, Canadian native people telling their myths) or what one reads of written retellings (as in the sophisticated narrative of Ovid), the manner of narration has certain constant features. I will deal mainly with Greek myth, which is still a vital source of imagery for archetypal process.[3]

Preceding chapters have endorsed a model of attentiveness to language that can enrich our reading and listening to the mythic, both for our own delight and for the benefit of analytical work at the soul face. One ear is always listening for the mythic in our practice, alert for parallels that give us a sense of living in a shared archetypal world, enlarging our sensibilities and connections. We all share Steiner's "primal impulse."

> The compelling affinities between the philosophic and the poetic modes, their twin inceptions in the primal impulse towards meaning, towards the attempts of the human consciousness to find a lodging in the given world—an attempt we call myth—have induced those conflicts of which Plato's *Republic* remains exemplary. The status of the fictive within the "truth-values" of analytic and systematic intellection, the status of the fictive within the "veracity-values" of morality, have been a fruitful irritant to epistemology and to ethics….Literature is a voracious and archaic beast.[4]

I am concerned with the project of unconscious experience to "find a lodging in the given world," a lodging in which to abide and to set-out-from. The myth stories are fabulous, yet simultaneously and paradoxically they are familiar in the mind's world, and in the world's mind. We hear them in our mother tongue, even when they are full of strange, alluring names of gods, heroes, and places, rooted in alien cultures, which are nevertheless universally resonant. Never-land is also Ever-land, located in realized worlds, improbably possible. I remember a powerful moment of recognition, as a child reading *Peter Pan*:

> Catch them trying to draw a map of a child's mind, which is not only confused, but keeps going round all the time. There are zigzag lines on it, just like your temperature on a card, and these are probably roads in the island; for the Neverland is always more or less an island, with astonishing splashes of colour here and there and coral reefs, and rakish-looking crafts in the offing,…and gnomes who are mostly tailors, caves through which rivers run….it would be an easy map if that were all; but there is also first day at school, religion, fathers, the round pond…and either these are part of the island or they are another map showing through,…Neverlands have a family resemblance.[5]

Each psychic map is created anew in each of us, in every succeeding era, with the oldest map of all *showing-through* maps of later mental and emotional discoveries. Myth is the most ancient layer of mind, expressing and recapitulating our containment in the archetypal world. Each human journey begins with this under-map in place, which we quickly begin to recognize as we discover and create subsequent charts that overlie but also rise out of the most archaic one.

WHITHER IN MYTH

One of our most fundamental myth maps is the odyssey, an inescapable trajectory always *from here to there, from whence to whither.* These adverbials hold each human story in a primordial archetypal stretch. *Here* is more stably knowable than *there*, since *there* shifts, and is often obscured between flashes of clarity. Until it can be found, it can only ever be imagined. Tennyson understood this, giving his ambivalent mythic voyager the words:

> Yet all experience is an arch wherethro'
> Gleams that untravell'd world, whose margin fades
> For ever and for ever when I move.[6]

We live-within and live-out myth, but we never possess it, never empty it, for it is always expanding and amplifying with each telling, each enactment, for ever and ever. It belongs to us and we to it. So the Greek Cavafy propels us to our own mythic voyage:

> As you set out for Ithaka
> hope your road is a long one…

He offers us his Ithaka, toward which we all might sail, meeting all Odysseus's hazards, especially en route home. He counsels that

> you won't encounter them
> unless you bring them along inside your soul,
> unless your soul sets them up in front of you.[7]

We have not yet played with the conjunction *unless*, which introduces conditional experience, but it is crucial to the archetype of setting off, taking to the road. For as Cavafy argues, "Without her you wouldn't have set out." And once she (Ithaka) has opened herself to the traveler as destination, "She has nothing left to give you now." Arriving *there* is our destiny, but it is the "marvelous journey" itself that Ithaka most valuably bequeaths. Only when we make the journey can we claim the promise, for "you'll have understood by then what these Ithakas mean." Ithaka is plural, Ithakas are places of departure and places of return, from where a new *there* can be envisioned. Ithaka is a meaning bigger than home. We live in the space between where-from and where-to; myth inhabits, grows out of, that gap. An analysand in midlife, a typical twenty-first-century agnostic, spoke of his "Nazareth years," a careless boyhood in a small town that preceded later times of trauma.

He acknowledged with surprise symbolic places in his psychic geography such as his Bethlehems, numinous moments of epiphany.

We do not lodge consciousness only in exotic distance. We might feel its roots in peasant earth close by:

> *There* is the source from which all cultures rise,
> And all religions,
> *There* is the pool in which the poet dips
> And the musician.
> Without the peasant base civilization must die,
> Unless the clay is in the mouth the singer's singing is
>   useless. (poet's italics)[8]

This chapter dips into this pool and listens to this song of peasant earth.

What was said of Daedalus's Cretan labyrinth might also be said of Odysseus's meandering round Aegean islands. There is no going-directly-to Troy, and certainly no going-straight-back home to Ithaka. Daedalus has built into the design of the labyrinth the very pattern of the mythic path,

> confusing the usual marks of direction, and leading the eye of the beholder astray by misleading paths winding in various directions. Just as the playful waters of the Maeander in Phrygia flow this way and that, randomly, as the river runs back on itself, flowing now towards its source and now towards the ocean, always changing course, so Daedalus constructed countless meandering paths and was himself hardly able to find his way back to the entrance, the maze was so deceptive.[9]

We have met this wandering in every chapter. How can we stabilize *where* or *there* when they wind *this* way and *that*, making full use of those arrogant demonstratives. Jung enacted the same oscillating compass: "I know nothing about a way. I can neither want this nor that since nothing indicates to me whether I want this or that."[10] This is not vague indecisiveness; it embraces the tension of the opposites till the way manifests. We must always honor such not-knowing in soul work.

Salley Vickers comments explicitly on this dilemma in her novel in which a mysterious narrator confronts Freud with the Oedipus myth. She asks,

> —Where to begin? Let's start with place. You know where you are with place. There is a particular place always in my mind when it comes to this story. A place in Greece in the region of Phokis, a place where three roads meet. A point where a road divides and one arm strikes northwest in a steep defile towards Delphi, while the other skirts the foot of Parnassus and winds eastward towards the fertile plains of Daulis. So, depending on your point of view, it could be a place of divergence or convergence.[11]

In our psychological discourse and psychic experience we constantly encounter the power of the affix *di-* or *con-*. We might see con-vergence as an archetypal expression of reconciliation of opposites and di-vergence as splitting. Either might be appropriate. Myths enact these options. Unsure which way to go, Oedipus consults the oracle. But Greek oracles are not like Bunyan's Evangelist, directing the path from here to a specified there. They do not make sense. (See Adam Phillips's remarks about nonsense, quoted earlier; see page 74.) Tiresias comes to the dying Freud, who wants to make sense of his journey:

> —I do not understand you. I have told you, I am not at all well. Speak sense or leave please.
> —Sense? To you of all people, Dr. Freud? I hoped to speak to you of something besides sense.
> —Please explain yourself.
> —It is of the senseless I would like to speak. A story without sense. No sense. Or maybe all sense.
> —What story? What is this nonsense?[12]

Through his blind but knowing visitor, we enter what Freud deemed the universal myth of self-knowledge and consciousness. Myth illuminates, it does not explicate. It is, as the seer alleges, something beside sense, sense-less-ness, or maybe all sense.

We might enter the mythic world through the compulsion of *bias*. Bias is ever active at the heart of our psychology, de-railing each planned expedition, disrupting intention, disturbing every therapeutic session. Jung comments that

> every period has its bias, its particular prejudice, and its psychic malaise. An epoch is like an individual; it has its own

limitations of conscious outlook and therefore requires a compensatory adjustment.[13]

Bias is most fierce in the activity of our complexes, like a magnet, drawing us to repetitions, both personally and collectively. But it also functions as a necessary compensatory adjustment, a corrective energy source from the depths of psyche. Bias as prejudicial influence resonates with the Greek goddess Bia (Βία), whose origins Hesiod describes:

> Styx the daughter of Okeanos was joined to Pallas and bare Zelos (Emulation) and trim-ankled Nike (Victory) in the house. Also she brought forth Kratos (Strength) and Bia (Force), wonderful children. These have no house apart from Zeus, nor any dwelling nor path except that wherein God leads them, but they dwell always with Zeus the loud-thunderer.[14]

Observe the company Bia keeps, preferably that of the supremely potent Zeus. She hangs around with Kratos (power), Nike (Victory), and Peitho (persuasion). The Greek word βίη means bodily and mental strength, force, might. Βία τίνος carried the sense of "against one's will," with the implication of "in spite of." Bia alone, as an adverb, has the sense of perforce, of necessity, and for that reason could be associated with Ananke, goddess of compulsion.[15]

In earlier remarks about mother tongue in unconscious material, I focused attention on adverbial and prepositional energies activated in our grammars, governed by Bia. I have suggested that their trajectories are essentially archetypal. I discussed briefly some key orientations that house and move us: the dimensions of up/down, above/below, in/out, before/after, inside/outside, then/now. Since the moment we stood upright as a species, we have perhaps felt the bias of up/down most keenly. The upright tree, so important to Jung, with its roots in the ground and its branches reaching up and out into the sky above, echoes our bio-psychic frames of reference. We know only too well in the analytical experience that the torture of *betwixt and between* must often be endured, lived into, before the energy or image of the transcendent function brings resolution. The weight of *down* outweighs *up*. Christian poets struggled with the same bias assailing the soul, as we found in Marvell's drop of dew. Western culture has attempted to negate the in-clination down. Hillman, however, sought to subvert the sky-driven paradigm that formed us, and this has also been the project of certain late-twentieth-century theologians. Donald Cupitt comments:

> In the long period dominated by Plato (c350 BCE – 1900 CE) when there was a sharp distinction between the sensuous world below and the eternal, purely intelligible world above, it was usually thought that whereas science is concerned with the lower world of the senses and empirical fact, philosophy is concerned with the higher world of a priori eternal truth. To do philosophy, you raised your sights.[16]

One might see this compulsion already challenged after Christ's ascension, when the forlorn disciples were asked, "Why do you stand gazing upwards?" This posture of looking up to the sky is still spiritually and psychologically active, despite protestations of indifference, if not of defiance. And it seems to be supported by dream phenomena. There is dynamic longing in the upward gaze toward something, someone, beyond self. Cupitt continues,

> the world above was eternal and the world below was temporal. The higher, noumenal world was a world of necessary truth, whereas the unstable phenomenal world below was a world of merely-short-term and contingent truths....The world above was a world of unchangeable Being, and the lower world was a world of everchanging Becoming.[17]

The twentieth century has sought to escape this model in its theology and in its secular thought, a development that is often expressed as a

> switch of religious attention from God to Man, from Yonder to Here and Now, from eternity to history...and in short, the full secularisation of Christianity into a form of radical humanism, the religion of life. Christianity brings God down to earth, for good.[18]

When Cupitt's formulation remains a conceptual reflection, it touches few. But this is exactly where myth serves us. Jung is vocal on this matter.

> Religions turned to myths for help, or rather, the myths always flung out bridges between the helpless consciousness and the effective *idées forces* of the unconscious. But you cannot, artificially and with an effort of will, believe the statements of myth if you have not previously been gripped by them.[19]

Mythic story offers bridges to archetypal compulsions and biases. So does the poet, whose imagery is so often mythic. So Yeats feels his way to Cupitt's disturbing act of consciousness.

> now that my ladder's gone,
> I must lie down where all the ladders start
> In the foul rag and bone shop of the heart.[20]

How provocative this *where* all ladders start! Of Yeats's image of the "rag and bone shop of the heart," Jung might have commented that "even on the dunghill the oldest and noblest treasures of the spirit are not lost."[21] He declares that to respond to myth, to recognize its truth, one must know its *grip*. The grammatical energies that I am exploring serve this grip. Through grammar, energy is exerted on consciousness, often subliminally. When we reflect on the difference, and the relationship, between the substantiveness of the symbolic world (making use of objects, creatures, events, and an infinite number of qualities of the materially given) and the non-substantial but purposefully driven world of prepositions, conjunctions, and adverbials, I am reminded of the theological distinctions in discussions of the Trinity by the Greek Church Fathers. They suggest that humankind can participate in the energy shared between the persons of the Trinity, the energy (ἐνέργεια) of God, rather than God's substance (οὐσία). We are concerned here with a purely dynamic principle.[22] Such an experience of Trinity depends on the properties of *between*.

Yeats's ladder evokes Jacob's ladder, that particular paradigm of spanning the gap, the gulf, between upper and lower, where up and down have been freighted with value. Given our shared shaping in the West by Platonic and neo-Platonic models espoused by the church, asserting that we ascend from the visible to the invisible, the image of the ladder, the *scala*, became inevitable. It is fascinating to look in the *English Short-Title Catalogue*, which lists books published from the reformation to 1800, to see how many titles include the word *Scala*. (Also, such words as Mirror, the *Speculum*.) Culture was preoccupied with ways of rising, raising the soul from mortal earth-clod to the eternal sphere of light.

Feeling terrestrial weight upon the soul, the gulf between it and the celestial realm was a source of anguish. How different the perception of the Irish poet, who perceives in women's gossip "earth to cool the burning brain of heaven."[23] Ways were needed to close the gap, to traffic between opposing realms of *here* and *there*. In addition to the *scala*, winged messengers were imagined, sometimes gods themselves, but always their agents. The work of Hermes was essential to the Greek imagination and still to ours. Angels of some sort have been felt necessary in most religious systems. They are messengers, those sent to communicate with the soul. Sometimes these messengers actually engage physically with human beings, as in Jacob's wrestling. The stretch between up and down, above and below, pre-occupies many of our world myths and folk traditions. I will reflect only on certain representative Western myths that have shaped us, whose dynamics we recognize not only from our own immersion in literature but also from our conscious and unconscious in-clinations.

However, many mythic figures prove unable to negotiate the gap, the space *between*. The technically skilful Daedalus manages it, largely through *technis*, but we should remember that he is implicated in the mortal failure of two boys. As his son Icarus fell, a bird reminded Daedalus of another fall. He had thrown his technically gifted nephew Talos from Minerva's tower, and the boy was saved only by Pallas's intervention. She valued the boy's mental agility and saved him by turning him into a partridge, a bird with limited flight. So it must stay close to earth, even in flight, an image of limited transcendence. One way of dealing with the gap, this might imply, is to ignore it, just to accept limitation.[24] The technician's own son fell to his death, unsaved by the gods. Icarus's story has been exploited moralistically to indict pride that precedes falling. Ovid tells the story differently, engaging with bias, the incitements that pull above and below, urges of a boy that feel qualitatively and quantitatively different from those of a mature man. Various translations emphasize more vividly than Ovid's sparse narrative the tension between up and down and the speed of moving through space. Seeing all routes from Crete blocked, Daedalus conceives of escape through flight, "but the sky is surely open to us: that is how we will go."[25] This is a potent mythic statement: *but* the skies are open to us mortals. How differently that assertion can be interpreted and lived. Once Daedalus has constructed wings, father advises son: "fly halfway between high and low," that is, travel between the opposites. Is he counseling compromise? The wings lift upward, and the boy flies higher. Adverbs and prepositions of vertical movement gather momentum, high and higher, until the final downward plunge.

The myth of Phaeton grows out of the same dilemma, the human quest to find a livable position in the space between earth and sky, divine and human, eternity and time. This is surely not boys' work. How this motif permeates our thought can be illustrated from a multitude of sources in Western literature. "Ah, but a man's reach should exceed his grasp, / Or what's a heaven for?" Robert Browning asks. Most of our myths in some way illuminate this reaching and grasping that mark us "half-men," half beast, half angel. In Andrea del Sarto's monologue, the Renaissance artist reflects on art's need for both earthly (human) craft and soul's aspiration (the divine reach).[26] This holds both in tension. It is not compromise.

Phaeton's status really is betwixt and between, for his father is a god, his mother mortal. Mythic mixed conceptions tell us a great deal about our human condition, and perhaps about the phenomenon of genius. Phaeton needs to have his paternity confirmed and goes to seek it from his father-god. He reaches the Sun's palace that "towered up, with sublime columns" and is asked by the god who sees all, "why have you come *here*?"[27] *Everything, anything* is promised as gift by the father, but the son asks for the one very thing Father would withhold, to ride his chariot of the sun. The syntax is tortuous in most translations, squirming between *but* and *however* and *if only* as the father tries to get out of his rash promise and make the son change his mind. The boy wins and father's subsequent advice is like that of Daedalus. Ted Hughes's poetic translation best catches the sense:

> Keep to that highway, follow the wheel ruts.
> Share your heat fairly
> Between heaven and earth, not too low
> And not crashing in among the stars. Too high
> You will set heaven aflame—and too low, earth.
>
> The middle way is best, and safest.
> And do not veer too far to the right
> Where your wheels might crush the Serpent, nor to the left
> Where they might be shattered against the Altar.
> Take a bearing between them.[28]

But of course the boy veered, unable to counter the bias of the poles. Pulled to the zenith, Phaeton looked-down on land far below. The horses were flung "this way and that way" in the vast sky, the balance of forces now completely lost. The myth stirs a sense of the dangers of precocity, not pride. Too soon, too soon. We often know this in our praxis. The wisdom of the fullness of time is always needed, when enough strength and discretion are assured. I remember a young doctoral student who wanted to engage with more philosophical second-half-of-life tasks before he had accomplished more mundane, ego-consolidating tasks of young manhood. He dreamed that he went fishing with Jung, the Wise Old Man. The dreamer caught a fish and excitedly showed it to his mentor, who told him kindly to throw it back into the river, for it needed to mature further before being brought to land.

Myths of rising and falling reach into the soul with a strong sense of recognition. Jung was constantly pre-occupied with the archetypal myths of knowledge and knowing, felt most keenly for him through Goethe's drama. The vertical yearning for ultimate knowledge was for Faust unbearable. Early in the play, watching the course of the sun, he laments, "Oh God, for wings to follow without fear." But such knowing *is* fearful, and he must confront his limitations, agonizing, as might Jung himself, as he confronted the horizons of the unconscious: "Alas! the wings that lift the mind cannot help to lift the body. And yet the delight of yearning forward and upward is born in every soul."[29] (Fig. 19) Our very instinct urges us to struggle upward to the heavens. Faust and Jung are doing what perhaps Midgley urges in unpacking the metaphor of height, which is

> a natural symbol for value. Before anybody thought of evolution, this was expressed in the idea of a Great Chain of Being—a scale of creatures reaching from the least to the most important....When people began to think about evolution, they made...no more changes in their way of thinking than they were forced to. They did not scrap the Great Chain of Being. Instead, they simply unhooked the top end from Heaven and slung it ahead into the Future. Its axis now was time. But its associations with value did not vanish. For good reasons and bad ones, they proved tenacious.[30]

Figure 19. Quarles, *Emblems,* Bk. 5.

We are still embedded in myths of verticality even when a temporal axis replaces the spatial. The myths that grip us perhaps help us reconcile the split. We are stuck down here with our load of distress, disappointment, and failure, with souls too big for our biological lives. Jung argued that "man's whole history consists from the very beginning [fall narratives, etc.] in a conflict between his feeling of inferiority and his arrogance."[31] So the whole network of upward and downward motion carries these mythic energies. In her neurobiological study *Changing Minds in Therapy*, Margaret Wilkinson reflects that bodily spatial orientation is used analogically for temporal dimensions. The physical dimensions of behind, backward, forward are transposed into properties of time. Myths engage with and enact such interchangeable perceptions. We mount or we fall through space and time, trafficking between heaven and earth. But we descend even below earth into death's kingdom. Some form of the *katabasis* (journey to an underworld) recurs in most mythologies. We encounter it in the myths of Persephone and Orpheus. Both are drawn into the lower depths through the agency of Eros.

Demeter, Goddess of Earth, works horizontally, but her child, the Kore, begins to live vertically. Demeter is always moving *over* the earth, inviting showers to fall upon it, turning its topsoil ("splitting open the grassland" in Hughes's translation), harvesting its produce, re-seeding. She only mounts upward in desperation to demand help from her partner-Sky-god and she sends Mercury/Hermes down under her earth to retrieve her daughter from the subterranean god. She is not concerned with eternity as such, but with seasonal and cyclic time, with continuity and forward movement through time. She is not concerned with *beyond* so much as with *here and now* life. The eternally cycling seasons cheat death. Then her daughter is snatched downward from emergent life to endless death, from the horizontal to the vertical. Ovid first sights the girl with her nymphs "flitting hither and thither…among the lilies and violets."[32] The demands of individuation can no longer support the innocently childish *hither and thither* that mother would love to prolong. The burgeoning girl is carried off in Pluto's chariot, his heart pierced by Cupid's arrow. Light pierces his under-ground through a crack, which brings him, enraged, above ground. There he sees Proserpina, whose flower plucking disturbed his soil and he is taken-over by passion and possesses the ripe girl. Not a little ominously we hear, "Meanwhile, the mother…" *Meanwhile* is an interesting measure of time-between, here registering foreboding. In terror, Ceres searches for her child, "through all the earth and sea"; with torch "she wanders, unquiet, through the bitter darkness." She rages over the land, "crossing it from end to end." Her prepositions are *through, along, over*, while those of Pluto are *below, under, underneath, beneath, downward*. Ceres's commitment to the horizontal is both strength and limitation. River nymphs like Arethusa have more flexibility and so see more: "So, while I glided underground down there, among Stygian streams, with my own eyes, I saw…" The fluidity of water allows movement on both planes, flowing over, along and downward, responsive to incline and inclination, able to negotiate multiple directions and gradients. This is perhaps why Jung uses the flow of water as analogy for the way energy moves in the psyche. The capacity to flow flexibly makes Arethusa's perspective more whole, accessing secrets above and below ground. Of Proserpina she reports:

> She was sad indeed, but though her face still showed fear, nevertheless she was queen, the queen among the world of shadows, the powerful consort, nevertheless, of the king of hell!

The nymph's language is measured, its sureness affirmed by her *indeed*; the paradoxicality of the new situation generated by the qualification *still* and the insistence of *but though*, and twice, the dynamic of *nevertheless*. Nevertheless/nonetheless assert something surprising, in contrast to, or in defiance of, what has gone before (*dennoch, trotzdem, nichtsdestoweniger*). *Nevertheless* can have even more energy than the adversative *but*, which halts or throws objections onto the path. In fact, the whole force of the *dénouement* of Proserpina's fate depends on this *but*. The ripening and hungry girl had engaged with Pluto through unconscious appetite. And now her release is assured *only if* she has not eaten *anything*. "But the Fates would not allow it, for the girl had broken her fast." *But* and *for* fight it out here. The *Homeric Hymns* stress that the act of eating seeds was also *against* her will, just as the initial snatching away had been, with all the force that the preposition *against* can exert, at least, consciously.[33] Having eaten by force of trickery, she remains connected to Pluto. Some reconciliation of the conflicting force of earth's life and death's imprisoning must be found. Jupiter intervenes between Ceres and Pluto and di-vides the "turning year equally," thereby securing a wholly new *and now. So many* months are now to be spent with mother above, and *just so many* with her subterranean spouse. Such a resolution does not sit well with the absoluteness of the mother-archetype, which by nature brooks no compromise.

Demeter/Ceres' ruthlessness when confronted with the threat of losing her child is earth-destroying: "The crops died as fresh shoots, destroyed by too much sun, and then by too much rain." Ceres in this aspect is the enactment of *too much*. In the *Hymn,* we are told that Demeter "fled like a bird over the nourishing land and the sea…she wandered about…" despite invitations from all the gods to ascend to Olympus. She would "never set foot there" and "never permit earth's grain to sprout, before regaining her daughter." She refuses Hades' *there* and that of Olympus, too, in her rage. Her *never* is unqualified. Only after the reconciling pact is Hades' *here* transformed, and a whole new dimension is created and perhaps introduced into Greek thought through the possibility of resurrection from death. Hades determines: "When you are here, you shall rule everything that lives," and then he will release her to the upper world of growth. Future tense auxiliaries emerge from the present tense indicative narrative. The promise from above ground is the same: *"You shall* go to the depths of the earth, to live there a third of the seasons of the year. Whenever the earth sprouts, *you shall* come up again from cloudy darkness." Demeter is enlarged by her daughter's descent and subsequent rising, as she is made to share life with death, accepting a vertical dynamic, the *anodos.* The mystery of descent and rising played a vital part in Eleusinian rituals.

Depth psychology invokes descent into far reaches of psyche. We have finished with height psychology. The depths had called for many decades, one most potent call downward felt by Jung personally. Constantly we encounter his *beneath, below, under* most potently and intimately in his biographical *Memories, Dreams, Reflections* and his autobiographical *Red Book.* In the latter, Jung's "I" encounters a "tramp," whom he met initially as "someone who does not look trustworthy," and to whom he does not want to be seen speaking. Jung's persona confesses almost enviously, "Incidentally, mustn't it be a peculiarly beautiful feeling to hit bottom in reality at least once, where there is no going down any further..."[34] This lowness is not the lowliness of Mary's *humilis* in her *Magnificat* (Luke 1), but it is related, psychologically, theologically, mythically. It is also the psalmist's life *de profundis*.

We have been experiencing specific energies that work through grammatical movement. In all languages, the power of certain conjunctives must be felt, often as hinge for a whole incident or action, as in Persephone's tale, where the remorseless narrative logic moves through *but* and *for*. In all our listening, we wait for *suddenly* or the intrusion of *however* or *nevertheless*, to hinder or initiate further action. Everything hangs on these overlooked context-driving lexical items.[35] It is in myth, fairytale, and dream especially that the rational *therefore* is deconstructed, our logical *because* decentered.

After exploring the valences of the up-down plane, I now engage with the myth of Narcissus. It is illuminating to look at the mechanisms of inflation and depression/diminution from that same vertical perspective. Like the fates of the two boys, Icarus and Phaeton, that of Narcissus has been amplified and distorted. In this story, in clinical practice, and in our own behaviors we work with processes that value and raise us, or diminish and push us down.

In the mythic imagination, the most blatant and absolute experience of magnification is transformation through apotheosis, projecting the idealized earthling into a new heavenly constellation. Here we rely on Latin/Greek prefixes.[36] Apo-theosis is charged with significant purpose in ancient myth. Consider the fate of Pollux and Castor, the *Dioscuri* representing the union or split between mortal and immortal.[37] For all his grandiosity, the fate of the inimitably beautiful Narcissus is not apotheosis into the heavens, but meta-morphosis into a groundling flower. Those who came to find his remains to re-duce him "to a handful of dust in an urn," found no corpse.

> But there, in the pressed grass where he had perished,
> A tall flower stood unbroken—
> Bowed, a ruff of white petals....[38]

How sure and provocative is the poet's early caesura after *but there* that makes us pause, behold this amazing sight. The yearning boy defies irredeemable diminution to an urn. Instead his form is changed into a flower of the soil.[39] Ovid's stark statement of fact works differently, with *nowhere* (*nusquam*) placed strongly in the first foot of the line, confronting us with absence of the expected. When they came to search, nowhere was there a body. The singularity of Narcissus is enforced from the beginning of his story by the negative diction that isolates him from surrounding life. No young men nor maidens touched him (*nulli illum iuvenes, nullae tetigere puellae*, l.355). The conjunction *nec* piles up clauses incrementally, ex-cluding the world around, rather like Marvell's dewdrop. "None dared be familiar, let alone touch him" (Hughes). This mechanism of ex-clusion, reinforced through the negatives, enacts the pull, the tense bias, between attraction and re-jection that is the undertow of the myth of pathological self-love. The Latin verbs *trahere* (to drag/carry) and *jacere* (to hurl/throw) act as poles for this experience of drawing near and pushing away, which were implicit in my chapter on the language of our analytical discourse. The nymphs around Narcissus are irresistibly attracted-to him and he persistently re-jects their overtures. This is most true of Echo, whose fate is inextricably tied to her re-jected love. Echo, who answers-back. Her very existence becomes bound and disembodied in the paring down of speech. She does not reply, but can only mimic as re-echo. Hughes catches this as Narcissus calls out to his companions,

"Where are you?"
"I'm here." And Echo
Caught at the syllables as if they were precious:
"I'm here," she cried, "I'm here" and "I'm here" and "I'm here."
Narcissus looked around wildly.
"I'll stay here," he shouted.
"You come to me." And "Come to me,"
shouted Echo. "Come to me.
To me, to me, to me."
Narcissus stood baffled,
Whether to stay or go. He began to run,
Calling as he ran: "Stay there." But Echo
Cried back, weeping to utter it, "Stay there,
Stay there, stay there, stay there."[40]

Stripped language, relying on repeated grammatical particles, articulates tantalizingly the withholding and refusing of communication. In supervision I have heard trainees' tapes of therapeutic sessions, supposedly demonstrating the process of mirroring, which sounded all too horribly like this.

Relationship is exercised through at-traction and re-pulsion. Narcissus's pre-occupation with himself defies all connection to another. His behavior arises out of the psychic mechanism of compulsion inward, presented in Ovid's telling of the tale through the verb *flectare*, to bend/curve. Hence the pervasive use of reflexives, the hallmark of narcissistic functioning. They haunt this narrative like a fugue. We know this from the beginning, when prophecy announces that he will live long, "If he does not come to know himself" (*si se non nouerit*). This is a momentous "if," perhaps the most poignant conditional in our experience at the soul-face, as is the yearning "if only," that dogs so many lives and hinders movement. Such an "if" seals Narcissus's fate, while offering escape from it simultaneously. He devotes his short life to dis-covering himself, mis-taking self-love for self-knowledge. He becomes conscious of what is happening, but is helpless to make use of that awareness. "Unknowingly he yearns for himself, and the one who admires is himself." The reflexive habit intensifies, "he is astonished by himself." Those whom he re-jected curse him: "So may he himself love, and so may he fail to possess what he loves!" He pro-jects his love into himself. "I stretch my arms out to you, you [stretch-out] yours. When I smile, you [smile-back]." Once he finds his own reflection, he never leaves his transfixed position, lying-above on the bank, looking-down-into the pond-mirror, mistaking surface for depth. "Flat on the ground adoring everything for which he is himself admired." The reaching-for self is entrenched; he cannot break out of it. "Reach" is a native English word used in many contexts with many nuances, the generative root of many phrasal verbs: reach-out, reach-into, reach-up, reach-for.[41] In our myths, our literature, in our idiomatic speech and praxis, we engage with the experience and language of reaching, especially of reaching-out, a core relational movement in therapy. Reaching aspires to touch. The aching of this gesture of soul is most effectively actualized through Narcissus. The myth's focal image is the boy, reaching-out-down-to-and-for his own reflection; he behaves visually just as Echo does aurally. He mimics himself, unable to make contact with the Self for whom he actually, but unconsciously, reaches. His reaching out/to/for accompanies gazing-upon, in Narcissus's case, even gazing-into. I have experienced this in analytical work where the analysand's involvement with self augurs well initially. There is capacity and will for self-discovery. But the person rests on his/her own surface and any attempt to delve more deeply is met with fierce resistance. This is often first experienced in the encounter with shadow, which dreams begin to personify, but with which or whom consciousness refuses to engage. In such cases, true knowledge of Self must be restricted, and what increases is knowledge only of an approved self.

Psychoanalysis has been enriched by the infant-parent work of Winnicott and Kohut. They offer a memorable image of the gaze, the mother gazing-down-into the eyes of her child, while the infant gazes-back-up-and-into the eyes of the mother, which function as mirrors of the child's own being and value. There is awe and wonder of the same intensity in reciprocal beholding of adult lovers, a psychic mechanism no doubt engendered in that early maternal erotic dyad. Mutual gazing demands and supplies simultaneously. It is not the gaze that subjugates or exploits, a dynamic exposed by feminist art critics.[42] The phenomenon of the gaze foregrounds the problem with Marvell's dew drop, which gazes back to the skies with one-way vision that eschews or is incapable of mutuality with earth.

The exchange within the maternal gaze is illuminated in numberless paintings of the Madonna and child imago that has shaped our cultural picture galleries, both outer and inner. The gazing dyads of Renaissance nativity paintings are particularly impressive. (Fig. 20) The whole history of the mother-infant experience can be appreciated through these Western cultural icons that underlie myths of motherhood. We see the infant beginning to turn its attention away from the mother (perhaps a turning-to*ward* kings or shepherds), a turning-away that offers crucial and positive development. However, there is potential developmental danger when the mother turns-away-from her child. Joan Marr's disturbing painting confronts us with the tragedy of the not-beheld. (Fig. 21) The trajectory of this gazing in the healthy maternal dyad is stable, if not fixed: the baby gazes-up, as

Figure 20. *The Virgin and Child (Madonna with the Iris)*. Workshop of Albrecht Durer. 1471–1528. (National Gallery, London).

Figure 21. Joan Marr, *Turning Away.*

mother gazes-down. In contrast, the myth of Narcissus lodges a potentially pathological gazing-on and reaching-toward the personal self for all time. Narcissus is only able to give and receive his own unproductive gaze: "I can gaze at what I cannot touch." His insoluble question is posed like a riddle that he does not even seek help to solve, for typically his speech only addresses himself. On the one hand, he acknowledges "What you search for is nowhere"; and yet even more of a conundrum is the realization, "Why do I search? What I want I have." This is the anguish of the personality locked into Narcissistic reflexivity. The story connects us to a necessary human relational bias toward oneself, rather than to an-other. There is a potent sense of strain in the telling of this myth. It is regressive, aching-back-and-into limited inner space. Much of the tension in this narcissistic dilemma is captured by function words.

Many myths elaborate a temporal straining-after akin to the spatially reaching arm. Rowan Williams sees this straining forward to what lies ahead as the "call to a future," central to Judeo-Christian thought.[43] He ponders the concept of *epektasis* (straining forward), a noun deriving from the verb used by St. Paul, when he speaks of "forgetting what lies behind, and straining forward to what lies ahead, I press on toward the goal."[44] This future to which the soul is called is a limitless yonder to which we have been responding, a yonder with no factually describable terminus. This might parallel ego's call to realize Self on the path of individuation along which we strain. Theologically, this journey into infinity, into God, represents a *synergeia* with God, a finally unrealizable experience of inexhaustible love and longing. It relates to Augustine's much-quoted claim about the purpose of restlessness, that it tortures and provokes us until we find rest in God. Or Gregory's longing for divine completion, *epithymia*. St. Bernard sees human yearning differently as "a searching never satisfied, yet without any restlessness…that eternal inexplicable longing that knows no dissatisfaction and want"; it is satisfying in and of itself.[45] All of this concerns the *extensus*, the universal, spiritual stretch with which humanity is endowed. We constantly lodge this in, project it onto, something that acts as transitional attractor.

Midgley sees a different mythic temporal pattern at work in our own time: the evolutionary myth, raised from exclusively biological ground. Speaking of the dissolution of the Great Chain of Being construct, she continues:

> Among good reasons was the desire to have values located somewhere. In an age of change it became increasingly difficult to locate them in the past; people could no longer confidently say, "It is good because our fathers did it." So they began to say, "it is good because our descendents will do it." Hence the bizarre cult of the Future itself as a kind of mythical subsistent realm enshrining value—a cult invented by Nietzsche, filled out by Wells and the Futurists, and still very influential.[46]

This is a very different extension, but equally a trajectory to the unknown, necessitating future verbal auxiliaries. But such a myth of progression can reinforce provisional living, psychic strategies to refuse here-and-now-ness of actual, present life.

All the shifts and turns through the time and space that is our life involve us in "the 'agonistics' of the actual human condition" lived *here*.[47] But always *there* pulls and pushes beyond here, and this beyond is drawn into the universal *agon*, quickened in myth. There is always a this-world and that-or-other-world that must be reconciled. Jung sees something of this bias in the myth of Prometheus and his brother, where the

> two tendencies get dissociated: the Epimethean attitude is adapted to the world as it actually is, but the Promethean is not, and for that reason it has to work for a renewal of life. It also produces a new attitude toward the world.[48]

It is probable that in all analyses, the Promethean myth has to be individuated in some way, the massive energy for each personal task concentrated into a mere stalk, the perennial and aromatic fennel. There often comes a moment when one special symbolic image carries the fire for transmutation, it might be a frog or a palm tree or a glass of wine. When we speak simply of alternatives, of *one or the other*, we posit a bias in one of two directions, an equal in-clination. Jung saw profounder wisdom in eschewing this sense of alternatives, the either/or of the limited ego. Sometimes myth embodies alternative as conflict, as in the monstrous option of Scylla or Charybdis, one attacking from the right, the other from the left. Sailors must find or make a way between the two destroyers. Odysseus made a conscious choice, risking a few sailors by sailing closer to Scylla, rather than consigning more of them to Charybdis's whirlpool. Jason was helped through by Hera, while tricky Aeneas made his way around. The myth of the either/or dilemma sometimes presents in the double bind that psyche finds intolerably exclusive. The Trickster Janus looks both ways; he is guardian of both entrance and exit. Kalsched brings him vividly to mind in his treatment of the "problem of Yahweh's right and left hands being either integrated or dissociated." And he reminds us of Winnebago trickster cycles where right hand fights with left, pointing out that the trickster "links things together or he tears them apart." Kalsched differentiates the containment of opposites from the ravages of Scylla and Charybdis in reflecting on the analyst's treatment of analysands who suffer such tension *between* warring parts of the personality. "Many treatments," he claims, "have been shipwrecked on the Scylla of too much confrontation or the Charybdis of too much compassion and complicity with the undertow of the patient's malignant regression." In this clinical crisis, he continues,

> If the patient's traumatized ego is to be coaxed out of its inner sanctum and inspired to trust the world again, a middle way will have to be found between compassion and confrontation.[49]

As so often in therapy, the myths offer us embodied wisdom and containment that is not merely compromise. The problematical fact is that we live *between*; it is our most poignant and productive preposition. Between heaven and earth, between birth and death, between continuous beginnings and endings, between hope and despair. We are continually crossing thresholds, building herms between *whence* and *whither*, forever crossing the wilderness toward *a*—toward *the*—land that feels promised. So much of our psychic experience feels liminal. The limen, the threshold, is a point of maximum tension between *before* and *after*, a temporal between that adds complexity and/or richness to the spatial between.

We keep encountering the ubiquitous pre-fix *trans-*, and we have considered the related paradigm of *from-to* in acts of trans-formation in fairytales and analysis. In *Transformation: Emergence of the Self*, Murray Stein elaborates the core image of the life cycle of the butterfly, from earth-bound caterpillar to soaring butterfly, to illuminate the individuation process, a natural image prompted by psyche in dream experience.[50] The myths of the world draw directly on such mechanisms of change, as in Ovid's encyclopaedic anthology. He was passionately engaged with these tales of shape shifting among gods and mortals, disturbingly fluid states where mortals mix with gods, where gods mate with, save and destroy, illuminate or blind mortals who attract their attention. Some humans may try to live like Thomas Hardy's rustics, who assume that it is safer just to get on with daily necessities, measuring one's years by the rhythms of "tatey-picking" like Christian Cantle, never raising one's mortal pate above the parapet to risk challenging the immortals.[51] This may constitute refusal of self-realization, but there may also be wisdom in accepting unexceptional ordinariness.

*Betwee*n lies enigmatically and variously in the gap between *from* and *to* in developmental process. This is the territory of the Greek prefix *meta-*, the processes of meta-noia, meta-phor, meta-morphosis. Plato defines *metaxy* as the in-between or middle ground. The *daimon* Eros crosses this between-space, frequently initiating liaison between gods and mortals, especially male gods and female mortals. The term was used to indicate the human dilemma of being placed between animal and god. Tacey comments that "psyche inhabits a middle area known as the metaxy, and is represented as subtle, elusive and metaphorical."[52] Crossing the in-between spaces is dangerous and disorienting, as Stein illustrates through case material. In praxis we occupy the *metaxy*, temporarily, in process of transformation. Such transformations might involve a conscious process of change, with some degree of intentionality, trans-lations to another state. Most transformations seem more a matter of accidental, incremental consequence than conscious intention.

Transformation can relate to passage across in many contexts. Dante begins his *Inferno* with the words, "In the middle of the journey of our life I came to myself in a dark wood where the straight way was lost."[53] He is bewildered by the many possible roads offered and afraid to go forward, wanting to turn-back rather than cross-over the river that lies in his way (Canto 111). Beatrice brings consolation and inspiration, speaking out of love: "I come from a place where I desire to return." The poet agrees to be led on by Virgil and immediately they come-to the River Styx. Seeing people on the shore, Dante wants to know "who these are: and what usage makes them seem so ready to pass over." An old man approaches with the words, "Hope not ever to see Heaven: I come to lead you to the other shore; into the eternal darkness; into fire and into ice." They do cross-over-to the *other* shore. Other heroes had made the same crossing, though not when dead, and had returned back to this earthly side. Virgil recalls the passage of Aeneas in detail.[54] None of the many translations of Dante can avoid the phrasal verbs of passing-over, crossing-over, and the energies of the pull toward, and repulsion against, that other side. Analysands also use this language to describe a sense of change, of having crossed over into different space and different time, as they begin to factor unconscious promptings into conscious life, often powered by the experience of unconscious dream fantasy. On the other side of what now feels like life lived literally and prosaically, they begin to experience the transforming power of the symbol active in their own inner life.

Crossing-over necessitated in transformational journeys can be illustrated in numberless world mythologies and the dream experience of most effective analyses. Today, famous bridges such as Tower Bridge and Golden Gate Bridge figure in important dreams, as well as minor crossings that have local significance. Such is Beggar's Bridge, a local Yorkshire dream site connected with a powerful legend of parted lovers straining to reach one another. All such crossings furnish metaphor for psychological conversion to new life, as do dream fords and ferries. Journeys of initiation are found in the many myths of the passage into death, as in the vessel of the sun barge in Egyptian mythology[55] or the carriage of the soul across the Styx by the boatman, Charon.[56] The prepositions *over* and *across* energize an essentially horizontal trajectory, though there can be a vertical pressure. In the *Red Book*, Jung makes several such passages. "And so I decided to cross over into lower and everyday life, my life, and to begin down there, where I stood."[57] He was fascinated by experiences of liminality, the place of transit between. The limen marks the between, a threshold between two conditions of being, two states of growth or consciousness in the necessary passage through stages of life. In many anthropological studies, we observe a crossing-over that is enacted through symbolic rites of *separation* followed by rites of *incorporation*.[58] What lies betwixt them are *transition rites*. There is no tension without *between*. We need to acknowledge its power and see how it is fulfilled, for psyche seems not to want to leave gaps. Such might be said of the creation of images of limbo, an active domain between two states that are felt to be incompatible, sinful earthly life and the pure innocence of heaven. In-between became a place of preparation and purging. In marriage rites, betrothal used to fill that *between* space. Developmentally, one stage of life merges with the next, but the space of merging is granted discrete status, marked with its own rites of passage, as in puberty.

Rites and experiences of crossing-over typically employ verbal compounds to effect the passage, as from slavery to freedom, so often couched in mythic rhetoric. Ex-odus and return from ex-ile are activated in rebellious times, at collective and personal levels. Such was the mythologizing rallying call of Martin Luther King. The great freedom spiritual, "Go down Moses," has been invoked by many seeking liberation. Going-to and flight-from unleash passionate archetypal forces. In Jewish and Christian liturgies that continue to be enlivened by the Exodus story, as in the Passover Seder or the Maundy Thursday Eucharist, the past is kept present, almost dispelling the time of between past and present. Through this re-living, imagination is re-vitalized and fresh hope released.[59] The prepositional trajectories of crossing-over have always compelled vigorous compounding, especially in German, as all the dictionary entries for *über* illustrate (*übergehen, übergeben, überholen, überfluten,* etc.).

Through the metaphoric language of exodus, emotion is aroused to fuel future possibilities. The language of movement inhering in such verbal and adverbial parts of speech is not merely prosaic. It can evoke and exert a strong kinesthetic sense. Responding to these stories that carry so much mythic sense, Walter Brueggemann comments that these poetic narratives become "models of liberated, liberating speech that stands in stark contrast to our conventional domesticated speech."[60] The actual lexical items need not be in themselves substantively symbolic. The poetry of movement can be generated in very domestic language, the maternal language of home and home-coming. When we want to move on from simply describing what is, and when we want to picture our trust that other things *might* be, we often assume that we should use more descriptive language. But the simply formulated command to Moses to *go-down-to* Egypt has significant emotional and imaginal potency. The use of the simple personal assertion, "I go to see X," was raised by an analysand who observed how often her dreams began in this way. It was not enough merely to say "I am with X," she must assert, I "go to be with X." I go up to, I go down, I go across. This going is our story and it often necessitates a going-across, an active entering into dream sites.

Most of the above references represent passages through space and time, progressions and conversions from an old state to a new. But in many myths, there seems often to be little in-between time or space. In the chapter on dreams, we saw how transformations from one condition into another can mystify and provoke contemporary dreamers. One mythic motif that is often recapitulated in analysis is the sudden shift from blindness to vision and the paradoxical archetypal construction of the blind seer, who needs outer eyes closed in order to see into things. At such times, the seer Tiresias or Saul of Tarsus are often invoked. Whenever the blindness/sight paradigm occurs, the transformative god/God is around.

We have paid attention to various biases or trajectories, dramatized in and by adverbs and ad-positions. One such scarcely resistible pull that in the psychological literature we encounter as regression might be imaged as looking-back. King Arthur's knights ride out, ride-forward, ride-through forests on their redemptive quests, in search of their own, or Camelot's, wholeness. Occasionally they lose heart and are tempted to turn-back to Camelot. Through various devices, some supernatural, they recover heart, like Sir Bors, who after his crisis "rode sorrowfully on his way" in search of the Holy Grail. This is always a crucial moment in analysis, when the horrible realization dawns that to turn-back is to lose oneself. There is no turning back. Sometimes analysands express that forlorn wish that they had never set out on this path to greater consciousness. It asks too much. And then the next night's dream will make it clear that if they do turn-back, their aliveness could well be turned solid to a pillar of salt. Such turning-back can actually be enforced by too much looking-back. We are not speaking here of the mechanism of *reculer pour mieux sauter*, the going/looking back in order to redeem or re-collect what has been lost, rejected, or ignored. One most moving myth that lodges our experience of yearning and looking-back is that of Orpheus. There are two occasions in Ovid's narrative when Orpheus looks-back, the first with disastrous results, the second with enhanced delight. In one condition, Orpheus may not do so, at another, he may.

Ovid indicates that Orpheus's destiny in love will be tragic by such omens as Hymen's inability to make the marriage torch burn brightly at his wedding ceremony.[61] Then his bride is killed by a snake bite and Orpheus's lament begins. Having mourned Euridice in the upper world, he goes-down-into the lower world to move Pluto and Proserpina to pity. He claims Amor as source of his grief,

> well known in the world above; whether he may be so *here* too, I do not know, but I imagine that he is familiar to you also and if there is any truth in that story of that rape long ago, then you yourselves were brought-together by Love.

Orpheus admits that in the end, every mortal will come down to this subterranean *here*; for "though we delay, sooner or later, we hasten home. *Here* we are all compelled, this is our final abode." Orpheus's plea causes even bloodless spirits to weep and Eurydice is released. Her lover is told "that he must not look back, until he emerged from the underworld, or she…would be taken from him." So "*up* the sloping path, through unspeaking silence, they made their way, *up* the steep track…till they had *almost* reached the surface of the earth." He comes this far in his errand of love, downward to retrieve life upward. Death has been momentarily overwhelmed by pity. Orpheus disobeys the command. He is *about to* lose his wife in a double loss. *Almost* within reach of the upper world, he stops. Almost is perhaps the most tantalizing adverb, representing painful experience of the *not quite*.

> Here, anxious in case his wife's strength should fail and urgent to see her, the lover looked behind him, and at once Eurydice slid-back-into the depths. Orpheus stretched-out his arms, straining to clasp her and be clasped; but the helpless man touched nothing but unresisting space. Eurydice dies again…falling-back once more into the same place from which she had come.

Orpheus looks-back, falls-back, and he tries to follow her back, but

> in vain did the poet desire and pray that he could cross the Styx again. The ferryman pushed him aside. For seven days, untidy and neglected, he sat on the river bank, without eating.

He determines never to love again and is rebuked, like Narcissus, for his refusal, rebuke followed by increasingly violent attacks by those he spurned. At first his music protects him, but then both instrument and harmony are destroyed. "*Then, at last* the stones grew scarlet with his blood."[62] Once dead, Orpheus descends legitimately to Pluto's kingdom.

> The ghost of Orpheus passed beneath the earth, recognizing everything he saw before. Searching through the fields of the Blessed, he found his Eurydice, and embraced her eagerly. There they walk together, side by side: or sometimes Orpheus walks behind while his wife goes before, sometimes he leads and looks-back at Eurydice as he can now safely do.

The same kinesthetic diction works through all the versions of the myth that I consulted, especially lively in poetic renderings. In German, Rilke's "Orpheus, Eurydice, Hermes," for example, plays fugally with *vor*, *voran*, *zurück*, with turning behind and around absorbed into verbs.[63] They are necessary to the very structure of the myth.

Looking or going back is psychologically ambivalent. As therapeutic remembering, it can be the source of new consciousness and integration. It is a keen and focal part of analysis, to return to a lost, hidden, or displaced self that was unable to live in the past because of overwhelming threats to its integrity. But the goal of such a return is to gather past life by re-imagining, to integrate and repossess what had to be repressed or dissociated, bring-back lost energy to the psychic store. I was much moved when an analysand found that as a compassionate adult he could tend some woodland where he had been traumatically molested as a boy. He was able to look-back and go-back to that place and find healing for old wounds. His action came from a very special insight into the mechanism of *then-and-now*. Such instances illuminate Kierkegaard's insight that *we live forward and understand backward*. Our inability to differentiate between *then*, *now*, *there*, and *here* is the work of our complexes. We might say that initially

Orpheus suffered from an immortality complex, unable or unwilling to accept loss and death. Desire for union on *this* side, or re-union on the *other*, are archetypally enforced.

Looking-back can also serve the practice of re-view, leading to a more comprehensive understanding of the past and its relation to the present, a means of celebration and thanksgiving, a tribute to past experience. It is helpful in ending analysis to look-back, to re-view what has been re-vised or re-stored over time. Looking-back-over past dreams can have the same value, when we see how images have formed and re-formed and how energies have been released and symbolic networks enlarged. What can exhaust psyche's energy is looking back with longing for that which cannot, and must not, be re-lived or re-possessed. This theme is explored with keen psycho-sociological insight in Tacey's work, where he diagnoses the "betraying of the *zeitgeist*," which he sees active in late-twentieth-century men's movements.[64]

In D. H. Lawrence's poem "She Looks Back," there is a memorable illumination of how the complex, especially the mother complex, can retard or prevent forward movement through this regressive bias.[65] It is a troubling exploration of the speaker's "deep burn or wound in his heart," a " curse against all mothers" that persists despite the *nevertheless* of his perceptive intelligence. The poem presents a partner's emotion, being abroad, enjoying the beauty of the world and the intimacy of a relationship with a woman who just cannot stop being mother to children left-behind. He observes how "that mother-love like a demon drew you from me / Towards England." They struggle "to be together," pronouns relating to you(rs) and my/mine intertwining. *There* and *here* register their separation:

> For you were straining with a wild heart, back,
> back again,
> Back to those children you had left behind, to all the
> aeons of the past.
> And I was here in the under-dusk of the Isar.

No matter how much they both wrestle with the complex and with each other, her assurances of presence feel deceptive. For

> The mother in you, fierce as a murderess, glaring to England,
> Yearning towards England, towards your young children…

This compulsion *backward-toward* inevitably evokes Lot's wife. He feels as though her salt has enveloped him, straining to produce *nevertheless* to engage her between their shared eros and her exclusive mother-love. He tries to reassure himself with the emphatic but unexceptional particles, "it is also well between us." The success of that consolation we can only guess from his final assertion "that you are with me in the end."

> That you never look quite back; nine-tenths, ah, more
> You look round over your shoulder;
> But never quite back.

These strained form-words that qualify his experience—*but*, *never*, and *quite*—are anti-climactically potent. The minimal diction evokes the hopelessness of the lover's envy and desire and the effort to escape the tyranny of that most powerful complex. These are the "stygian depths" of the Mother archetype.[66] "It is just this massive weight of meaning that ties us to the mother and chains her to her child, to the physical and mental detriment of both."[67] The tying-to in early life can excite the pulling-back-to in subsequent life. Jung describes these two "ineluctable" urges in the human psyche, the urge to self-realization and the oppositional pull back to containment in the mother. These indomitable forces collide and collaborate in the process of individuation. They fight it out. Fighting it out between them is an apt translation of the formulation of the individuation process as "*auseinander–setzung mit der unbewußtsein*," where the pileup of prepositions and suffixes carries the load and the relations. The energy of this process can be fiercely dia-logic and dia-lectical.[68]

Looking-back and going-back are related to the yearning associated with the English verb hark/harken (or hearken), etymologically related to OHG *horchen*. To harken is more than simply to hear; it is straining to hear. It is an old hunting term for the action of the hounds when they have lost the scent. They harken back along the path until they find the old scent. Tacey speaks about using the theory of the unchanging archetypes to re-inforce old patterns, diagnosing how it can affirm psychological attitudes that are "reactionary, conservative and backward looking." In his work on remaking men, he explores such phenomena as the "Iron John" culture, which harken back nostalgically to archaic male models like warrior, king, magician—old forms it seeks to enliven by going down into the unconscious and awakening the so-called Hairy Wildman.[69] He argues that this is to mis-use archetypal theory. Archetypes are not powers to be gone-back-to, fulminating below consciousness, waiting to be re-constellated in the same forms. They are energies that open up and envisage inexhaustible possibilities, new forms arising out of eternal paradigms, always moving in hitherto unrealized directions, constantly being individuated afresh in individual lives, collectives, and cultures. We do not have to harken-back to in order to repeat. We can disengage, leave soul's home for a time, be broken down and re-membered and return in transformed relationship to archetypal patterns. This is the shape of myth. We might see it enacted in the Prodigal Son mytheme. The son rebels against even the good father, claims his inheritance, descends into his own particular depths to a traumatic phase of wasting and loss required by his pursuit of wholeness. Only then can he return to the father as his own man. Coming back need not be a refusal of going forward, it can be a coming home to live from oneself in new ways. Harken is related to hanker, a verb always needing a preposition, hanker-after, hanker-for. The boy hankered after life apart from father. And when he had discovered more of himself, using up his natural inheritance, he hankers for home. To pine, to have longing in German is *sich sehnen*, or *verlangen haben*. This takes us back to the hart harkening-after, longing-for, the streams, already felt. Hart and heart hankering after that which gives life. Contemporary Christian agnostics speak of a "God-shaped hole" in the human being that longs to be filled.[70]

One of the starkest of human reality principles, Freud insistently reminds us, is the dialogue with death, involvement with *thanatos*. This is the stuff of myth, as we saw in the tale of Orpheus. In a poem ironically titled "Aubade," Phillip Larkin echoes Orpheus's reluctant admission of the ineluctability of death. The poet acknowledges that though "things may never happen: this one will"[71]—three pounding, monosyllabic function-words. "This one will." Things, the mundane life, stand in contradistinction to this immutable one thing, death. Larkin's aubade is written, ironically, in the tradition of the morning song; but for this poet every dawn announces only "unresting death, a whole day nearer now." In each day's new light he sees "*what's really always there*," recording his obsessive awareness of death's invasive reality, "but how / And where and when I shall myself die." Such thinking makes thought impossible. Thinking forever about "the sure extinction that we travel to / And shall be lost in always." It feels that in such existential moments, language is reduced to the utterly minimal and works through negation. "Not to be here, / Not to be anywhere, / And so on; nothing more terrible, nothing more true." And later, he offers himself the paradoxical, perhaps contradictory comfort, of a numb form of the mystic's *apatheia*.

> No rational being
> Can fear a thing it will not feel, not seeing
> That this is what we fear—no sight, no sound,
> No touch or taste or smell, nothing to think with,
> Nothing to love or link with,
> The anaesthetic from which none come round.[72]

Larkin explores a version of the *here* with which I am pre-occupied. His *here* is the land of the living; his *there* is death itself as extinction of life, body, and consciousness. The earlier Christian paradigm of the inferior earthly here, waiting for the superior there, is refused, and death becomes not only not-being-here, but not-being-anywhere. We encounter this kind of agonizing in myth and works of the imagination in and through paradigms of *elsewhere* and *hereafter*. They are archetypal spaces that myth fills in culturally diverse ways. Larkin's cool poetic agon is a way of striving for equanimity, striving to maintain psychic equilibrium.[73] This is the energic process with which this whole study is concerned, a psychic dynamism that underlies our grammar and lexical relationships. The most terrible reality for Larkin is the loss of instinctual experience, and his poetry reflects this with aching intensity through the very sinew of grammar.

In his paper "On Psychic Energy," Jung posits the existence of a spiritual principle that enables a man "to set up a spiritual counterpole to his primitive instinctual nature, a cultural attitude as opposed to sheer instinctuality."[74] This is a function of symbolic systems and of myth, imaginally and imaginatively to assist and enact the "transition from the biological to the cultural attitude, for the transformation of energy from the biological form to the cultural form."[75] Tacey is also pre-occupied with this field of exchange.

> The two poles of our archetypal experience, spirit and nature, have collapsed into one and this is a fraught and untenable situation. It is not that Jung is promoting a rigid dualism above the idea of a unitary reality. He is saying that a necessary polarity between spirit and nature has to be maintained and this has been subverted in our time. Just as electricity requires tension between polarities to function at all, so our minds work best when spirit and nature are held in dynamic tension. When we live between spirit and matter, heaven and earth, we live correctly.[76]

Tacey sees these as "spiritual factors in the psyche," not merely cultural accretions or constructions. Man's religious appetite is a "prejudice of being human" that we cannot escape. The movement *between* often feels slippery; we slide between, not knowing or understanding how we made the passage.

This bias, these biases, can be construed in many different ways, being constantly reformulated and perhaps updated. Derrida, for example, conceives of our bias to construct and conceive of the world in terms of oppositions, or "antagonisms." He sees them embedded in our language, in our habitual either-or categories, and he questions whether our experience dictates the antagonistic language, or whether our far-from-innocent language dictates our perceiving.[77] His project is de-constructive. He de-rails conceptual oppositions and hierarchical systems of thought that are the thinking tools we in the West inherit. A massive weight of meaning bulges from either/or, both/and pairing. These innocent particles engage the philosophic as well as the psychological mind. It is a speech we cannot escape.

In all our agonizing, our finding and making our way through labyrinths, across rivers or oceans, into forests, below the earth, beyond visible horizons, we might say that in such pathless wastes the gods of myth provide our "psychic co-ordinates."[78] They must be no more than that, despite our sometimes frantic desire to find or create a "portable God," or at least, an instantly accessible and possess-able god. Symbols point to something beyond themselves and link us to archetypal reality, but they are not it. Nevertheless it may be the only way to point to that ineffably whole reality.

I end this chapter with a reflection from Jung's own mythic surrender to his hankering spirit, which actually led him back-into ordinary living.

> My spirit reflected on everything rare and uncommon, it pried its way into unfound possibilities toward paths that lead into the hidden, toward lights that shine in the night. And as my spirit did this, everything ordinary in me suffered harm without my noticing it, and it began to hanker after life, since I did not live it. Hence this adventure. I was smitten by the romantic. The romantic is a step backward.[79]

Postlude

"between the dictionary and the horizon"[1] "we walked into a new vocabulary."[2]
—Seamus Heaney, "An Invocation";
Jackie Kay, "Holy Island"

—genealogies and nominations echo the primal Adamic deed of naming in Eden. They enact an instinctual but also ontological impulse to make.[3]
—George Steiner, *No Passion Spent*

What we need in order to feel at home in the world, is certainly not a belief that it was made for us. We are at home in this world because we were made for it. We have developed here, on this planet, and are adapted to live here. Our emotional constitution is part of that adaptation. We are not fit to live anywhere else.[4]
—Mary Midgley, *Beast and Man*

I have ranged widely over many experiences of language, spoken and written, following prepositions in many directions to numberless destinations, being moved by adverbials in ways they needed to conduct us, surrendering to demands of auxiliaries, relating through conjunctive connection, being arrested by interjection, directed by affixes, and regulated by intensifiers. So where have we reached in this exploration of the language of the Jungian field?

I wanted to explore that *somewhere* "between the horizon and the dictionary." This is for me exciting psychic territory, between the dictionary as lived words and a horizon after which language strains. Since I began work as an analyst, I have walked into a new vocabulary, or at least, into a new relationship with the vocabulary of psychotherapeutic exchange and a more urgent engagement in communication itself. It would seem that the lexis to which we have been paying attention, perhaps absurdly, is a most accessible soul language. It is primary. And yet it is in many ways more sophisticated than Alice's "nice grand words."[5] It is language as psychic locomotion.

Jung suggested that "the concept of libido in psychology has functionally the same significance as the concept of energy in physics."[6] The grammatical dynamics in sentence forms to which we have been responding are natural currents of soul, grammatical libido that we might associate with Hitchings's "syntactic magnetism."[7] We might also think of it as James does in distinguishing between substantive and transitive. Introducing the phenomenon of the "stream of consciousness," he designates these "states of mind."

> Let us call the resting-places "substantive parts," and the places of flight the "transitive parts," of the stream of thought. It then appears that our thinking tends at all times towards some other substantive part than the one from which it has just been dislodged. And we may say that the main use of the transitive parts is to lead us from the one substantive conclusion to another.[8]

Bell claims that the "transitive elements of that stream have as much meaning and impact as the substantive points, which denote entities."[9] Energy is the core concept in Jung's theory, radiating out to everything else. This energy, in praxis, is mediated through experience and exchange, trans-ferring and counter-trans-ferring libido and image. Even in peaceful dia-lectic, she speaks-*to* him and he listens-*to* her. *To* carries the exchange between. I can hear passively on waking as I am met by morning birdsong. But then I might start to listen-to it keenly, as Keats attends to the nightingale: "Darkling I listen." This is listening-*to*. This is tuning-*in* with intention. One key problem for Miller's "gifted child" is that her antennae are always out to the world, desperate to listen-*to* any necessary signal about the needs of others, those others she is never heard-*by*. In all this we may be talking-*about* language, but we are entering-*into* speech, responding to the generation of linguistic spirit, the generous capacity of language to effect communication.

There is a conventionally assumed simplicity in the language I am befriending, a primitive patterning of experience that is elusive to definition. What do I mean, or rather, what do I want to implicate, in simplicity? There has been a tendency to see words as simple just because they are little and constantly repeated. Grammars collude with this inference. As far back as Aristotle, there has been a tendency to give some words more value than others.

> Of words, some are single, by which I mean composed of parts not significant; and some double: of which last some have one part significant and the other not significant, and some both parts significant. A word may also be triple, quadruple, etc., like many used by those who love hard words, as *Hermocaïcoxanthus*. Every word is either common or foreign, or metaphorical, or ornamental or invented, or extended, or contracted or altered.[10]

The material expression of Jung's psychology, tales of psyche in the form of dreams, myths, and fairytales, is richly textured, and often it seems that the grandiloquence of the archetypal story can pass by the work done by bread-and-butter words of the word-hoard. These particles shy away from content as such, but indicate or modulate direction, in-clination, tendency, in-tensity, ex-tensity. They are often the carriers of archetypal dynamics in their grammatical motion. In these relations between words, we might sometimes see "the restlessness of the complex" in action.[11] In our pre-occupation with them, we should heed Hillman's counsel:

> A new angelology of words is needed so that we may once again have faith in them....How can anything of worth and soul be conveyed from one psyche to another, as in a conversation, a letter, or a book, if archetypal significances are not carried in the depth of our words?[12]

I would also add to this my conviction that "Among your earthiest words the angels stray." This is Patrick Kavanagh, "In Memory of my Mother," acknowledging what I would regard as backyard language.

And to Hillman's depths of words I would add the dynamics and dynamisms in-between words. These chapters have considered the relations *between* words, valuing every speech act as a psychic event. Kugler's imaginative work on language is different from mine in this study, but one vital comment that he makes serves my purpose.

> The move from libido to psychic energy, from a theory based on the primacy of substances to one founded on the primacy of relations, allowed Jung to adopt a structural approach to the collective layer of the personality.[13]

Syntax might be seen as libidinous, in that it seeks to animate semantic affinities. As Jung says, "Libido is…tied to definite forms or states. It appears as the intensity of impulses, affects, activities."[14] In the grammar and the syntax of language inhere psyche's energy; in each language event psychic forces are released. Grammar is attuned to psyche's bias, two forces in tension: the exclusive bias of either/or (a one-sidedness that enforces neurosis) and the bias toward wholeness, encompassing the both/and that Jung sees governing our whole psychic system, despite the limitations of ego's capacity to contain contradiction, or experience it paradoxically. I am fascinated by what I experience as a linguistic kinesis, a vital motion or change. It is in this grammatical movement that Psyche can reveal herself at work. Stein's discussion of energy in his map of the soul also affirms that "to speak of energy is to be concerned with the relation between objects, rather than with the objects themselves."[15] I think of syntax as a current flowing rather like electricity or water. Once one pays attention to this movement, one can perceive even in dream records "the fluctuations of psychic balance" and feel a psychic process along which consciousness "slides."[16] The energy of the archetype is not "at the disposal of the conscious mind"; it manifests through conscious and unconscious manipulations of grammar. I ask at the end of all this, do syntax and all the grammatical directions I have been illuminating express and convey what Jung values as sense of purpose? "By finality I mean merely the immanent psychological striving for a goal. Instead…one could say, 'sense of purpose.'"[17] The language this study has foregrounded is thoroughly, irresistibly, purposive.

There are many adverbial and prepositional phrases that we have encountered that capture this motion, enacting the behavior of the complexes. We experience it in the cadences of the syntax, in the depicting of Christian's paralysis: "he looked this way and that way as if he would run; yet he stood still, because…he could not tell which way to go."[18] Here the very rhythm of the syntax acts out the blockage, enforced by the hindering conjunctions. We hear this rhythm in the speech of complex-blocked analysands: "I just keep going both ways, so I go nowhere." "I am utterly blocked. I just don't know what I should do." "I just can't decide which way to go." "I do this and I do that but it just makes no difference." The intensifier *just* acts intensely, just as an intensifier should. The restlessness of the complex is typically kinetic in confessional or imaginative speech. It is often manifest in *The Red Book*.

> The door of the Mysterium has closed behind me. I feel that my will is paralysed and that the spirit of the depths possesses me. I know nothing about a way. I can neither therefore want this nor that, since nothing indicates to me whether I want this or that. I wait, without knowing what I'm waiting for. But already in the following night I felt that I had reached a solid point.[19]

Jung and Bunyan's pilgrim are in similar places, using similar language, harnessing sub-lexical energies to go in the ways that they must go, both bewildered by the many possibilities. Jung is engaging with his own observations about energy, which "is always experienced specifically as motion and force when actual, and as a state or condition when potential."[20] So syntax halts and directs.

Despite my sympathy for Hillman's concern that our Western pre-occupation with grammar might hinder our attention to the image, I have been elaborating grammar and syntax as agents of archetypal motion, defending grammatical particles, befriending *but* and *into* as friends of the image, defending psyche's imaginal speech. Hillman insists that

> our usual ways of speech may keep us from hearing what the image is saying. And a main determinant of the volume of an image resides in the multiple implications of its words. To get at this volume, this amplification, we have to break through the roles assigned to words by grammar and syntax; we must break the literalism of the parts of speech. For we have been sentenced by our sentences. In grammar and syntax is lodged the

> fundament of our collective unconscious and its non-imaginal singleness of mind. We are unconscious in the very instrument of consciousness: our speech.[21]

I would dispute that non-imaginal singleness of mind is always lodged in grammar and syntax. I respond more positively to the parts of speech, finding in them potential currents of locomotive imagery. I am also sympathetic to the *fascinosum* of *if* and *can*, the "ifs and cans" that philosophers value as "protean words, perplexing both grammatically and philosophically." Austin's opening question is, "Are cans constitutionally iffy?"[22] These optatives and subjunctives engender confusion, the philosopher claims. But the literary response and psyche's response are different. They "engender life" even though they may be "logically recalcitrant." Steiner sees these qualities as "fundamental energies of adjustment between language and human need."[23] Language is a servant of human complexity and need.

Freud had urged liberation of the personality "from the ego's, or rather, the super-ego's grammatical constraints," also claiming that the unconscious disregards all words with grammatical functions, especially conjunctions, because dreams

> have no means at their disposal for representing these logical relations between dream thoughts that they take over and manipulate. The restoration of the connections which the dream work has destroyed is a task which has to be performed by the interpretative process.

Such was Freud's idealized trust in the conscious interpretive work of the analyst to restore grammar to the dream image.[24] But this is often already achieved in translation, as the dream ego hands over dream experience to the waking speech-animal.

There are many lexical items that we have not considered. *Beside*, for example, as preposition (with its logical extension to the adverb, *besides*, meaning *furthermore, except for*), might have been considered in any one of the foregoing chapters. *Beside* is an egalitarian position, while *above* is hierarchically privileged. *Beside* governs the horizontal axis, it is *alongside*, to right or left, it is lateral. Many vital figures sit beside the road in fairytales, like the first girl in "Mother Holle," who sits there spinning. To be beside the road is to be ready for the journey. Helpful creatures appear beside the way for those already en route.

Being beside can be a strangely soothing, reflective modality. Being *beside* the psalmist's still waters is a posture of companionship, a gestalt of mutuality. Not ahead, not behind, but beside. If Orpheus had walked out of Hades staying-beside Eurydice, he would not have lost her. One can look forward and be beside; one can sense beside-ness, not needing visual re-assurance. It is a good model for analytical presence. Jung insisted on "face to face" therapy, rejecting the potently knowledgeable but not-knowable analyst *behind* a couch. Face-to-face encounter is a special composition, sitting opposite and yet feeling beside. Analysands sometimes need to look-*away*, and sometimes they need the analyst to look-*away*. See me, but give me the option not to be seen, and certainly not to feel exposed.[25]

It often seems that as the mystery and the inexplicable intensify, language becomes more elemental. We can see this happening in the immensities created by the poets out of lexically minimal effects. Many literary climaxes come to mind, compounded of these humble particles that have seduced me. Shakespeare either knew this, or practiced it unknowingly—King Lear's painful acceptance of the existentially human hither and thither: "men must endure / Their going hence, even as their coming hither: / Ripeness is all,"[26] that teasingly voluminous *all*, an all that relates to the promiscuous, expansive, and inclusive *It*, reminiscent of Lacan's *thing*. One thinks of Prufrock in his love song, aching for communication but able only to utter words that convey his isolation: "I shall tell you *all.*" If one, settling a pillow by her head, should say, "*That is not what I meant at all. That is not it, at all…*"[27] In contrast, Donne, in the ec-stasy of climactic communion, asserts that this union makes "one little room an everywhere."[28] And Auden's expensive, delicate ship on the Icarian sea, an amazing something, nevertheless, is compelled by the somewhere to which it must go, and sails onward undisturbed.[29] How feckless and indifferent that limitless *somewhere to get to*. Utterly banal and unbearable, in breathtaking contrast with "something amazing." Even more formidable, the ultimate expression of divine compassion in the words from the cross, "Father, forgive them, for they know not what they do." *What* they do. These words resound down the centuries with massive charge. What is it really that they do? In the languages with which I am familiar, this has the same understated enormity. The conjunction *for* that encompasses the theology of forgiveness, symbolized by a primitive wooden cross.[30] *For*, in this sense of because, is perhaps our deepest response to our deepest interrogations: *why, who, when, where*? On those few stark letters so much depends. I remember a child who thought a sufficient answer to any interrogation was a bald *because*. Pure *ipse dixit* explanation and excuse. Freud presented the child's first questioning, "Where do babies come from?" as our first curiosity, our first intellectual project. This emerges again in analysis. *Who am I? Where am I? Where have I come from and where am I* heading? *Why do I* suffer *like this?* In bereavement, Rilke grieved that death could steal till-then from ever-since (*das Bisdahin—vom Seither*), thereby robbing his friend of her future's history. Such enigmas of time were fittingly caught in stark temporal particles.

It is fascinating to see how this minimalist, reduced language is used, and has always been used, in various discourses. So commonly in theological writing, one comes up against that "bullying by the infinite" that comes to a truce in such statements as Williams's

> the negativity is less a matter of an absolute "this is not it"—which might suggest that there could in principle be a standard by which the accuracy of a proposition about God could be measured—than of "this is not, and can never be, all," since there is an infinity of excess in the being of God beyond what can ever be expressed.[31]

Merest particles of utterance are re-loaded to assist the speaking of the unspeakable in theology as in psychology at depth. In all literature of thought, one comes across remarks such as Jacques Maritain's "how things are not only what they are," how "they give more than they have."[32] It offers one more way of trying to "get the better of words" in the attempt to "raid [on] the inarticulate." Eliot adopts a posture of discontent with the capacity of language to serve the poet adequately, it is "shabby equipment always deteriorating."[33] This is always the dilemma in probing psychic depths. "What should I say?" Jung asks, "This is beyond words."[34] For that which is beyond words, we reach for figurative language and for full-words that carry so much ready-loaded content, so often overlooking the power of mere function-words. In experiences of *here* in psychological communication, we accede to

Jung's, "Here something wants to be uttered."[35] As we experience soul, we see not only that we want to go after the saying of the *something*, but that *something* wants to be made conscious in speech. *Something* comes after us to be said, then it often flowers into *something else*. We do know what we cannot yet say.

In this uttering, in what we might describe as domestically banal diction, we must enroll as well as ensoul the ego's parts of speech generously, not grudgingly. We have explored pronominal necessities. This is the stuff of therapeutic work, the "holy trust between you and me," an inter-psychic and an intra-psychic bond. We are wired for relationship, and our work relies on empathy, imagining that I am you in a process of "co-experiencing." Recent neurological research affirms this wiring in the activity of mirror neurons, affording such vivid phrases as the "mystery of resonance."[36] Over his whole career, Jung was involved with encounters of ego-self and Self, as well as other/Other. The urge to discriminate between the two identities involves the profoundest dialectical experience, intense self-questioning such as that in the crucial opening of Jung's "Scrutinies":

> I resist. I cannot accept this hollow nothing that I am. What am I? What is my I? I always presuppose my I. Now it stands before me—I before my I. I speak now to you, my I.[37]

Such wrestling with one's complex inner identities is reminiscent of Shakespeare's typically tortuous soliloquy.[38] Pronominal play reaches deeply into soul's grammar. For all shaped by Judeo-Christianity, the Exodus words from the burning bush, God's self-revelation, "I am that I am," are charged with numinous ambiguity. This "single immensity," an untranslatable tautology, reduces language to a rawness that has "numbing singularity" (Meister Eckhart). What can it mean? I am what I am or, perhaps, simply, I am / I am. We cannot translate it yet alone understand it. But that prepositional play is what concerns all analyses, where all ask, like Lear, "Who is it that can tell me who I am?"

Somehow, something, somewhere are often needed when we struggle to lay hold of what cannot yet be reached, when we are groping for what lies outside formulation. As in all dream experience, the elusive somebodies of the *Red Book* slowly acquire form, substance, identity, even names. But first they needed to be experienced as unknown energies and agents (*jemand*). They evolve presence. We see this in unconsciously prepared encounters when *somebody* comes-*toward* the experiencing *I*:

> As I moved toward the East, one from the East hurried toward me and I strove toward the sinking light. I wanted light, he wanted night. I wanted to rise, he wanted to sink....And so we hurried toward each other; he, from the light; I, from the darkness; he, strong; I, weak; he, God; I, serpent; he, ancient; I, utterly new; he, unknowing; I, knowing....But we were both astonished to see one another on the border between morning and evening.[39]

The individuation process demands a constant discovering of the other, the others, within—every *someone* who appears actively in imagination. At the same time, there is continual movement between collective and individual persons, shifting *from me* to *we*, for no one can individuate alone. There is significant danger of merging *between me and us* in family cloning, a point echoed by the political theologian Volf, who warns that a "disappearance of the I into the we" is "characteristic not only of totalitarian regimes but of many cultural movements and family relations."[40] "Nobody stands 'nowhere' for we think and act as 'encumbered selves.'" These are not non-imaginal words. *Nowhere* and *no-one* are endlessly evocative, throwing self's encumbering into relief. We encounter such substantial nothings in the nursery as in the dream. I am still haunted by the nursery rhyme:

> As I was going up the stair,
> I met a man who wasn't there.
> He wasn't there again today.
> I wish that man would go away.[41]

Such remarkably unremarkable language communicates the palpable terror of the unknown. In his autobiographical writing even more than in discursive, theoretical texts, Jung presses these words into service of soul.

> My soul speaks to me in a bright voice: "The door should be lifted off its hinges to provide a free passage between here and there, between yes and no, between above and below, between left and right."[42]

POSTLUDE

All these busy particles have been much used throughout this book, and I hope that such re-valuing of them now pays dividends in reading such imaginative texts as this. (One might note the many auxiliaries that follow this quotation.) We search for the concealed and secret, and overlook the obvious, the mundane. But it is through such words that we "fall into the mystery," a complex process of self-discovery concentrated between an explanatory *therefore* and culminating *thus*:

> Therefore I no longer wanted to seek myself outside of myself, but within. Then I wanted to grasp myself and then I wanted to go on again, without knowing what I wanted and THUS I fell into the mystery.[43]

This is a highly sophisticated use of language that we grow into from infancy. Grammar has potential to create a linguistic soul home, re-visioning the very ordinary, even the banal, a known language we still have to grow into. I was surprised to realize how children have to learn spatial and temporal directions. I remember sharing certain early picture books with my children that enacted these parameters. In *Rosie's Walk*, the bare story is simply that Rosie the hen went for a walk, and got back in time for dinner. But her farmyard expedition took her "*across* the yard, *around* the pond, *past* the mill, *through* the fence, *under* the beehives," each venue posing a threat of which she was sublimely unaware. She should have been clobbered but evaded every danger.[44] These same prepositional directions were travelled in the second narrative, *We're Going on a Bear Hunt*, in which children overcome natural obstacles to go *through,* and *not over, round or under*, in making their way to a cave, where they find a bear. In terror they retreat, retracing the outward path exactly.[45] Through to the source of their fear, back again. This kind of imaginative writing prepares children for more ex-tensive fiction like *The Wind in the Willows*, where the trajectory is from the familiar riverbank or hole in the ground, off into the wild wood, out to the wide world, then back to *dulce domum*.[46] All of these animals are exposed to the "spirit of divine discontent and longing" that pulls them from the riverbank's *here* through *over there* to a distant *yonder*, enthusiastically pursued by the extravertedly voracious Toad. This is a much remembered English story, and like Milne's *Winnie the Pooh* fantasies, provides many dreamers with profuse inner imagery. Rat, Mole, and Badger are attached, even neurotically attached, to their holes, while the swallows fly high and free from attachment, far and near, between north and south. We meet them all in therapy. These creatures are "bullied by infinity," pulled beyond *over-there* to a further dimension. The fugal use of these words in Jung's own work is intriguing. Heed them in these very typical narrative experiences from *Red Book* imaginings.

> It is agonizing as a sleepless night to fulfill the beyond from the here and now, namely the other and the opposing in myself....But here you may not stop—do not place your disgust between your here-and-now and your beyond. (p. 264)

> So the path of my life led me beyond the rejected opposites, united in smooth and—alas!—extremely painful sides of the way that lay before me. I stepped on them but they burned and froze my soles. And thus I reached the other side. (p. 279)

> You need to undertake only half of the way, he will undertake the other half. If you go beyond him, blindness will befall you. If he goes beyond you, paralysis will befall him. Therefore, and insofar as it is the manner of the Gods to go beyond mortals, they become paralyzed and become as helpless as children. Divinity and humanity should remain preserved, if man should remain before the God, and the God remain before man. (p. 281)

> I have united with the serpent of the beyond. I have accepted everything beyond into myself. From this I have built my beginning. When this work was completed I was pleased and I felt curious to know what might lie still in my beyond. So I approached my serpent and asked her whether she would not like to creep over to bring me news of what was happening in the beyond. But... (p. 322)

Jung's whole massive undertaking moves between an early and urgent self questioning—"I wandered for many years, so long that I forgot that I possessed a soul. Where were you all this time? Which Beyond sheltered you and gave you sanctuary"[47]—to a final interrogation by the serpent—"You have the whole wide earth. What do you want to ask the beyond for?"[48] One might see all of Jung's work answering these questions.

Whereas all the time-adverbials indicate rate of process, *never/ nevermore* denies it, asserting stasis at the very least. And while that negation can be absolute and unambiguous, unlike "occasionally" or "soon," it can also open up uncertainty and doubt. That sense erupted in me at a recent Gauguin exhibition when confronted by his painting with that title, "Nevermore." The title and subject allude to Poe's "The Raven," and perhaps represent the poignancy of lost love and beauty and efforts to reach out beyond death. The actual affirmation, *nevermore* or equivalent, echoes in every final line of every stanza of Poe's poem.[49] The imaginal potential of such adverbial reaction signals can be realized in dreams. For example, what might we do with a dream that has *only* the emphatic words, "No! No way!" This dream came with a sharp sense of the exclamation mark, the analysand insisted. And the qualifier *only* was also keen. But she thought that a dream without an image was no dream. This study challenges such an attitude. There may be no obvious image, no strictly eidetic content in a conventional sense. "No. No way!" *And yet*! (I have come to trust even that minimalist assertion.) Might there be a silent, submerged image here, too? I think so. The dream reflected a turning point in the analysis. The cry of pain and outrage that enacted the soul's protest against its own tyranny brought with it hosts of more visually enforced memories, crowds of protesting students whom she could never join, her beating heart in face of her father's will. It was a moment of passion. Such negatives carry massive energies in innocent sentences. "No way."

Affirmation works in equally declarative ways using closed-category lexis. *Yes* can command absolute spiritual authority. St. Paul uses it so: "All the promises of God find their yes in him" (1 Cor. 1:20). Of course, the poet conjures this yes most illuminatingly, as in Walcott's poem quoted above in chapter 1.[50] And the novelist, John Updike, writing in the person of the painter, is also driven to attest,

> When I paint, I just have to believe that beauty will emerge. Painting is abstract, you don't have a pretty landscape or bowl of oranges to lean on; it has to come purely out of you. You have to shut your eyes, so to speak, and take a leap. You have to say yes.[51]

Jung was always in quest of soul's *yes*. And yet. "It's all yes and no," he declares to the Serpent, affirming the reconciliation of opposites. "It is all yes and no. The opposites embrace each other, see eye to eye, and intermingle."[52]

Though so many such lexical items have been neglected, I hope that the work done to imagine and re-animate them will make you reach out to them. The archetypal current of directionality lies behind much of my exploration. In Jung's first mandala of 1916, when he was still "wholly unconscious of what it meant," he found a form to bring together all the directions active in his psyche, up, down, right, left, inside, outside.[53] As we see in the quotation from the *Red Book*, a critical wandering hither and thither in the unconscious imagination and the dispersing of his many selves is drawn together. I end this study with the language of these peregrinations.

It would be a relief to have space to elaborate many more psycholinguistic possibilities, as, for example, to circum-ambulate the psychological implication of certain adversarial conjunctives that broker balance in the psychic system; or further to explore verbal auxiliaries—*might, should, could, will, shall*—in representing or activating the "applied field of the will."[54] But waves go on coming to shore, the tide never stops moving them. So the last wave will be a final assertion from *The Red Book* that illuminates the un-ending-ness and fluctuations of speech. Jung's "I" is in dialogue with the Anchorite, who has already warned him that "words should not become Gods," and that he should "guard against being a slave to words." Jung had approached him questioningly, "eager to experience and understand what you think about the meaning of the sequence of words."[55] So Jung's un-learning evolves.

> You cry out for the word which has one meaning and no other, so that you escape boundless ambiguity....The word is protective magic against the daimons of the unending....You are saved if you can say at last, that is that and only that.[56]

In this certainty we must be disappointed. In psyche's largesse it cannot only be this *or* that, but the wholeness of it all, the fullness of *all that*. I hope that all the little atoms of speech are now fully primed for more intense communication.

At the end of this long process, measuring many weeks in coffee spoons, the question looming for me remains simply, What was all this for? A good Jungian interrogation of the whole project, all those hours thinking, writing, all that lifetime of reading and responding. I realize that in large part it is *just* so that I can listen more keenly when analysands speak, be more responsive to details so familiar and unpretentious that they are hardly noticed. So that I might respond more imaginatively to soul speech, from the heart's home and the heart's loom.

The goal of this study is practical, arising from a desire to make myself and perhaps my audience more sensitive to language at the soul face, a soul vernacular that we recognize in dream and in poetry, those innocent but bulging particles in any language. I give Rilke the last words, where he opens up worlds through the meager "thus only and no otherwise."

> Du willst die Welt nicht anders an dich halten
> als so, mit dieser sanftesten Gebärde.
> Aus ihren Himmeln greifst du dir die Erde
> und fühlst sie unter deines Mantels Falten.
>
> [With this gentlest of gestures you would hold
> the world, thus only and no otherwise.
> You lean from out its skies to capture earth,
> and feel it underneath your mantle's folds.][57]

The poet feels, as every analysand can feel, the massive, soul-easing relief of *just* having said it, experiencing that mysterious power of *just* expressing it against all the inexpressible odds, that sense of deliverance, feeling expressed. *I've got it out*, and in speech accessible to all. This is a true magic of words.

Notes

PRELUDE

1. John Hill, *At Home in the World: Sounds and Symmetries of Belonging* (New Orleans: Spring Publications, 2010).
2. *Ibid.*, p. 27. The Parker MS reads, "*þrie Scottas common to Ælfrede cyninge, on anum bate butan ælcum gereþrum of Hibernia, þonon hi bestælon forþon þe hi woldon for Godes lufan on elpiodignesse beon, hi ne rohton hwær.*" *Two Saxon Chronicles,* Year 891, vol. 1 (Oxford: Clarendon, 1965), p. 82.
3. Typically assumed into 1611 King James version.
4. cf. Vulgate's *unde* and *quo:* Whence and whither also used in the Douai-Rheims Catholic translation. German, *woher* and *wohin*; Swedish, *varav/varifrån* and *vart än*; Dutch, *waar vandaan* and *ewaats/waarheen*; French, *d'ou* and *Ou, la ou*; Italian, *Donde* and *Dove*.
5. It is impossible to document all the dialectal variants, but common early AS forms are *hwanon* and *hwyder*.
6. Hill, *At Home*, p. 28.
7. C. G. Jung, *Memories, Dreams, Reflections* (New York: Random House, 1962, 1989), p. 274. Hereafter cited as *MDR*.

8. Margaret Wilkinson, *Coming into Mind: The Mind-Brain Relationship: Jungian Clinical Perspective* (London: Routledge, 2006). Wilkinson says: "Perhaps as yet speculative, nevertheless it may be inferred that the therapeutic process and the evolving symbolizations associated with it can develop new neural pathways in the brain, and in particular can develop the fibre trace known as the corpus callosum that is the major highway between the two hemispheres, shown to be reduced through the effects of trauma" (p. 11). Quoting Daniel J. Siegel, *Coming into Mind*, p. 12: "When one achieves neural integration across the hemispheres one achieves coherent narratives." Quoting Regina Pally, *Coming into Mind*, p. 74: "By containing within them sensory, imagistic, emotional and verbal elements, metaphors are believed to activate multiple brain centers simultaneously."
9. Daniel Bell, *The Cultural Contradictions of Capitalism* (New York: Basic Books, 1976), p. 114.
10. *Have, be, do, are*, and auxiliaries are primary verbs. In the prepositional field, the words relate to space, destination, passage, cause, agency. They support or oppose, except or include. They also relate to time, duration, or direction of time's flow. They serve to orientate us in lived life. See Randolph Quirk et al., *A Comprehensive Grammar of the English Language* (London: Longman, 1985). See section on word classes, i.e., parts of speech.
11. Adam Phillips, *Darwin's Worms* (London: Faber and Faber, 1999), p. 43.
12. Seamus Heaney, *New and Selected Poems: 1966–1987* (London: Faber & Faber, 1990), "Station Island V1," p. 177.
13. Henri Nouwen, *The Way of the Heart: The Spirituality of the Desert Fathers and Mothers* (New York: Harper Collins, 1981), p. 45.
14. Phillips, *Darwin's Worms*, p. 46.
15. Henry Hitchings, *The Language Wars: A History of Proper English* (London: John Murray, 2011), p. 304.
16. *Ibid*, p. 305.
17. *Ibid*, p. 303. Hitchings discusses John Horne Tooke's work.
18. *Ibid*, p. 134. Insisting that "the first aim of language was to communicate our thoughts: the second, to do it with dispatch."

NOTES

19. David Tacey, *Remaking Men: Jung, Spirituality and Social Change* (London: Routledge, 1997), p. 55.
20. C. G. Jung, "Transformation Symbolism in the Mass," in *Psychology and Religion* (1977), vol. 11 of C. G. Jung, *Collected Works*, ed. Sir Herbert Read, Michael Fordham, Gerhard Adler, and William McGuire, 20 vols. (London: Routledge and Kegan Paul, 1953-1983), §442. Hereafter cited as *CW*.
21. Jonathan Swift, Gulliver's Travels, Project Gutenberg, bk. 3, chap. 5. Available at http://www.gutenberg.org/ebooks/829. First published 1726.
22. The splendid ARAS project (Archive for Archetypal Research) attempts to avoid this. See its publication, *The Book of Symbols: Reflections on Archetypal Images,* (New York: Taschen Books, 2010).
23. E. A. Bennet, *What Jung Really Said* (New York: Schocken Books, 1983), pp. 40, 42.
24. Paul Kugler, *The Alchemy of Discourse: An Archetypal Approach to Language* (London: Associated University Presses, 1982).
25. C. G. Jung, *Letters* (Princeton, NJ: Princeton University Press, 1973), vol. 2, p. 70 (my italics).
26. Sonu Shamdasani, *Jung Stripped Bare by His Biographers, Even* (London: Karnac, 2005), p. 48. No doubt we lose much in understanding Jung's intentions by reading his work in English translation.
27. Ben Jonson, "Timber, or Discoveries," in *Critical Essays of the Seventeenth Century*, ed. J. E. Spingarn (Bloomington, IN: Bloomington University Press, 1968), vol. 1, p. 36.
28. 1667. Quotations can also be found in Spingarn, *Critical Essays*, vol. 2, p. 116. Their project was to eradicate "luxury and redundance of speech" and all "ornaments of speaking" for language had "degenerated from original usefulness," for which poetry was largely to blame, with its "vicious…abundance of Phrase, this trick of Metaphors, this volubility of tongue, which makes so great a noise in the world." So the Royal Society "exacted for all their members a close, naked and natural way of speaking, positive expressions, clear senses, a native easiness,…and preferring the language of Artizans, Countrymen and Merchants, before that of Wits or Scholars."

29. George Steiner, *No Passion Spent: Essays 1978-1996* (London: Faber & Faber, 1996), p. 215.
30. Ian McEwan, *The Child in Time* (London: Vintage, 1992), p. 7.
31. Charles Baudelaire, *Les Fleurs du Mal*. Available at https://www.gutenberg.org/ebooks/6099.

> Ailleurs, bien loin d'ici! trop tard! *jamais* peut-être!
> Car j'ignore où tu fuis, tu ne sais où je vais,
> Ô toi que j'eusse aimée, ô toi qui le savais! ("À une passante," XC111, p. 137.)
> [Elsewhere, far from here, too late! perhaps never!
> For I know not where you flee, you know not where I go,
> You whom I might have loved, you who indeed know it!]

32. Rainer Maria Rilke, *Das Stundenbuch*, Project Gutenberg. Available at https://www.gutenberg.org/ebooks/24288.

> Du willst die Welt nicht anders an dich halten
> als so, mit dieser sanftesten Gebärde.
> Aus ihren Himmeln greifst du dir die Erde.
> und fühlst sie unter deines Mantels Falten.
> ("Es lärmt das Licht im Wipfel deines Baumes")
> [With this gentlest of gestures you would hold
> the world, thus only and no otherwise.
> You lean from out its skies to capture earth,
> and feel it underneath your mantle's folds.]

33. Murray Stein is of course one of the editors of this Spring series.
34. T. S. Eliot, "The Love-Song of Alfred J. Prufrock," in *The Complete Poems and Plays* (London: Faber & Faber, 1970), p. 14.
35. Phillips, *Darwin's Worms*, p. 42.

Chapter 1

1. John Milton, *Paradise Lost*, bk. 9, line 467ff. There are numberless editions of Milton.
2. "Yonder" is an archaic word in other European languages.
3. I have been preoccupied with this issue since my lectures on "The Language of the Dream" at the Jung Institute, exploring the language in which we tell and talk about dreams and the language used inside the dream.

4. Seamus Heaney, "Mint," in *The Spirit Level* (London: Faber & Faber, 1996), p. 6.
5. See Stephen Ullman's still valuable *Words and Their Use* (London: Muller, 1951); Quirk's *Comprehensive Grammar*.
6. Kugler, *Alchemy of Discourse*.
7. German, *Substantiv/Hauptwort*; Dutch, *naamwoord*; French, *le substantif*; Greek, οὐσιωτικός/ὄνομα; Latin, *nomen/ substantivum*. The sub-stantive stands alone, Latin *sub-stare*. Newspaper headlines often proliferate noun clusters, eliminating verbs, a practice leading Hitchings to speculate that we are becoming such a sedentary society that we feel little need for active verbs! Hitchings, *Language Wars*, p. 332.
8. Seamus Heaney, "In Illo Tempore," in *New and Selected Poems*, p. 206.
9. *Ibid.*
10. George Steiner, *After Babel: Aspects of Language and Translation*, 3rd ed. (Oxford: Oxford University Press, 1998), p. 3.
11. Jung, "Studies in Word Association," in *CW* 2, §8.
12. Jung, "Association, Dream and Hysterical Symptom," in *CW* 2, §857.
13. Per ipsum, et cum ipso, et in ipso, est tibi Deo Patri omnipotenti in unitate Spiritus Sancti, omnis honor et gloria. Per omnia saecula saeculorum.
14. Steiner, *No Passion Spent*, p. 61.
15. *Ibid.*, p. 318.
16. England's current first female Poet Laureate.
17. Carol Ann Duffy, *Selected Poems* (London: Penguin Books, 2006), p. 105.
18. *Ibid.*, p. 107.
19. *Ibid.*, p. 87.
20. G. K. Chesterton, *Autobiography* (London: Arrow Books, 1959), p. 41.
21. Wolfgang Giegerich, "Love the Questions Themselves," in Robert and Janis Henderson, *Living with Jung: "Enterviews" with Jungian Analysts*, vol. 3 (New Orleans: Spring Journal Books, 2010), p. 279.
22. I remember a child whose first words were "terminal moraine," though she had no knowledge what such sounds signified. Too

close for comfort is Gilbert and Sullivan's cheeky ditty, where the aesthetic poet pronounces that "the meaning doesn't matter if it's only idle chatter of a transcendental kind." Psychological discourse can sometimes sound like that!
23. See the discussion in Kugler, *Alchemy of Discourse*, p. 6.
24. Judith Plaskow, *Standing Again on Sinai* (San Francisco: HarperSanFrancisco, 1991), p. 144. See Mary Daly: "naming God as a dynamic verb": "God is not a Being, in fact, not a noun at all. Rather, God is being, the most active of verbs." *Beyond God the Father* (Boston: Beacon Paperback, 1985), p. 33.
25. See work on the doctrine of correctness by grammarians like S. A. Leonard.
26. Shakespeare, *Julius Caesar*, Act 2, sc. 6.
27. Shakespeare, *Macbeth*, Act 2, sc. 2.
28. In the poem, there are 79 form-words, 53 full-words, and one proper noun. *Happenings 2*, ed. Maurice Wollman and Alice Austin (London: Harrap, 1972), p. 80.
29. Fyodor Dostoevsky, *The Devils*, Project Gutenberg. Available at https://www.gutenberg.org/files/8117/8117-h/8117-h.htm.
30. Derek Walcott, *Midsummer*, LIV (London: Faber & Faber, 1984), p. 74. Consider also the use of "yes" as the final word of James's *Ulysses*.
31. Sigmund Freud, *The Psychopathology of Everyday Life* (Harmondsworth: Penguin Books, 1978), vol. 5, p. 271.
32. e e cummings, *Complete Poems, 1904-1962* (New York: Liveright, 1991).
33. Shakespeare, *Hamlet*, Act 3, sc. 1, and *Othello*, Act 5, sc. 2.
34. George Herbert, "Sacrifice" and "The Pulley," in *The Works of George Herbert* (Oxford: Clarendon, 1959), pp. 30, 159.
35. William James, *Psychology: A Briefer Course* (London: Macmillan, 1923), p. 165. First published 1892.

Chapter 2

1. I use the term rhetoric for the art of effective communication, suggesting that psyche adopts and adapts common language to its specific and associative purposes.

2. James, *Psychology: A Briefer Course,* p. 165.
3. Jung, "Preface to Answer to Job," in *CW* 11, p. 358.
4. Jung, "Concerning the Archetypes," in *CW* 9/I, §111.
5. Heaney, "Oysters," in *New Selected Poems,* p. 92.
6. Plato, *Symposium* (Harmondsworth: Penguin Books, 1951), p. 81.
7. Gerard Manley Hopkins, "The Leaden Echo and the Golden Echo," in *The Poems of Gerard Manley Hopkins,* Wikisource. Available at https://en.wikisource.org/wiki/Poems_of_Gerard_Manley_Hopkins.
8. David Tacey, *Edge of the Sacred* (Einsiedeln: Daimon Verlag, 2009). "Even energies are not mechanical, predictable, objective, but changing, mystical and affected by the subject who observes them," p. 127. Jung's comment is found in *CW* 5, §189.
9. German yonder/*jenseits, diesseits*/this side; *jenseits*/far side. *Dort drüben* (direction) is more or less obsolete.
10. George Lakoff and Mark Johnson, *Metaphors We Live By* (Chicago: University of Chicago Press, 2004), p. 14.
11. Herbert, "Time" and "Prayer (1)," in *Works of George Herbert,* pp. 51, 122.
12. Yann Arthus-Bertand, *La Terre Vue du Ciel* (Paris: Éditions de la Martinière, 1999).
13. See work of biblical commentators like Marcus J. Borg and J. Dominic Crossan.
14. J. W. T. Redfearn, *My Self, My Many Selves* (London: Academic Press for the Society of Analytical Psychology, 1985).
15. Bell, *Cultural Contradictions of Capitalism.*
16. Tate Modern, London, November 2009.
17. Quoted in Tate Modern gallery notes.
18. Swift, *Gulliver's Travels.* Lewis Carroll, *Alice's Adventures in Wonderland,* first published 1865.
19. Hannah Arendt, *Eichmann and the Holocaust* (London: Penguin Books, 2005), p. 103.
20. Jung, "Phenomenology of the Spirit in Fairy Tales," in *CW* 9/I, §408.
21. Jung, *Aion, CW* 9/ii, §223.
22. Jung, "The Psychology of the Child Archetype," in *CW* 9/I,
    §289 (italics in original).

23. Richard Crashaw, "A Hymn of the Nativity as Sung by the Shepherds," in The Complete Works of Richard Crashaw, ed. William B. Turnbull (London: John Russell Smith, 1858), 37-41.
24. William Wordsworth, "Intimations of Immortality from Recollections of Early Childhood," in *Poetical Works* (London: Oxford University Press, 1959), p. 460.
25. *Ibid.*, "Tintern Abbey," p. 163.
26. Theodore Roszak, *Voice of the Earth: An Exploration of Ecopsychology* (Grand Rapids: Phanes, 2001), p. 183.
27. Bell, *Cultural Contradictions of Capitalism*, p. 47.
28. Jung uses this expression "beyond good and evil" in a letter to the *Listener* (January 21, 1960), responding to mail he received after a BBC broadcast, when he ventures the "illegitimate hypostasis of my image, I would say, of a God beyond good and evil just as much dwelling in myself as everywhere else." Quoted in Bennett, *What Jung Really Said*, p. 169.
29. Michael Maine, *To Trust and to Love* (London: Darton, Longman, Todd, 2010). p. 163.
30. C. G. Jung, "The Castle in the Wood," in *The Red Book*, "Liber Novus," ed. Sonu Shamdasani (New York: Norton, 2009), 9/10, p. 264. Hereafter cited as *Red Book*.
31. Lakoff and Johnson, *Metaphors We Live By*, p. 42.
32. Andrew Marvell, "To His Coy Mistress," in *The Complete Poems* Project Gutenberg. Available at https://www.gutenberg.org/ebooks/26288.
33. Miroslav Volf, *Exclusion and Embrace: A Theological Exploration of Identity, Otherness and Reconciliation* (Nashville: Abingdon, 1996).
34. Steiner, *No Passion Spent,* p. 24.
35. Michael Payne and John Schad, eds., *Life. after. theory: Interviews with Jacques Derrida, Sir Frank Kermode, Toril Moi and Christopher Norris* (London: Continuum, 2003), p. ix.
36. *Wie der Hirsch schreit nach frischem Wasser, so schreit meine Seele, Gott, zu dir. Meine Seele dürstet nach Gott, nach dem lebendigen Gott.*
37. Jung, *Red Book*, p. 100.
38. *Ibid.*, p. 326.
39. *Ibid.*, p. 329.
40. *Ibid.*, p. 272.

41. Payne and Schad, *Life. after. theory*, p. 54.
42. George Steiner, *Errata: An Examined Life* (London: Orion Books, 1998), p. 5.
43. Theodore Dalrymple, *Our Culture, What's Left of It: The Mandarins and the Masses* (Chicago: Ivan Dee, 2005); Richard Holloway, *Doubts and Loves: What Is Left of Christianity* (Edinburgh: Canongate Books, 2001).
44. Mark Vernon, *After Atheism: Science, Religion and the Meaning of Life* (London: Palgrave Macmillan, 2007). Also see Alasdair MacIntyre, *After Virtue: A Study of Moral Virtue* (Notre Dame, IN: Notre Dame University Press, 2007).
45. Steiner, *No Passion Spent*, p. 24.
46. Shamdasani, *Jung Stripped Bare*, p. 117.
47. Marilynne Robinson, *Absence of Mind* (New Haven: Yale University Press, 2010), p. 21.
48. Hesiod traces the degeneration of human beings from an age of gold, through five stages: gold, silver, bronze, the age of heroes, and so to iron. Ovid eliminated the age of heroes.
49. Mario Jacoby, *Longing for Paradise* (Boston: Sigo, 1985).
50. Steiner, *Errata*, pp. 84-85.
51. See, for example, Ann Holm, *I Am David* (Orlando, FL: Harcourt, 2004); Robert Swindells, *Brother in the Land* (London: Penguin, 1988). And see the work of Adrienne Kertzer, "Do You Know What 'Auschwitz' Means? Children's Literature and the Holocaust," *Lion and the Unicorn* 23/2 (April 1999).
52. Steiner, *After Babel*.
53. *Ibid.*, p. 53.
54. *Ibid.*, p. 58.
55. *Ibid.*, p. 60.
56. *Ibid.*, p. 110.
57. Susan Rowland, *Jung as a Writer* (London: Routledge, 2005).
58. Lakoff and Johnson, *Metaphors We Live By*, p. 40. See also: "Thus UP is not understood purely in its own terms but emerges from the collection of constantly performed motor functions having to do with our erect position relative to the gravitational field we live in. Imagine a spherical being living outside any

gravitational field, with no knowledge or imagination of any other kind of experience. What could UP possibly mean to such a being?" p. 57.
59. Epistle to the Romans 7:19.
60. Christopher Marlowe, *The Tragicall History of Dr. Faustus*, Project Gutenberg. Available at www.gutenberg.org/ebooks/779. First published 1604. Faustus continues:
> See, see where Christ's blood streams in the firmament:
> One drop would save my soul, half a drop! Ah, my Christ,
> Ah rend not my heart for naming of my Christ.
>   Yet will I call on him, oh! spare me Lucifer!
>   Where is it now? 'tis gone,
> And see where God stretches out His arm,
> And bends His ireful brows! (Act V, sc. ii)

61. Mary Midgley, *Beast and Man: The Roots of Human Nature* (London: Routledge Classics, 2002), p. 188.
62. Heaney, "The Swing," in *Spirit Level*, p. 48.
63. Donald Cupitt, *Above Us Only Sky: The Religion of Ordinary Life* (Santa Rosa: Polebridge, 2008).
64. Shakespeare, *King Lear*, V.ii.
65. Francis Quarles, *Emblems Divine and Moral: Together with Hieroglyphics of the Life of Man* (London: Printed for Alexr. Hoggs, 1728).
66. Greek prepositions, *kata* (toward), *apo* (away from). Most simply, Kataphatic theology is affirmative, describing what/who God *is*. Apophatic theology is negative, describing who/what God is *not*.
67. Steiner, *After Babel*, p. 138.
68. *Ibid.*, p. 168.
69. Rowland, *Jung as a Writer*, p. 155.
70. Roszak, *Voice of the Earth*, p. 121.
71. *Ibid.*, p. 172.
72. Marvell, ""On a Drop of Dew," in *Complete Poems*, p. 102.
73. Jung, *Red Book*, p. 262.
74. *Ibid.*, p. 266.
75. Patrick Kavanagh, "Lough Derg," in *Collected Poems* (London: Penguin Modern Classics, 2004), p. 97.

76. Jung, "Symbols and the Interpretation of Dreams," in *CW* 18, §589.
77. Lakoff and Johnson, *Metaphors We Live By*, p. 132.
78. Consider the Greek prepositions absorbed into our vocabularies: *ana, anti, amphi, apo, dia, ek, epi, kata, meta, para, peri, pro, huper,* etc.
79. James, *Psychology: A Briefer Course*, p. 165.
80. Lewis Carroll, "The Walrus and the Carpenter," *Alice in Wonderland: Through the Looking Glass* (New York: Norton, 1971), p. 142. First published 1871.
81. Jung, "Symbols and the Interpretation of Dreams," in *CW* 18, §543.
82. Jung, "Child Development and Education," in *CW* 17, §102.

Chapter 3

1. James, *Psychology: A Briefer Course*, p. 162.
2. John Bunyan, *Pilgrim's Progress* (Harmondsworth: Penguin, 1972), p. 1.
3. Compare the rhetoric of Charlotte Brontë's heroine in *Villette* Project Gutenberg, Chapter 4, pg. 52. Available at https://www.gutenberg.org/ebooks/9182. "What was I doing here alone in great London? What should I do on the morrow? What prospects had I in life? What friends had I on earth? Whence did I come? Whither should I go? What should I do? ...A strong, vague persuasion, that it was better to go forward than backward, and that I *could* go forward—that a way, however narrow and difficult, would in time open, predominated over other feelings."
4. Consider Dale Mather's formulation of meaning disorders: *An Introduction to Meaning and Purpose in Analytical Psychology* (Hove: Brunner-Routledge, 2001).
5. The person setting out on the spiritual journey in Ignatius of Loyola's *Spiritual Exercises*, a discipline that attracted Jung's attention.
6. Alfred Plaut, *Analysis Analysed: When the Map Becomes the Territory* (London: Routledge, 1993).

7. CORE: Clinical Outcomes in Routine Evaluation. Questions include "My problems have been impossible to put on one side," "unwanted images or memories have been distressing me," and 34 more items.
8. Jung, "Psychology of the Transference," in *CW* 16, §400.
9. John Keats, "On First Looking into Chapman's Homer," and Alfred Lord Tennyson, "Ulysses."
10. Jung, *Red Book*, Cap. 1, p. 259.
11. Hill, *At Home in the World*, p. 165.
12. Jung, "On Psychic Energy," in *CW* 8, §75.
13. Jung, *Aion*, *CW* 9/ii, §2.
14. Bell, *Cultural Contradictions of Capitalism*, p. 47.
15. Herbert, "Affliction IV," in *Works of George Herbert*, p. 89.
16. Coltman's "but": quoted in chapter 1, above.
17. Jung, "The Psychology of Eastern Meditation," in *CW* 11, §939.
18. Adam Phillips, *Terrors and Experts* (London: Faber & Faber, 1995), p. 87.
19. A-ttachment/de-tachment, col-lusion, sub-con-scious, dia-gnosis, de-pression, anti-thesis, syn-thesis, and so on.
20. Heaney, "Bone Dreams," in *New Selected Poems*, p. 62.
21. Jung, "Archetypes of the Collective Unconscious," in *CW* 9/i, §80.
22. Jung, "Symbols of the Mother and Rebirth," in *CW* 5, §344.
23. Jung, "The Phenomenology of the Spirit in Fairy Tales," in *CW* 9/i, §397.
24. Herbert, "The Flower," in *Works of George Herbert*, p. 165.
25. Dale Mathers, ed., "Introduction," in *Vision and Supervision: Jungian and Post-Jungian Perspectives* (London: Routledge, 2009).
26. Some say the word *metaphysics* was so called because, in the standard ordering of Aristotle's writings, it followed "Physics," hence meta-physics. If true, a lovely misdirection of Western culture.
27. See Ernst R. Curtius, *European Literature and the Latin Middle Ages* (London: Routledge & Kegan Paul, 1979).
28. T. S. Eliot, "Four Quartets, 'East Coker V'," in *Complete Poems and Plays*, p. 182.
29. Jung, "On the Relation between Analytical Psychology and Poetry," in *CW* 15, §105.
30. Jung, "Psychological Types," in *CW* 6, §814.

31. Jung, "On the Relation between Analytical Psychology and Poetry," in *CW* 15, §119.
32. Wolfgang Giegerich, *The Neuroses of Psychology: Primary Papers towards a Critical Psychology* (New Orleans: Spring Journal Books, 2005). See his later comments: "Transference with all its intellectual uncleanness, is the landmark of psychology. It embroils patient and therapist, theory and practice, psychology and soul-process, general validity of the intellectual doctrine and personal confession in one another" (p. 162).
33. Jung, "General Aspects of Dream Psychology," in *CW* 8, §519.
34. Jung's *aber, doch*, and *dazu* play with particular force. And constructions such as *nichtsdestoweniger / dessen ungeachtet: jedoch, und doch*, etc., in *CW* 11, §400.
35. Jung, "The Structure of the Psyche," in *CW* 8, §314.
36. Steiner, *After Babel*, p. 243.
37. Jung, "On the Psychology of the Trickster Figure", *CW* 9i. §484.
38. Jung, "On Psychic Energy," in *CW* 8, §14.
39. Jung, "Psychological Types: General Description," in *CW* 6, §557 and §633.
40. James, *Psychology: A Briefer Course*, p. 153.
41. Giegerich, *Living with Jung*, p. 278.
42. Rowland, *Jung as a Writer*, p. 157.
43. Alexander Pope, "Essay on Man: Epistle 11," in *Collected Poems* (London: Dent, 1961), p. 189.
44. Richard Wainwright, "Representation, Evocation, Witness," in *Vision and Supervision*, ed. Dale Mathers (London: Routledge, 2009), p. 120.
45. Heaney, from *Stations*, "England's Difficulty," in *New Selected Poems*, p. 43.

Chapter 4

1. James, see epigraph to chapter 2.
2. English has no adequate adjectives deriving from dream. Dreamy, dreamlike have rather negative implications. The number of words in Greek suggest a more imaginative respect for the realm of Oneiros (Ὄνειρος), given the status of god.

3. Steiner, *No Passion Spent*, p. 217.
4. Walter Brueggemann, *The Hopeful Imagination: Prophetic Voices in Exile* (Philadelphia: Fortress, 1986), p. 98.
5. Cf. Descartes's *cogito ergo sum*. "Tesco" is the name of a British supermarket.
6. Jung, *MDR*, pp. 11-12.
7. Sherlock Holmes, the fictional detective then appearing in a new television series in which he was intriguingly "anorexic and analytical."
8. John Beebe, *Integrity in Depth* (College Station: Texas A & M University Press, 2005), p. 90.
9. Jung, *MDR*, p. 12.
10. Jung, "On the Nature of Dreams," in *CW* 8, §542.
11. Steiner, *After Babel*, p. 69.
12. *Ibid.*, p. 247.
13. Murray Stein, *Transformation: Emergence of the Self* (College Station: Texas A & M University Press, 1998), p. 5.
14. Jung, "On the Nature of the Psyche," in *CW* 8, §407.
15. Jung, "On Psychic Energy," in *CW* 8, §96.
16. Jung, "On the Nature of the Psyche," in *CW* 8, §414.
17. Midgley, *Beast and Man*, p. 188.
18. Explored in my unpublished contribution to a Festschrift for Sonja Marjasch's seventieth birthday.
19. Murray Stein, *Map of the Soul: An Introduction* (Chicago: Open Court, 2003), p. 127.
20. Donna Williams, *Somebody Somewhere: Breaking Free from the World of Autism* (London: Jessica Kingsley Publishers, 1999).
21. Jung, "Psychological Aspects of the Kore," in *CW* 9/i, §314.
22. Exodus 3:14: God said to Moses, I am HE WHO IS:...Thus shalt thou say unto the children of Israel, HE WHO IS hath sent me to you.
23. Donald Kalsched, *The Inner World of Trauma: Archetypal Defences of the Human Spirit* (London: Routledge, 1996), p. 66.
24. Steiner, *Errata*, p. 71.
25. Redfearn, *My Many Selves*.
26. Jung, "A Review of the Complex Theory," in *CW* 8, §203.
27. Jung, "Psychology of the Transference" in *CW* 16, §454.
28. James Hillman, *Thought of the Heart and Soul of the World* (Dallas: Spring Publications, 1981), p. 22.

NOTES

29. Rowland, *Jung as a Writer*, p. 162.
30. *Ibid.*, p. 155.
31. Jung, "The Transcendent Function," in *CW* 8, §187.
32. Jung, "Civilization in Transition," in *CW* 10, §292.
33. Joseph F. Rychlak, "Jung as Dialectician and Teleologist," in *Jung in Modern Perspective*, ed. Renos Papadopoulos and Graham Saayman (Middlesex: Wildwood House, 1984), p. 47.
34. Renos Papadopoulos, "Jung and the Concept of the Other," in Papadopoulos and Saayman, *Jung in Modern Perspective*, p. 58.
35. Jung, *MDR*, p. 32.
36. Quoted in Phillips, *Darwin's Worms*, p. 107.
37. Stein, *Transformation: Emergence of the Self*, p. 69.
38. *Ibid.*, p. 79.
39. Murray Stein, ed., *The Interactive Field in Analysis* (Wilmette: Chiron Publications, 1995); Mathers, *Vision and Supervision*.
40. Kalsched, *Inner World of Trauma*, p. 193.
41. T. S. Eliot, "The Love-Song of J. Alfred Prufrock," in *Complete Poems and Plays*, p. 16.
42. See Evelyn Underhill's work on mysticism.
43. Herbert, "The Clasping of Hands," in *Works of George Herbert*, p. 57.
44. Shakespeare, *The Tempest*, 5.1.204-212.
    > Was Milan thrust from Milan, that his Issue
    > Should become kings of Naples? O rejoice
    > Beyond a common joy, and set it down
    > With gold on lasting pillars: in one voyage
    > Did Claribel her husband find at Tunis,
    > And Ferdinand her brother found a wife
    > Where he himself was lost: Prospero his dukedom
    > In a poor isle; and all of us ourselves,
    > Where no man was his own.
45. Mark P. Hederman, *Walkabout* (Dublin: Columba Press, 2005), p. 23.
46. Kalsched, *Inner World of Trauma*, p. 5.
47. Josephine Evetts-Secker, "The Prick of Consciousness: On the Psychology and Art of Arousal," *Harvest: Journal for Jungian Studies* 39 (1993.

48. Stein, *Jung's Map of the Soul*, p. 183.
49. Jung, "General Aspects of Dream Psychology," in *CW* 8, §462.
50. Jung, *Red Book*, p. 263.

Chapter 5

1. W. J. Ong, *Orality and Literacy: The Technologizing of the Word* (London: Routledge, 1982). Leonard Shlain reports the African's response to a library in *The Alphabet Versus the Goddess: The Conflict between Word and Image* (London: Allen Lane, 1998), p. 4.
2. Josephine Evetts-Secker, *The Barefoot Book of Mother and Daughter Tales* (Bristol: Barefoot Books, 1996, 2011).
3. Heaney, "Mint," in *Spirit Level*, p. 6.
4. Aristotle, *Politics and Poetics,* trans. Benjamin Jowett and Thomas Twining (New York: Viking Press, 1969). p. 232.
5. See Ong, "Some Psychodynamics of Orality," in *Orality and Literacy*.
6. See Max Luthi, *The European Folktale: Form and Nature* (Bloomington: Indiana University Press, 1986).
7. Ursula Le Guin, *Dancing at the Edge of the World: Thoughts on Words, Women, Places* (London: Harper Collins, 1992), p. 147.
8. Heaney, "Station Island, VI," in *New Selected Poems*, p. 177.
9. Le Guin, *Dancing*, p. 147.
10. Shlain, *Alphabet Versus the Goddess*, p. 7.
11. Rowan Williams, *Lost Icons: Reflections on Cultural Bereavement* (London: T & T Clark, 2003), p. 91.
12. E. M. Forster, *Aspects of the Novel* (Harmondsworth, Middlesex: Penguin Books, 1870), p. 93.
13. Le Guin, *Dancing*, p. 165.
14. *Ibid.*, p. 167.
15. *Ibid.*, p. 39.
16. *Ibid.*, p. 169.
17. My Jung Institute thesis many years ago bore the title, *The Errant Mode: Alliance and Misalliance of Self and Ego*—written on the road, conceived during a game of *Balderdash* when the word "gyrovague" accidentally pricked psyche. The gyrovague was an errant, reputed to be arrant, monk, who wandered (*vagus*) in circles (*gyro*), refusing settlement in the cloister. Undirected

wandering (deviant straying) was condemned in a culture giving priority to purpose, the goal-oriented life. Errantry in that paradigm relates to error, though the Latin verb *errare* originally only suggested wandering.
18. Roszak, *Voice of the Earth,* p. 96.
19. Marilynne Robinson, *The Death of Adam* (New York: Picador, 1998), p. 243.
20. The same observations relate to any translation of Grimms's German text.
21. "The Sleeping Beauty," by Owen, Wilfred (1893-1918). The Estate of Wilfred Owen. *The Complete Poems and Fragments of Wilfred Owen* edited by Jon Stallworthy, first published by Chatto & Windus, 1983. Preliminaries, introductory, editorial matter, manuscripts and fragments omitted. Via First World War Poetry Digital Archive, accessed February 24, 2020, http://ww1lit.nsms.ox.ac.uk/ww1lit/collections/item/3362.
22. Le Guin, *Dancing,* p. 68.
23. Roy Daniells, "Deeper into the Forest." Quoted in *The New Wind has Wings: Poems from Canada* (Tontonto, Oxford: Oxford University Press, 1984), p. 16.
24. Le Guin, *Dancing,* p. 117.
25. OED. Here = in this place, where the person is speaking; there = in that place pointed to, away from the speaker.
26. See my "*Orphanos Exoikos*: The Precarious Possibility of Wholeness", Guild of Pastoral Psychology Lecture 272, 2000.
27. Jung, "The Origin of the Hero," in *CW* 5, §299.
28. *Grimms Kinder-und Haus Märchen,* Erste Band (München: Eugen Diederichs Verlag, 1990), p. 116.
29. Jung, "On the Nature of the Psyche," in *CW* 8, §429.
30. Le Guin, *Dancing,* p. 44.
31. See *One Eye, Two Eyes and Three Eyes.*
32. Midgley, *Beast and Man,* p. 51.
33. Jean-Paul Sartre, *Les Mots* (Paris: Éditions Gallimard, 1964), p. 39. "The teller's voice seems to come from a statue….who was speaking and to whom? My mother disappeared…I was an exile….I didn't recognize her language….from where did she get that confidence? I suddenly understood…it was the book that spoke."
34. "About the woodcutter, what he'd done and why the sisters liked him best, and would he approve of Babette's punishment?"
35. Jung, "Liber Secundus," in *Red Book,* 6/7, p. 262.

Chapter 6

1. Holloway, Doubts and Loves, p. 58.
2. Salley Vickers, *Where Three Roads Meet* (Edinburgh: Canongate Press, 2007), pp. 23, 28.
3. Tacey, *Remaking Men*, p. 34.
4. Steiner, *No Passion Spent*, p. 109.
5. J. M. Barrie, Peter Pan and Wendy (London: Pavilion Books, 1988), p. 13. First published 1911.
6. *Tennyson, "Ulysses."*
7. C. P. *Cavafy*, "Ithaka," in *Collected Poems* (London: Chatto & Windus, 1990), p. 29.
8. Patrick Kavanagh, "The Great Hunger, XIII," in *Collected Poems* (London: Penguin Modern Classics, 2004), p. 85.
9. P. Ovidi Nasonis, *Metamorphoses* (Oxford: Oxford University Press, 2004), Book 8, p. 221. I will translate and adapt various versions.
10. Jung, *Red Book,* p. 259, cap. 1.
11. Vickers, *Where Three Roads Meet*, p. 29.
12. Ibid., p. 18.
13. Jung, "The Spirit of Man in Art and Literature," in *CW* 15, §153.
14. Hesiod, *Works and Days, Theogony and the Shield of Heracles* (New York: Dover, 2006), p. 383ff.
15. *Aeschylus, Prometheus Bound.*
16. Cupitt, Above Us Only Sky, p. 33.
17. Ibid., p. 42.
18. Ibid., p. 99.
19. Jung, *Mysterium Coniunctionis*, vol. 14 of *CW*, §751.
20. W. B. Yeats, "The Circus Animals' Desertion," in *Last Poems* (Irish University Press, 1939).
21. Jung, "*Ulysses*: A Monologue," in *CW* 15, §196.
22. Rowan Williams, *The Wound of Knowledge* (London: Dartman, Longman & Todd, 1990), p. 56.
23. Kavanagh, from "Lough Dergh," in *Collected Poems*, p. 97.
24. Ovid, *Metamorphoses*, trans. Mary Innes (London: Penguin, 1955), bk. 8, p. 186.

NOTES

25. *Ibid.*, p. 184: *Ovid's more compact original is Terras licet…et undas obsturat, at caelum certe patet; ibimus illac.* The tension here comes through "but," Latin's insignificant *at*.
26. Robert Browning, "Andrea del Sarto: Called the Faultless Painter," in *Selections of the Poems and Plays of Robert Browning*, Project Gutenberg. Available at https://www.gutenberg.org/files/28041/28041.txt.
27. Ovid, *Metamorphoses*, bk. 2.
28. Ted Hughes, *Tales from Ovid* (London: Faber & Faber, 1997), p. 33.
29. Johann Wolfgang von Goethe, "Outside the City Gate," in *Faust*, Parts 1, 2.
30. Midgley, *Beast and Man*, p. 152.
31. Jung, "Phenomenology of the Spirit in Fairy Tales," in *CW* 9/i, § 420.
32. Hughes, Tales from Ovid, bk. 5, p. 57.
33. "Hymn to Demeter" in The Homeric Hymns, trans. Apostolos Athanassakis (Baltimore: Johns Hopkins University Press, 1976).
34. *Jung*, "One of the Lowly," in *Red Book*, p. 265, cap. iii.
35. German; *nichtsdestoweniger, dessen ungeachtet, jedenfalls, und doch*; Greek: ἔμπης; Latin: *tamen, verumtamen*; French: *malgré, néanmoins, meme si, pourtant*; Italian: *malgrado, tuttavia*; Dutch: *niettmin, toch, ofschoon, hoewel*; Scandinavian: *likväl, emellertid, men, utan*.
36. English vocabulary can only offer stock multipurpose verbs: change-into, turn-into, alter. Latin verbs serve too well. German is richer: *umwandeln, unformien, umgestalten*.
37. Pollux was granted immortality by Zeus, then allowed to share the gift with Castor. They spent alternate days on Olympus (as gods) and in Hades (as deceased mortals). At the death of Castor, Zeus transformed them into the constellation of Gemini.
38. Hughes, *Tales from Ovid*, p. 84.
39. How tellingly Hughes elaborates this dynamic in his translation of Ovid's spare iamque quassasque faces feretrumque parabant: / nusquam corpus erat; croceum pro corpore florem/invenient, p. 83.
40. Hughes, *Tales from Ovid*, p. 76.

41. The verb has a long history in Germanic languages: OE *ræccan*; HG *Reichen*.
42. This predates art historians' work on the "gaze as male fantasy projected onto the female figure…said to connote a *to-be-looked-at-ness*." Mulvey, quoted in Adams and Gruetzner, *Gendering Landscape Art* (Manchester: Manchester University Press, 2000), p. 3.
43. Williams, *Wound of Knowledge*, p. 54.
44. Philippians 3:13: Ἐπεκτεινόμενος.
45. St. Bernard, Serm. V. in Cant. 2. Quoted in Williams, Wound of Knowledge, p. 114.
46. *Midgley, Beast and Man,* p. 152.
47. *Cupitt, Above Us Only Sky, p. 45.*
48. Jung, "Psychological Types: The Type Problem in Poetry," *CW* 6, §301.
49. Kalsched, *Inner World of Trauma*, p. 39.
50. The initiating dream in Stein, *Transformation*, quoted in chapter 4.
51. Thomas Hardy, *The Return of the Native*.
52. Tacey, *Edge of the Sacred*, p. 154.
53. Dante, *The Divine Comedy: Inferno*, Project Gutenberg, Canto 1. Available at https://www.gutenberg.org/ebooks/41537.
54. Virgil, The Aeneid, bk. 6.
55. Andreas Schweitzer, "The Sun God's Journey through the Netherworld: An Egyptian Vision of Death and Renewal," in Creation and Destruction (New Orleans: Spring Journal Books, 2010), p. 131.
56. The ferryman is a crusty old character in Tom Stoppard's twentieth-century play The Invention of Love (London: Faber & Faber, 1997).
57. Jung, "Divine Folly," in Red Book, cap. 14, p. 293.
58. See the work of Arnold Van Gennep, *The Rites of Passage* (London: Routledge & Kegan Paul, 1977); Victor Turner, *The Ritual Process: Structure and Anti-Structure* (Ithaca, NY: Cornell University Press, 1977, 1991).
59. See works like Mircea Eliade, *Cosmos and History: The Myth of the Eternal Return* (Princeton, NJ: Princeton University

Press, 1954) and *Rites and Symbols of Initiation* (London: Harvill, 1958).
60. Brueggemann, *Hopeful Imagination*, p. 98.
61. Ovid, *Metamorphoses*, bk. 10, 1-85.
62. Ovid, *Metamorphoses*, bk. 11, p. 246.
63. Rainer Maria Rilke, *Selected Poetry* (London: Picador, 1987), p. 48.
64. Tacey, *Remaking Men*, p. 3.
65. D. H. Lawrence, "She Looks Back", in *Look! We Have Come Through*, Internet Archive, https://archive.org/stream/havecomelookweth00lawrrich/havecomelookweth00lawrrich_djvu.txt.
66. Jung, "Psychological Aspects of the Mother Archetype," in *CW* 9/i, §158.
67. *Ibid.*, §172.
68. It would be interesting to consider this poem in relation to Lawrence's novel *Sons and Lovers*, where the son is as disabled as the mother by the collusive complex. Jung asserts: "Whoever sunders himself from the mother longs to get back to the mother," "Symbols of the Mother and Rebirth," in *CW* 5, §§351-352.
69. Tacey, *Remaking Men*, p. 88.
70. Mark Vernon, *How to Be an Agnostic* (Basingstoke: Palgrave Macmillan, 2011).
71. Compare the words Stoppard gives Charon: "Everyone is here, and those that aren't will be." (*The Invention of Love*, Act 1).
72. Phillip Larkin, "Aubade," in *Collected Poems* (London: Faber & Faber; Marvell Press, 1988, 2003), p. 190.
73. Jung, "Psychology of the Types: Introduction," in *CW* 6, §3.
74. Jung, "On Psychic Energy," in *CW* 8, §111.
75. *Ibid.*, §113.
76. David Tacey (in press), *The Darkening Spirit: Jung, Spirituality, Religion* (London and New York: Routledge, 2012), p.15.
77. See Hitchings, *Language Wars*, p. 310.
78. Charles Poncé, Working the Soul: Reflections on Jungian Psychology (Berkeley: North Atlantic Books, 1988), p. 38.
79. *Jung, Red Book*, "Liber Secundus," p. 263.

Postlude

1. Heaney, "An Invocation," in *Spirit Level*, p. 27.
2. Jackie Kay, "Holy Island," in *Fiere* (London: Picador, 2011), p. 32.
3. Steiner, *No Passion Spent*, p. 46.
4. Midgley, *Beast and Man*, p. 186.
5. Carroll, *Alice in Wonderland*, p. 8.
   > "Down, down, down. Would the fall never come to an end? 'I wonder how many miles I have fallen by this time?' she said aloud. 'I must be getting somewhere near the centre of the earth. Let me see; that would be four thousand miles down, I think—' (for, you see, Alice had learnt several things of this sort in her lessons in the school-room, and though this was not a very good opportunity for showing off her knowledge, as there was no one to listen to her, still it was good practice to say it over) '—yes, that's about the right distance—but the I wonder what Latitude or Longitude I've got to?' (Alice had not the slightest idea what Latitude was, or Longitude either, but she thought they were nice grand words to say.)"
6. Jung, "Symbols of Transformation: Introduction," in *CW* 5, §189.
7. Hitchings, *Language Wars*, p. 176.
8. James, "The Stream of Consciousness," in *Brief Course*, p. 160.
9. Bell, *Cultural Contradictions of Capitalism*, p. 113.
10. Aristotle, *Poetics*, "On Language," p. 249.
11. Jung, "The Psychology of Dementia Praecox," in *CW* 3, §181.
12. James Hillman, *Re-Visioning Psychology* (New York: Harper & Row, 1975), p. 9.
13. Kugler, *Alchemy of Discourse*, p. 68.
14. Jung, "The Dual Mother," in *Symbols of Transformation*, *CW* 5, §505.
15. Stein, *Jung's Map of the Soul*, p. 70.
16. Jung, "On the Nature of the Psyche," in *CW* 8, §408 and "On the Nature of Dreams," §554.
17. Jung, "General Aspects of Dream Psychology," in *CW* 8, §456.
18. See p. 63, above.
19. Jung, "The Red One," in *Red Book*, Cap. i., p. 259.
20. Jung, "On Psychic Energy," in *CW* 8, §26.

21. James Hillman, "Further Notes on Images." (This will appear in the forthcoming volume 4 of the uniform edition of Hillman's work, *From Types to Images*, to be published by Spring in 2012).
22. J. L. Austin: "Ifs and Cans, 1956 Annual philosophical lecture," Henriette Hertz Trust, British Academy, 1956. In response, C. P. Goodin interrogates the auxiliary "would" and "wouldy."
23. Steiner, *After Babel*, p. 226.
24. Sigmund Freud, *On Interpretation of Dreams* (Harmondsworth, Penguin Books, 1978), vol. 4, p. 422.
25. Evetts-Secker, *Noli and Ecce: Dis-covering Psyche* (London: Guild of Pastoral Psychology, 1994, 2004), Guild Lecture 254.
26. Shakespeare, *King Lear*, Act V, sc. 2.
27. T. S. Eliot, "The Love-Song of J. Alfred Prufrock," in *Complete Poems and Plays*.
28. John Donne, "The Good Morrow," in *The Poems of John Donne* (London: Oxford University Press, 1957), p. 7.
29. W. H. Auden, "Musée des Beaux Arts," in *Collected Shorter Poems, 1930-1944* (London: Faber & Faber, 1959), p. 19.
30. *Car ils ne savent ce qu'ils font*; want zij weten niet, wat zij doen; for de vet ikke hvad de gjør; non enim sciunt quid faciunt.
31. Rowan Williams, *Dostoevsky: Language, Faith and Fiction* (London: Continuum, 2009), p. 222.
32. Rowan Williams, *Grace and Necessity: Reflections on Art and Love* (London: Continuum, 2005), p. 26.
33. T. S. Eliot, "East Coker," in *Complete Poems and Plays*, p. 182.
34. Jung, *Red Book*, p. 290.
35. *Ibid.*, p. 37.
36. Quoted by Heuer in Mathers, *Vision and Supervision*, p. 175; Gottfried Heuer, "Spooky Action at a Distance: Parallel Process in Jungian Analysis and Supervision."
37. Jung, *Red Book*, "Scrutinies," p. 333.
38. Shakespeare, *Richard 3*:
    > What do I fear? Myself? There's none else by:
    > Richard loves Richard; that is, I am I.
    > Is there a murderer here? No—yes, I am:
    > Then fly. What, from myself? Great reason why—
    > Lest I revenge. What, myself upon myself!
    > Alack, I love myself. Wherefore? For any good

> That I myself have done unto myself?
> Oh, no! Alas I rather hate myself
> For hateful deeds, committed by myself!
> I am a villain; yet I lie, I am not. (Act V, sc. iii)

39. Jung, *Red Book*, p. 280.
40. Volf, *Exclusion and Embrace*, p. 144.
41. Form-words in the nursery canon deserve attention.
42. Jung, *Red Book*, p. 302.
43. *Ibid.*, p. 254 (emphasis mine).
44. Pat Hutchins, *Rosie's Walk* (New York: Macmillan, 1968).
45. Michael Rosen, *We're Going on a Bear Hunt* (London: Walker Books, 1989).
46. Kenneth Grahame, *The Wind in the Willows* (1908; New York: Scribner, 1961). Jung, *Red Book*, p. 322.
47. Jung, *Red Book*, p. 233.
48. *Ibid.*, p. 319.
49. Gauguin exhibition, London, Tate Modern, 2010. Quotations from Poe: "Only this, and nothing more; Nameless here for evermore; This it is, and nothing more; Darkness there, and nothing more; Merely this and nothing more; 'Tis the wind and nothing more!; Quoth the raven, Nevermore; With such name as Nevermore; Then the bird said, Nevermore," and so on.
50. Walcott, *Midsummer*, LIV.
51. John Updike, *Terrorist* (New York: Alfred Knopf, 2006), p. 91.
52. Jung, *Red Book*, p. 317.
53. *Ibid.*, Appendix A, p. 364.
54. Stein, *Jung's Map of the Soul*, p. 98.
55. Jung, *Red Book*, 16/17, p. 268.
56. *Ibid.*, 20/21, p. 270.
57. Rilke: *Das Stundenbuch*, "Es lärmt das Licht im Wipfel deines Baumes":
    > With this gentlest of gestures you would hold
    > the world, thus only and no otherwise.
    > You lean from out its skies to capture earth,
    > and feel it underneath your mantle's folds. (p. 35; trans. Babette Deutsch)

Appendix

The Leaden Echo and The Golden Echo: *Gerald Manley Hopkins*

The Leaden Echo

HOW to kéep—is there ány any, is there none such, nowhere
    known some, bow or brooch or braid or brace,
    láce, latch or catch or key to keep
Back beauty, keep it, beauty, beauty, beauty, … from vanishing away?
Ó is there no frowning of these wrinkles, rankéd wrinkles deep,
Dówn? no waving off of these most mournful messengers,
    still messengers, sad and stealing messengers of grey? —
No there's none, there's none, O no there's none,
Nor can you long be, what you now are, called fair,
Do what you may do, what, do what you may,
And wisdom is early to despair:
Be beginning; since, no, nothing can be done
To keep at bay
Age and age's evils, hoar hair,
Ruck and wrinkle, drooping, dying, death's worst, winding
    sheets, tombs and worms and tumbling to decay;

So be beginning, be beginning to despair.
O there 's none; no no no there 's none:
Be beginning to despair, to despair,
Despair, despair, despair, despair.

The Golden Echo

Spare!
There ís one, yes I have one (Hush there!);
Only not within seeing of the sun,
Not within the singeing of the strong sun,
Tall sun's tingeing, or treacherous the tainting of the earth's air,
Somewhere elsewhere there is ah well where! one,
Oné. Yes I cán tell such a key, I dó know such a place,
Where whatever's prizéd and passes of us, everything that's
    fresh and fast flying of us, seems to us sweet of us
    and swiftly away with, done away with, undone,
Undone, done with, soon done with, and yet dearly and dangerously sweet
Of us, the wimpled-water-dimpled, not-by-morning-matchèd face,
The flower of beauty, fleece of beauty, too too apt to, ah! to fleet,
Never fleets móre, fastened with the tenderest truth
To its own best being and its loveliness of youth: it is an ever-
    lastingness of, O it is an all youth!
Come then, your ways and airs and looks, locks, maiden gear,
    gallantry and gaiety and grace,
Winning ways, airs innocent, maiden manners, sweet looks,
    loose locks, long locks, lovelocks, gaygear, going gallant,
        girlgrace—
Resign them, sign them, seal them, send them, motion them with breath,
And with sighs soaring, soaring síghs deliver
Them; beauty-in-the-ghost, deliver it, early now, long before death
Give beauty back, beauty, beauty, beauty, back to God, beauty's self and
    beauty's giver.
See; not a hair is, not an eyelash, not the least lash lost; every hair
Is, hair of the head, numbered.
Nay, what we had lighthanded left in surly the mere mould
Will have waked and have waxed and have walked with the
    wind what while we slept,

APPENDIX

This side, that side hurling a heavyheaded hundredfold
What while we, while we slumbered.
O then, weary then why should we tread? O why are we so
     haggard at the heart, so care-coiled, care-killed, so fagged,
     so fashed, so cogged, so cumbered,
When the thing we freely fórfeit is kept with fonder a care,
Fonder a care kept than we could have kept it, kept
Far with fonder a care (and we, we should have lost it) finer, fonder
A care kept.—Where kept? Do but tell us where kept, where.—
Yonder.—What high as that! We follow, now we follow.—
     Yonder, yes yonder, yonder,
Yonder.

Prayer (1): *George Herbert*

PRAYER the Churches banquet, Angels age,
     Gods breath in man returning to his birth,
     The soul in paraphrase, heart in pilgrimage,
The Christian plummet sounding heav'n and earth ;
Engine against th' Almightie, sinner's towre,
     Reversed thunder, Christ-side-piercing spear,
     The six daies world-transposing in an houre,
A kinde of tune, which all things heare and fear;
Softnesse, and peace, and joy, and love, and blisse,
     Exalted Manna, gladnesse of the best,
     Heaven in ordinarie, man well drest,
The milkie way, the bird of Paradise,
     Church-bels beyond the stars heard, the souls bloud,
     The land of spices ; something understood.

Index

A

above and below 171–2
Above Us Only Sky (Cupitt) 50–1
across 48, 81
ad 41
Adamic vernacular 46
adverbial energies 170
adversative conjunctions 61, 117–18
advertisements 141
Aeneas 188
affirmation 213–14
affixes 20, 75
after 40–1, 42–5
after-Auschwitz 40–1
again 127, 155
against 118
agon 187
Aion (Jung) 55, 60–1
alchemy 72
Alchemy of Discourse (Kugler) 14
Alice, Wonderland 17, 30, 32illus, 86
aloneness 152
always 126–7
amphi-ballein 83
analogy 115
analytical dyad 84
and 61–2
angels 173
Anglo-Saxon 19
Answer to Job (Jung) 24
antagonisms 199
anti- 118
any- 109

apotheosis 180
archetypes
  of direction 23
  energy of 204
  as irrepresentable 82
  Mother 196
  nature of 18, 197
  rhetoric of 45
  transformative possibility 72
Arethusa 178
Aristotle 136–8
artistic communication 20
Ascent of Mount Carmel (St. John of the Cross) 66, 68illus
At Home in the World (Hill) 1
atonement 85–6
attentiveness 165
"Aubade" (Larkin) 197–8
Auden, W.H. 13, 207
autism 113–14
auxiliaries 11, 156, 159, 179

B

Babel 46–7
back 27, 127
back-tracking 71–2
Bakhtian, Mikhail 48
banality 58, 163–4
Beebe, John 97
before-after 72, 77–8
Beggar's Bridge 190
behind 101–3, 101illus
being at home 1
being lost 152

Bell, Daniel 29, 38, 73, 202
Bennet, A.E. 8
beside 206–7
besides 206
between 45–8, 61, 62, 83, 119, 189, 191
betwixt 73
beyond 28, 38–40, 69, 81–2, 102
Beyond Good and Evil (Nietzsche) 38–9
Beyond the Pleasure Principle (Freud) 39
beyond words 208
beyond-yonder 38, 40
bi-lingualisms 75
Bia 170
bias 87–8, 169–70, 173, 187, 199, 204
big dreams 98–100, 115–16
birth, rituals 51
blindness/sight paradigm 192
"Bone Dreams" (Heaney) 75
borrowing, of language 19–20
"Briar Rose/Sleeping Beauty" 144–7
bridges 61–2
Browne, Anthony 151, 158
Browning, Robert 174
Brueggemann, Walter 191
Buber, Martin 8, 122
Bunyan, John 63–4, 71, 91, 205
but 18–19, 61, 117, 119, 145
"but" (Coltman) 18–19

C

Camelot 192
Castor and Pollux 180
Cattelan, Maurizio 35
"Caul" (Duffy) 16–17
Cavafy, C.P. 167
centers 147–9
Ceres 177–9
Changing Minds in Therapy (Wilkinson) 177

characters, in dreams 120–1
Chesterton, G.K. 17
child, value of 36–7
children's stories 211
Christ 71, 85–6, 207
Christ of St John of the Cross (Dalí) 58, 59illus
Christianity 109
clang associations 17
closed-class words 4
Cognitive Behavior Therapy (CBT) 66
collective unconscious 92
Coltman, Paul 18–19
communication 20, 47
comparative, use of 36
conceit 93
conjunctions 61–2
consciousness 88–9
contra- 85, 118
convergence 169
conversion 45, 78
CORE questionnaire 66, 69
cost 38
counter- 79, 85
counter-transference 85
couplings 61
Crashaw, Richard 37
crossing over 190–2
crucifixion 46
cultural mediation, symbols 47–8
cummings, e.e. 20
Cupitt, Donald 171
curiosity 208

D

Daedalus 173–4
daimon 24–5
Dalí, Salvador 58
dancing 129–30
Daniells, Roy 147–8
Dante 189–90
Darwin, Charles 5, 12

INDEX

death 48, 51, 112, 197–8
deep into woods 148illus
Del Sarto, Andrea 174
Demeter 177–9
democratization, of language 20
depth psychology 179
Derrida, Jacques 199
desire 62
Devils (Dostoevsky) 19
dia- 61
direction 21, 23
dis- 61
disappearance, of I 210
divergence 169
Donne, John 207
Dostoevsky, Fyodor 19
down 48–50
drama, Aristotle's view of 137–8
drawings 35–6
dream commentary, use of comparative 36
dream ego 122–3
dream-I, and ego 118–19
dream reports 91–113, 35illus, 101illus, 102illus
  ascent dream 94
  biting snake 108
  black horse 119–20
  blackberries 104
  capture/imprisonment 114
  casts of characters 120–1
  colors 117
  conference dream 92–3
  crocodiles 106–7
  death 129
  Einstein 111
  elevator 104
  end of the world 115
  eucharist 112–13
  fish swimming in wine 94–5
  fishing with Jung 175
  horizontal and vertical movement 99–104
  Jung, C.G. 95–6, 109
  kiln 128
  menace 110–11
  metamorphosis 99–101
  mouse/emerald 116
  moving through building 135
  nursing home 112
  polarity 105–6
  positioning 99–103
  prison 128
  religion 104–5
  shape shifting 107–8
  snakes 96–7
  supermarket trolley 95, 132
  swans 108–9
  three women 133
  transfiguration 98–9
  travelling with baby 133
  uprightness 96–7
  Vita 103–4
  white seal 98
dream yonders 91
dreams
  authorial 12
  big 98–100, 115–16
  Freud on 206
  Jung on 96–7
  metamorphosis 99–101
  temporality 127
  translation 48
dualism, of language 9–10
Duffy, Carol Ann 16–17, 21
dyad, analytical 84
dynamic 31, 35
dynamo 130
dystopia 43

E

"East Coker" (Eliot) 82–3
ego, and dream-I 118–19

Eliot, T.S. 12, 82–3, 130, 208
elsewhere 27
empathy 209
enantiodromia 78
encumbrance 210
energic model 85
energies, adverbial and prepositional 170
energy 23–4, 202, 204
English, as global language 5–6
entgeg 41
enumeration 29
epektasis 186
epithymia 186
equilibrium 78–9
Eros 24–5, 189
ET (Spielberg) 70
even though 144
ever 126
ever after 143
evolution 55
evolutionary myth 186–7
exclusion and inclusion 47
exercitants 66
exodus 191
expectation 3
experience, psychology as 24
explaining 74
explication 74
exploration, of language 201–2

F

face-to-face therapy 207
fairytales
   "Briar Rose/Sleeping Beauty" 144–7
   fathers 157
   "The Golden Bird" 157
   "The Handless Maiden" 163
   "Hansel and Gretel" 149–52, 150illus, 153illus, 155, 158–9
   "Jorinda and Joringel" 142–3
   lack of unity 138
   language of 139
   "Mother Holle" 143–5
   narrative strategies 138
   resolution 136
   setting-out 156
   "The Seven Ravens" 155
   "The Singing Soaring Lark" 157–8, 159–60
   "The Six Swans" 152–5
   structure 137
   temporality 143, 145
   "Water of Life" 160–1
faith 118
   see also religion
father tongue 138–9
fathers, fairytales 157
Faustus 49, 175
feminine, enclosure of 146–7
finding a lodging 166
flood myths 44
folk tradition, possible origins 135
for 207–8
form-words 14, 15, 20–1, 26
Forster, E.M. 140, 141
Freud, Sigmund 3, 8, 20, 39, 197, 206, 208
Friedrich, Caspar David 69
from-to dynamics 30–1, 37, 48, 52–3, 55–6, 107, 109, 127
from-to narrative 100–1
from-to perspectives 30
full-words 14
function-words 14, 126
funerals 51

G

gaps, negotiating 173–4
gaze 183
geography, physical and spiritual 126
German 19, 84
Giacometti, Alberto 30, 31illus

Giegerich, Wolfgang 17, 84, 88–9
gifted child 202
gifts 62
globish 5–6
goal, as idea 69
God 17–18, 51–2, 114–15, 209
  longing for 54illus
grace 78
gradior 71
grammar 204, 205–6
grammatical particles, role of 3–4
Great Chain of Being 187
Greek 19
Gregory 186
grumpy old men 43
Gulliver's Travels (Swift) 7, 30, 33illus

H

Hades 179
Haggard, Rider 66–7
Hairy Wildman 197
Hamlet (Shakespeare) 20
handless maiden 155, 156–7
hanker 197
"Hansel and Gretel" 149–52, 150illus, 153illus, 155, 158–9
Hardy, Thomas 189
hark/harken 196–7
he 123
Heaney, Seamus 4, 14–15, 24, 50, 75, 89, 201
heaven 49–50
Hebrew script 16
height, metaphor of 175
hence 23
hence-hither 60
Herbert, George 28–9, 52, 73, 80, 125, 243
here 127, 152, 157–8
here-and-now 66
here-there 56
Hermes 62

heroic dominance 140
Hesiod 170
Hill, John 1, 2
Hillman, James 13, 45, 50, 71, 170–1, 203, 205–6
Him (Cattelan) 34illus
hinauf 41
History of the Royal Society (Spratt) 9
Hitchings, Henry 5, 6, 202
hither-and-thither 66
Hitler, Adolf 34illus, 35
holocaust, living after 44
Holy Grail 192
Holy Spirit 130
home 157
home-coming 161
homing instinct 158
Hopkins, Gerard Manley 25–7, 72–3, 91, 241–3
horizon 69
horizontal plane 102–3
however 61
Hughes, Ted 174, 181–2
humankind, as dialectical 60–1
Husserl, Edmund 89
hybridity 108–9

I

I 119–22, 210
I am 114–15
I and Thou (Buber) 122
Icarus 173
idiolect 98
images 60, 62
inclusion and exclusion 47
indicative, writing in 156
indistinctness 112
individuation 23, 55, 65, 72, 126, 154, 196, 210
infant-parent work 183
Inferno (Dante) 189–90
infinity 38

inflation, linguistic 4–5
inside/outside dynamics 131–2
insider/outsider paradigm 47
instead of 85–6
instinct, and spirit 106
inter- 81, 124
inter-ference 83
inter-pretation 47, 74
Internet 81
Ireland, geography 126
Iron John 196–7
it 24, 124–5
Ithaka 167

J

Jacob's ladder 172
James, William 21, 23, 61, 63, 88, 91, 202
Janus 188
Jason 188
John 3:8 1–2
Johnson, Mark 28, 40, 48, 60
Jonson, Ben 9
"Jorinda and Joringel" 142–3
journeys 51, 70–1, 126, 147–9
Julius Caesar (Shakespeare) 18
Jung, C.G.
   on African travel 2
   on ambiguity 8–9
   Answer to Job 24
   beyond 39–40
   beyond words 208
   on bias 169–70
   contrasting urges 196
   crossing over 190
   depth psychology 179
   dream reports 95–6, 109
   on dreams 96–7
   enantiodromia 78–9
   energic model 85
   face-to-face therapy 207
   goal as idea 69
   image as dynamic 60
   introversion/extraversion 87–8
   language 6–7, 210, 212
   on libido 27, 202, 204
   living after 42–3
   mandala 214
   on maturation 51
   nach 41–2
   nature of history 177
   necessity of relationship 60–1
   nothing-but 86
   otherwise 86–7
   on Prometheus 187
   Red One 69–70
   reductive method 77
   on relatedness 121
   religion and myth 171–2
   on roots 55
   on self 73–4
   self-questioning 209
   sense of authority 122
   soul's yes 213–14
   spatial and temporal relations 36, 37
   spectrum 106
   spiritual principle 198
   surrender to spirit 200
   symbolism 8
   transformation 76–8
   truth in banality 58
   un-learning 214
   on value of child 36–7
   why and wherefore 131
   Word Association Experiment 15
Jung Stripped Bare (Shamdasani) 42–3
just 114
just as 147

K

Kabbala 16
kairos 136
Kalsched, Donald 118, 124, 127, 188

INDEX

katabasis 177
Kavanagh, Patrick 203
Kay, Jackie 201
Keats, John 69
Kermode, Frank 42
Kierkegaard, Soren 194
King Lear (Shakespeare) 51, 207
King, Martin Luther 191
King Solomon's Mines (Haggard) 66, 67illus
kinship libido 123–4
Kohut, Heinz 183
Kugler, Paul 14, 204
Kuhn, Thomas 44–5

L

La Terre Vue du Ciel (Arthus-Bertand) 29
Lacan, Jacques 207
ladders 172–3
Lady Macbeth 18
Lakoff, George 28, 40, 48, 60
language
  democratization of 20
  dualism of 9–10
  exploration 201–2
  heroic 138
  as home 161–2
  specialized 47
langue 10, 75
Larkin, Phillip 197–8
Latin 6, 19
Lawrence, D.H. 195–6
Le Guin, Ursula 138–9, 140–1, 142, 147, 149–50, 156
l'enfant divin 36
levels, in dreams 103–4
Lewis, C.S. 141
libido 27, 202, 204
life 48
Life. after. Theory (Schad and Payne) 41, 42
limen 188, 190–1

linguistic exploration, soul in 163
linguistic inflation 4–5
listening to 202
Little Red cap 147
liturgy 14–15
living after 45
looking-back 193–5
Lot's wife 196
love, Socrates' view of 24–5
"Lovesong" (Eliot) 12
Luther, Martin 2, 41
lysis 136

M

Macbeth (Shakespeare) 18
Madonna and child 183, 184illus
Magnificat 180
Magritte, René 30
maps 66, 166–7, 204
Maritain, Jacques 208
Marr, Joan 183, 185–6
Marvell, Andrew 40, 56–8, 181, 183
masculine power 156
maternal gaze 183, 184–5ilus
Mathers, Dale 81
maturation 51, 108–9
McEwan, Ian 10–11
meaning 77, 98
measurement 28
memory 52–3, 55
menace 110–11
Mercurius 62
meta- 81–2, 189
meta-language 75–6
metamorphosis dreams 99–101
metamorphosis, from-to dynamics 107
metanoia 82
metaphors 3–4, 28, 40, 82, 175
metaxy 189
Midgley, Mary 49–50, 109, 158, 175, 186–7, 201
Miller, Alice 202

Milton, John 13
mirror neurons 209
mono-language, desire for 5–6, 46
monosyllabism 19
mood 79–81
morphing 18, 19–20, 108
mortality 3
mother complex 195–6
"Mother Holle" 143–5
Mother, pull to 196
mother tongue 138–9
motion, capturing 204–5
multo in parvo 16
must 152
My Self, My Many Selves (Redfearn) 29
mythic, listening for 165
myths 44
    Aeneas 188
    creatures 108
    Daedalus and Icarus 173–4
    embodied wisdom 188
    evolutionary 186–7
    as fabulous and familiar 166
    Faustus 175
    Janus 188
    Jason 188
    Narcissus 180–6
    Odysseus 167–8, 188
    Oedipus 168–9
    Orpheus 193–5, 207
    Phaeton 174–5
    Prodigal Son 197
    Prometheus 187
    Proserpina 177–9
    and religion 171–2
    of self-knowledge 169
    of verticality 177
    verticality 179

N

nach 41–2
naming 21, 35

Narcissus 180–6
narrative, construction of 140
narrative strategies, dreams and fairytales 138
narrative trajectory 65
neo 43
networks 29
neuroscience 3
never 126, 127–8, 213
never again 127, 155
Neverland 166
nevermore 213
"Nevermore" (Gauguin) 213
nevertheless 61, 85–6, 178
Newton, John 45
Nicodemus, and Christ 71
Nietzsche, Friedrich 38–9
nominalism 6–7
nominals 17, 21
nonetheless 178
nothing 113
nothing-but 86
Nouwen, Henri 4
novels 121
now 127

O

Odysseus 188
odyssey 166–8
Oedipus 168–9
On a Drop of Dew (Marvell) 56–8
"On Psychic Energy" (Jung) 198
"On the Formation of Mould" (Darwin) 5, 12
"On the Nature of the Psyche" (Jung) 23–4
Ong, W.J. 135
only 50
open-class words 6
opposites, in self 122
opposition 55
orientational metaphors 28

INDEX

orientations 170–1
Orpheus 193–5, 207
Othello (Shakespeare) 20–1
others, discovery of 210
otherwise 44, 86–7
outside/inside dynamics 131–2
Ovid 173, 181–2, 189, 193
Owen, Wilfred 146

P

Palestrina 41
paradigm shift 44–5
paradigms, of analysis 78
Paradise Lost (Milton) 13
parole, and *langue* 10
particles 21, 211
Payne, Michael 41, 42
perhaps 128
peri-peteia 137
Persephone 177–9
Peter Pan (Barry) 166
Phaeton 174–5
Phillips, Adam 5, 74
phrasal verbs 49
Plato 24–5, 189
Plaut, Alfred 66
plot 137, 140
Pluto 177–9
Poetics (Aristotle) 137
poets 13, 18
polarity 105–6, 122, 151
Pollux and Castor 180
polysyllabism 19
Pope, Alexander 89
post- 44–5
power, masculine 156
praxis, words in 14
prayer 28, 52
"Prayer" (Herbert) 28, 243
precocity 175
prepositional energies 170
prepositions 160

primal impulse 165–6
printing 135–6
pro-spection 77
Prodigal Son 197
progress 71–2
Prometheus 187
pronouns 119–26
Proserpina 177–9
Prufrock (Eliot) 130, 207
Psyche 76–7, 86, 87, 88, 163
psychic maps 166–7
Psychology: a Briefer Course (James) 23
psychology, as experience 24
punctuation 16

Q

quantity 38
Quarles, Francis 51–2
Queen Mother 156
questionnaires 69
quests 66
Quirk, Randolph 89

R

re-cycling 109
re-gression 71–2, 76–7
reality, accommodating 80
Red Book (Jung) 41, 58, 69–70, 86, 131, 163–4, 179, 190, 205, 212
Redfearn, J.W.T. 29, 120
reductive method 77
reflexives 182
regression 192
reification 17
relatedness 121–2
relationality 83
relationship, necessity of 60–1
religion 104–5, 109, 171–2
  see also faith
religious conversion 45
resistances 149

revaluing, of particles 211
review 195
rhetoric of archetypes 45
Rilke, Rainer Maria 208, 215
rites, of transition 191–2
ritual 51
"River" (Duffy) 17
Robinson, Marilynne 43, 143
roots, importance of 55
Rosie's Walk (Hutchins) 211
Roszak, Theodore 38, 56, 143
Rowland, Susan 48, 55, 89, 121
Rychlak, Joseph 122

S

sandplay 8
Sartre, Jean-Paul 162
satiety 157
Saussure, Ferdinand de 10
scala 172–3
scale, use of 35–6
Schad, John 41, 42
scientific writing, aims and ideals 9
"Scrutinies" (Jung) 209
Scylla and Charybdis 187–8
Self 73–4, 114, 120, 122
self-discovery 211
self-infinitizing 73
self-questioning 209
self-realization 196
setting-out 156
Shakespeare, William 18, 20–1, 98, 125, 209
Shamdasani, Sonu 42–3
shape shifting 107–8
she 123
"She Looks Back" (Lawrence) 195–6
sicut 86
Sicut cervus desiderat ad fontes aquarum (Palestrina) 41
sideways 98–9
Sidney, Phillip 49

silence 154
simplicity 203
simultaneity 116, 117
size, relative 36, 37–8
"Sleeping Beauty" (Owen) 146
Socrates, on love 24–5
some- 109, 115
somebodies, emergence 209–10
somehow 111, 112, 115, 116–17, 118, 128, 209
someone 112, 120
something 28–9, 110–13, 127–8, 209
sometimes 127
somewhere 112, 209
soul
  anchoring 60
  Giegerich on 84
  in linguistic exploration 163
  longing of 52
  speaking 163
soundplay 17
space, transitional 73
spectrum 106
spirit
  energy 130
  and instinct 106
  personal 124
  surrender to 200
spiritual principle 198
Spratt, Thomas 9
St. Augustine 49, 186
St. Bernard 186
St. John of the Cross 66, 71
St. Paul 49, 80, 213
"Stages of Life" (Jung) 51
Stein, Murray 110, 123–4, 130, 188–9, 204
Steiner, George 5, 15, 41, 42, 44, 46–7, 52–4, 86–7, 91–2, 118, 132, 165–6, 201, 206
Stevens, Anthony 83
stories, as stratagems of mortality 141

INDEX

story, primacy of 74
storytelling, temporality 140–1
straining forward 186
stream of consciousness 202
sub- 49
subjunctive 156
suddenly 100, 102, 128
suffering, meaning 77
Sufism 61–2
super- 49
supervision 81, 124
surrender 89
swans 108–9
Swift, Jonathan 7
symbolism, of regression 71
symbols 8, 47–8, 72, 78, 83
  up/down 53illus
Symposium (Plato) 24–5
synergeia 186
syntax 87, 204–6

T

Tacey, David 6, 27, 189, 195, 198–9
Talos 173
technical language 75
technology 81
temporality 37, 84, 140–1, 143, 145
Tennyson, Alfred Lord 69, 167
tenses 52, 55
tension 20–1, 81, 87, 130, 191
Tertullian 118
text, as homeland 132
thanatos 197
"The Clasping of Hands" (Herbert) 125
The Cultural Contradictions of Capitalism (Bell) 29
"The Fitcher's Bird" (Kalsched) 124
"The Golden Bird" 157
"The Handless Maiden" 163
"The Leaden Echo and the Golden Echo" (Hopkins) 25–7, 72–3, 241–3

"The Phenomenology of the Spirit in Fairy Tales" (Jung) 78–9
The Pilgrim's Progress from this World to That Which Is to Come: Delivered under the Similitude of a Dream 63–5, 142, 205
"The Raven" (Poe) 213
"The Seven Ravens" 155
"The Singing Soaring Lark" 157–8, 159–60
"The Six Swans" 152–5
The Spirit Level (Heaney) 50
The Spirit of Geometry (Magritte) 30
"The Stream of Consciousness" (James) 88
The Tempest (Shakespeare) 126
The Wind in the Willows (Grahame) 211–12
then 127
then-and-now 80, 194–5
thence 137
thence-thither 60
theology 125, 171
theory 41–2
therapeutic remembering 194
there 56
there-ness 52
Therrien, Robert 30, 32illus
thither 137
though 117
thresholds 188, 190–1
time 40, 126
time-adverbials 213
"Tintern Abbey" (Wordsworth) 37
too 130
Tooke, John Horne 6, 7
towards 41–2
training 124
trans- 62, 75–8, 81
transference 83–4
transformation 76–7, 108–9, 115–16, 145–6, 189–90

Transformation: Emergence of the Self (Stein) 188–9
"Transformative Relationships" (Stein) 123–4
transition rites 191–2
transitional space 73
transitivity 15
translation 47, 48
transmutation 72
trauma, living after 44–5
tribal memory 55
tricksters 188
truth 58, 118
turning-back 192–3
Tyndale, William 1–2
tyranny, of language 7–8

U

über 84
un-learning 214
underclass, linguistic 14
unification 121
union 125
Unitive Way 125
unity 87
unreadiness 146–7
up 48–52, 80
up/down 171–2
    emblems 53illus
uprightness 97

V

"Value after Theory" (Kermode) 42
value of, words 203
values 58, 89
Van Lier, Leo 10
verb structures 130–1
verbal compounds 191
vernacular, Adamic 46
vertical plane 103–4
verticality, myths of 177, 179
Vickers, Salley 168–9

viewpoints 29
vocabulary 202
Volf, Miroslav 40, 210
von Franz, Marie-Louise 137

W

waiting 70
Walcott, Derek 19
wandering 142, 166–8
Wanderwegen 12
"Water of Life" 160–1
we 122–3
wellness 69
We're Going on a Bear Hunt (Rosen) 211
what 113
what for 74
whence 1–2, 13, 23, 66
whence-to-whither 66
wherefore 131
whether 119
whither 1–2, 13, 23, 66, 136, 137
why 131
Wilkinson, Margaret 3, 177
Williams, Rowan 139, 186, 208
Winnicott, Donald 30–1, 124, 156, 183
Winnie the Pooh (Milne) 211
wit 93
Wonderland 17
Word Association Experiment 15
words 13–14, 42, 203
Wordsworth, William 37
would 10–11

Y

yearning 186
    upward and forward 176illus
Yeats, W.B. 172–3
yes 19, 213–14
yet 55
yonder 13, 27–8, 38, 45, 65, 69, 91, 102